MW00983534

Praise for No Place Like Home

"C. J. Janovy promises the reader lessons to be learned from a detailed study of recent activism, and she more than delivers. Using a wide array of fascinating individuals to demonstrate the necessity of acting locally, organizing, and using a variety of leadership styles, Janovy reminds us that we LGBT people are indeed 'everywhere.' No Place Like Home is an important contribution to the overdue but growing number of studies of 'flyover' America."

—**Vicki L. Eaklor**, author of Queer America:
A People's GLBT History of the United States

"With fine prose and a big heart, No Place Like Home reminds us—once and for all—that flyover country is destination travel for those of us interested in contemporary American LGBT life. In Janovy's beautiful book, curious readers encounter wide-ranging responses to a queer 'Kansas lifestyle' as it politically evolved over the past two decades. The individuals that she painstakingly chronicles across these pages will not be forgotten anytime soon."

—**Scott Herring**, author of Another Country: Queer Anti-Urbanism

"What's the matter with Kansas? Pretty much the same thing that's wrong with most of America these days: irrational fear, willful ignorance, and a pervasive sense of resentfulness that seems to bring out the worst in everybody at some point or another. As C. J. Janovy's No Place Like Home makes perfectly clear, however, there's much to admire about the Sunflower State, including the tireless resolve of its many, many LGBT citizens and activists. A meticulous and thoroughly engrossing account of queer Kansans' fitful and often inspiring journeys through the maelstrom of the contemporary culture wars."

—**Colin R. Johnson**, author of Just Queer Folks:
Gender and Sexuality in Rural America

"A work of both meticulous research and heartfelt experience, No Place Like Home tells the story of the fight for justice for LGBT people, and does so with passion, insight, and wisdom. Using the Sunflower State as the bellwether for the country's long struggle for human rights, C. J. Janovy's book shows us that the moral arc of the universe is long—and it bends toward Kansas."

—**Jennifer Finney Boylan**, author of *She's Not There: A Life in Two Genders* and *Long Black Veil: A Novel*

"At heart, all politics are local. *No Place Like Home: Lessons in Activism from LGBT Kansas* is invaluable for insisting we understand that the battle for LGBT rights is vibrantly enacted and fought at the state and local levels, as well as nationally. C. J. Janovy has written a compelling, meticulously researched, and sweeping tapestry of heroic moments—small and large—as women and men stand up to their municipalities, friends, colleagues, and neighbors to do the right thing. *No Place Like Home* is a masterful account of how issues such as marriage equality, AIDS, discrimination, transphobia, and anti-LGBT violence shape the lives, politics, and actions of these brave everyday activists. This is a vital addition to the ever-growing body of literature on LGBT history."

—**Michael Bronski**, author of *A Queer History of the United States*

"If you read *What's the Matter with Kansas?* and thought that there must be more to the story, read C. J. Janovy's *No Place Like Home*, a moving tale of generations of LGBTQ Kansans brilliantly fighting conservative attempts to legalize discrimination. Janovy lovingly and vividly portrays quiet, determined advocates who contradict the stereotypes and stand as exemplars of American democracy."

—**Carol Mason**, author of *Oklahomo: Lessons in Unqueering America*

"This close-to-the-ground account of the battle for LGBT rights in twenty-first-century Kansas brings this recent history alive through the stories of ordinary people who bravely fought for justice against tremendous odds. As Janovy demonstrates, defeats transformed them into tireless activists who took risks, spoke out, found each other, built community, and changed Kansas. Their stories are inspiring."

—**John D'Emilio**, author of *Lost Prophet: The Life and Times of Bayard Rustin* and coauthor of *Intimate Matters: A History of Sexuality in America*

NO PLACE LIKE HOME

NO PLACE
LIKE HOME

LESSONS IN ACTIVISM
FROM LGBT KANSAS

C. J. JANOVY

UNIVERSITY PRESS OF KANSAS

323.3264
JAN

© 2018 by the University
Press of Kansas

All rights reserved

Published by the University
Press of Kansas (Lawrence,
Kansas 66045), which was
organized by the Kansas
Board of Regents and is
operated and funded by
Emporia State University,
Fort Hays State University,
Kansas State University,
Pittsburg State University,
the University of Kansas,
and Wichita State
University.

Library of Congress Cataloging-in-Publication Data
Names: Janovy, C. J., author.
Title: No place like home : lessons in activism from LGBT
    Kansas / C.J. Janovy.
Description: Lawrence, Kansas : University Press of Kansas,
    2018. | Includes bibliographical references and index.
Identifiers: LCCN 2017052558 | ISBN 9780700625284
    (cloth : alk. paper) | ISBN 9780700625291 (ebook)
Subjects: LCSH: Gay rights—Kansas. | Gays—Political
    activity—Kansas. | Sexual minorities—Political
    activity—Kansas. | Kansas—Politics and government—
    21st century.
Classification: LCC HQ76.8.U5 J36 2018 |
    DDC 323.3/26409781—dc23
LC record available at https://lccn.loc.gov/2017052558.

British Library Cataloguing-in-Publication Data is available.

Printed in the United States of America

10 9 8 7 6 5 4 3 2 1

For Matthew Shepard

CONTENTS

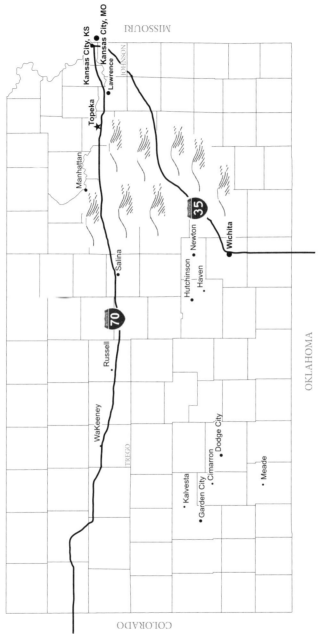

Major locations of people and events in *No Place Like Home: Lessons in Activism from LGBT Kansas. Credit: Emily Levine*

A STRANGE FEELING IN MIDDLE AMERICA

When I was a kid growing up in Nebraska, during summer and Christmas vacations my parents loaded us into a brown Ford Country Squire station wagon and pointed it due south toward Oklahoma City, where my grandparents lived. The trip was eight tedious hours, most of them on two-lane Highway 15 through Kansas.

I came to know the towns along the way only as time stamps on a long drive. Three hours in, Clay Center, the first real town, looked like a Norman Rockwell painting. Forty minutes later, when for a while the highway was also the main drag of Abilene, my dad would pull into an A&W Drive-In where a teenaged girl dressed in orange and black polyester and wearing a change belt delivered Papa Burgers, Mama Burgers, Baby Burgers, and root beer floats to the station wagon window. Back on the road we passed billboards advertising the Dwight D. Eisenhower Presidential Library and Museum and the Greyhound Hall of Fame, though we never spent precious daylight stopping to check them out. An hour and a half farther south, the highway joined Interstate 35 and we finally picked up speed, zooming around the vast edge of Wichita, where people lived in trailers with yards big enough for horses. From there it would be two more agonizing hours to my grandparents' house in Oklahoma City, but the air was starting to feel warmer, thicker, with the smell of iron-red dirt.

In those days Kansas was a place to get through, and if I was lucky I would sleep for most of it. This is not to say that the state was boring, just that no kid has patience for a long drive. But in those hours when I couldn't sleep, I'd be mesmerized by the passing landscape. It was not so different from Nebraska: farm fields on both sides of the road; rows of tall green corn in the summer and lines of stalk stubble poking up from the snow in the winter; sections marked by stands of cottonwood farther out, where I pictured creeks running; white frame houses where I imagined people like my grandparents lived—soft, gray-haired women who kept their candy dishes full and tanned, pipe-smoking men who drove pickup trucks and would take a girl pond fishing and give her sips from a cold Schlitz can. I'd read my obligatory *Little House on the Prairie*, which hadn't made that landscape sound like a place you'd want to live, but when I looked out at the wide-open horizon it was cowboys I thought about, their toughness and free spirits. Out here, a girl could go anywhere.

So I left. By the time I was eighteen my feelings about the Midwest were much less romantic, my feelings for women much more so. Like so many other gay kids from mid-America, I lit out for the promised land of San Francisco. A college degree later, I headed for the East Coast. Grad school seemed like a reasonable excuse to hang out in Boston, where I would also discover the gay vacation mecca of Cape Cod's Provincetown. But as soon as I got the credentials I aimed my little pickup truck—a '75 Ford Courier, mustard orange, holes in the floorboards—back toward the West Coast. I got halfway.

Stopping in Kansas City was a strategic decision: I had spent a lot of time in gay bars on both coasts and had grown friendly with some of the beer-drinking athletes who competed every year in the national Gay Softball World Series. There were teams from all over the country, and everyone said Kansas City had the prettiest girls. This turned out to be true enough, but it was the prairie, I remembered, that I'd always been in love with. Is it so inconceivable that a gay girl would give up the endless supply of lesbians and the utopian politics of the Bay Area for the straight, repressed Midwest, for no other reason than summers are supposed to be hot and humid? Home is a complicated thing.

I arrived in Kansas City in 1990 and began building a career as an alt-weekly journalist. As a reporter for and later editor of the *Pitch*—owned for part of that time by Village Voice Media—I worked for an organization dedicated to advocacy journalism, and my staff and I were intimately familiar with all manner of characters and dynamics, political as well as cultural, in a metropolitan area that sprawled across a state line: Missouri to the east and Kansas to the west.

It's never been an easy border. In their beginnings, Missouri was a slave state and Kansas was a free state. Civil War skirmishes in these parts remain legendary, and the region still fights variations of those battles. In the 1960s and 1970s, when black kids began to outnumber white kids in public schools in Kansas City, Missouri, the typical white flight wasn't just to suburbs but to suburbs in Kansas: being in another state allowed these citizens to distance themselves even further, psychologically and politically, from their metropolitan area's racial concerns. When the University of Kansas Jayhawks play the University of Missouri Tigers, local sportswriters call it a "border war." So do politicians when one of the states dangles tax breaks in an attempt to lure a big employer to the other side. All of which is to say: it's a great place for journalism, and one of the places where we did our best work, and had the most fun, was Topeka. The capital city of Kansas was stocked with legislative characters who enjoyed stoking turn-of-the-twentieth-century culture clashes.

We weren't the only ones watching, of course. Thomas Frank's *What's the Matter with Kansas?: How Conservatives Won the Heart of America* provided the nation with a prescient, bestselling crash course on how conservative politicians wielded social issues to convince people to vote against their own economic interests. As Frank entertainingly noted, the state wasn't always a stronghold for far-right conservatives. In the mid-to-late nineteenth century, he writes, the place "crawled with religious fanatics, crackpot demagogues, and alarming hybrids of the two, such as the murderous abolitionist John Brown, who is generally regarded as the state's patron saint, and the rabid prohibitionist Carry A. Nation, who expressed her distaste for liquor by smashing saloons with a hatchet."[1] Frank lifted his book's title from fabled Emporia, Kansas, newspaper editor William Allen White's 1896 essay of the same name, a screed against the state's populists who in those days were leftish. The widely circulated socialist newspaper *Appeal to Reason* was published in the small town of Girard, where Eugene Debs accepted the Socialist Party's nomination for president in 1908.

It's fun to imagine an alternate history in which Kansas remained the intellectual home of America's leftist activity. But the next Kansas-grown presidential candidate was the state's Dust Bowl governor, Alf Landon, a liberal Republican who had the misfortune of running against Franklin D. Roosevelt in 1936 and "gained lasting fame for his landslide defeat," according to his *New York Times* obituary.[2] Landon had won only eight electoral votes, from Maine and Vermont, losing even his home state. By this point, writes Kansas historian Craig Miner, "there were signs . . . that the rest of the country found Kansas and Kansans more humorous than profound."[3] Miner is talking about politicians, editorial writers, and real-life events, but we all know it was a South Dakota fiction writer who cemented the state's unending status as a joke, thanks to another Depression-era phenomenon.

L. Frank Baum published *The Wonderful Wizard of Oz* in 1900, but the movie came out in 1939 and to this day, "not in Kansas anymore" remains a punch line, one with particular relevance for LGBT people. Dorothy's journey from the boring black-and-white farm and its traditional family to the Technicolor big city, accompanied by weird companions initially considered defective but ultimately becoming heroic examples of self-acceptance, is less a metaphorical than a literal representation of the gay experience in the twentieth century. Almost as soon as the movie came out, "Are you a friend of Dorothy?" became a coded question to help gay men identify each other.[4] And gay men's well-documented love for Judy Garland deserves all due respect for its role in the Stonewall Riots, when patrons of the fabled bar, mourning Garland's death and in no mood to be harassed, decided they would no longer tolerate police raids. Certainly "Somewhere over the Rainbow" would be a contender for the gay national anthem if there were such a thing. But embracing the story requires being in denial about its ending. For countless LGBTs who left loving families seeking brighter futures among more diverse populations, "home" is likely fraught with unpleasant memories and other painful emotions.

That's certainly true for Sandra Stenzel, who grew up on a farm in rural Trego County, Kansas. In the mid-eighties, a career move took her to Austin, Texas, which felt like "the most wonderful place in the world."[5] When her father died and she inherited his land, Stenzel went back to the place she loved—only to find that her home was now a dangerous place. "The Oz crap," Stenzel said,

> haunts those who leave as well as those who stay. It makes it easy not only to trivialize the state as populated by a bunch of hicks—which it is—but it also trivializes and stereotypes the people who manage to escape and never look back. I always had to fight that image. Even as a seasoned professional, once people found out I was from Kansas, I was immediately pigeonholed.

It's not as if the state hasn't produced figures of great national esteem, including one president, Dwight D. Eisenhower, and another legitimate presidential candidate, Senator Bob Dole, both pillars of moderate Republicanism and neither particularly jokeworthy (except during Dole's brief role as a Viagra spokesman, which even he joked about[6]). In fact, lost to the state's reputation at the turn of the twenty-first century as a laboratory for far-right fiscal and social causes is the previous half century it spent being a model of moderation, governed as often by Democrats (two of them women) as it was by Republicans. It's a state that sent another moderate Republican, Nancy Landon Kassebaum (Alf Landon's daughter), to the US Senate for nearly twenty years.

Kassebaum left the Senate in 1997, the same year Sam Brownback arrived there, elected in a special election to fill Dole's old seat. Brownback had spent just two years in the US House of Representatives. In November 2015, Kassebaum, then eighty-three, told *Wichita Eagle* reporter Beccy Tanner that she "saw change coming, and not just in Kansas."[7] Kassebaum had returned to her family farm in Morris County after the death of her second husband, Senator Howard Baker. "If she were to run for office now, she said, she doubts whether she would make it out of the primary," Tanner wrote. Kassebaum blamed social media. Its users' fixation on finding statements that could be twisted out of context had turned campaigning into *Entertainment Tonight*, she said, adding, "That's why Donald Trump has caught on." Dole had made a similar observation a couple of years earlier, telling *Fox News Sunday* host Chris Wallace in 2013 that neither he nor Ronald Reagan would have "made it" in the current Republican Party.[8]

It's too soon to know, fully, how America's political evolution has been influenced by the Koch family, which may turn out to be the state's most significant contribution to global history. The family has grown exponentially more powerful and sophisticated than it was in 1980, when David Koch ran as the Libertarian Party's candidate for vice president (or in 1958, when patriarch Fred Koch helped found the John Birch Society, hosting local chapter meetings in his home). Amid the emerging body of journalism on this topic, two books serve as primers: Daniel Schulman's *Sons of Wichita: How the Koch Brothers Became America's Most Powerful and Private Dynasty*, from 2014, and Jane Mayer's *Dark Money: The Hidden History of the Billionaires behind the Rise of the Radical Right*, from 2016. Both books show how brothers Charles and David have, as Mayer puts it, "altered the nature of American democracy."[9]

Using Kansas as the rooster atop his national weathervane, Frank dates the Republican Party's extreme rightward swing to a series of events five years before Dole's unsuccessful 1996 campaign for president. "The push that started Kansas hurtling down the crevasse of reaction," Frank argues, "was provided by Operation Rescue, the national pro-life group famous for its aggressive tactics against abortion clinics."[10] One of those clinics was run by George Tiller (murdered by Scott Roeder in 2009) in Wichita. In what is now known as the 1991 "Summer of Mercy," tens of thousands of abortion opponents descended on the city for protests, arrests, and, most significantly, organizing. In Frank's account, the pro-lifers took over the state's Republican Party infrastructure, ultimately allowing conservatives to wage a class war disguised as a culture war.[11]

The Republican Party marched rightward, with abortion providers and LGBT people its primary targets. So it was no surprise in 2005 when 70 percent of Kansas voters passed a constitutional amendment banning gay marriage; that percentage was essentially the same as a similar vote in Missouri a year earlier. That it was predictable made it no less painful.

A few weeks after the Kansas vote, I headed to a family gathering in Oklahoma City. In adulthood I'd made my own drives south through Kansas dozens of times. From my home in Kansas City, the route to Oklahoma City was a couple of hours shorter and more diagonal than the straight line my parents had taken from Nebraska, and it was interstate the whole way. Instead of that two-lane highway through Clay Center and Abilene, I-35 took me through the starkly beautiful Flint Hills, that vast stretch of rolling tallgrass prairie, once the bottom of an ocean, now studded with cliffs of the limestone and shale that made it inhospitable for growing crops—and thus preserved the last remnant of what the Great Plains looked like before it became America. This landscape had always felt sacred.

Now it felt hostile.

Like tens of thousands of other gay Kansans—and hundreds of thousands of LGBT people in all of the states that banned same-sex marriage in those years—I was heartbroken.

Every once in a while, politicians here will reinforce their red-state worthiness by tossing out "San Francisco" as a synonym for "gay." The Kansas Secretary of State, a Republican named Kris Kobach (architect of controversial voter-fraud myths and anti-undocumented-immigrant laws around the country) did this in 2012: "If a person wants to live in a San Francisco lifestyle, they can go there," he told the *Kansas City Star*. "If they want to live a Kansas lifestyle, they can come here."[12] Whatever "a Kansas lifestyle" is, shouldn't LGBT citizens be allowed to live it just like straight people? Are we crazy for wanting to? *No Place Like Home* answers those questions.

Given Kansas's backwater reputation, readers outside the state, and maybe even inside it, might be surprised to learn that its proportion of LGBT people in the population is not dramatically different from bigger states with larger cities. The Williams Institute at the UCLA School of Law, a think tank that compiles extensive data on LBGT populations as part of its policy research, teamed up with Gallup in 2013 to survey adults across the country to estimate LGBT population percentages by state. They put Kansas at 3.7 percent, in the same league as Indiana, New Jersey, and New Hampshire; just above Ohio (3.6 percent); and just below Illinois, Michigan, and New York (3.8 percent). LGBT people make up a full 10 percent of the population in the District of Columbia; they are the most lonesome in North Dakota, at just 1.7 percent.[13] With Kansas's overall population of 2.9 million, this would put the state's LGBT population at 107,300.

A growing body of work is beginning to document, analyze, and contextualize the histories and contemporary lives of LGBT people far from the coastal big cities with which we have historically been associated. In the academy, a handful of scholars are liberating us from the idea that our movement could only have happened because of, or owes its progress solely to, the much-documented and discoursed twentieth-century concentration of gay populations and cultures in big cities. In *Another Country: Queer Anti-Urbanism*, Scott Herring sets out to chart, through analysis of various literary, artistic, and other cultural artifacts and phenomena, how "non-urban identified queers . . . have coped with, navigated, mourned, side-stepped, muddled through, menaced, and rearticulated the onslaught of queer urbanisms through the twentieth century." Kansas shows up in the fiction of Willa Cather, where Herring finds characters whose emotional choices signify "freedom from metronormative constraints."[14] The LGBT Kansans I came to know while researching for *No Place Like Home* were in general less "antiurban" than simply proud of their prairie or small-town homes—perhaps they're beneficiaries of a foundation laid by Herring's more aggressive antiurbanists, who, he concludes, "have been making every space—not always the metropolis—a Lesbian and Gay space."[15]

That's a point Carol Mason approaches from the opposite direction in *Oklahomo: Lessons in Unqueering America*, which contextualizes some notorious examples of homophobia in, and nationally known homophobes produced by, Kansas's neighbor to the south. Most intriguingly and entertainingly is Anita Bryant, whose "Save Our Children" campaign made a bizarre stop in Wichita in 1978. Mason comes to an admittedly "meandering conclusion" regarding economic and cultural forces that inspired Christian conservatives to adopt "an antigay identity . . . by decentering supposedly urban attitudes and glorifying white-washed small-town life," an identity that now purports to represent all of America—falsely, because, as Mason shows, "*country is always a little queer*."[16]

How Kansas's own most notorious homophobe and his extensive family assisted, if indirectly, in Mason's Christian "unqueering" of America gets close examination in *God Hates: Westboro Baptist Church, American Nationalism, and the Religious Right*. Rebecca Barrett-Fox spent extensive time inside the Westboro compound, learning the Phelps family's ways and even traveling across the country to their funeral pickets. She applies deep knowledge of religious history and doctrine to explain the far-reaching influence of Kansas's most notable cultural export. By employing tactics most observers found despicable, Westboro actually gave cover to a generation of religious leaders whose homophobia sounded acceptable compared to the Phelpses'. "The Religious Right has deployed multiple strategies to distance itself from Westboro Baptist Church," Barrett-Fox notes. "Its goal is to use the Westboro Baptist Church as a foil to construct itself as compassionate to gay people but critical of gay sex. In other words, by characterizing Westboro Baptists as 'haters,' the Religious Right can recalibrate the scale of homophobia so that its own homophobia is seen as moderate—as, indeed, compassion rather than hate."[17] Politicians, I would add, used the same tactics, and much of that homophobia is now codified in public policy.

Other pioneering scholarly work includes Mary L. Gray, Brian J. Gilley, and Colin R. Johnson's Queering the Countryside: New Frontiers in Rural Queer Studies (in which Lucas Crawford's essay, "Snorting the Powder of Life: Transgender Migration in the Land of Oz," finds Baum's The Marvelous Land of Oz [a sequel to Wizard] to be "a compelling tale of transgender and mobility, one that replaces Kansas-loving Dorothy with gender-crossing and soon-to-be rural-expat Tip")[18] and Johnson's Just Queer Folks: Gender and Sexuality in Rural America. Other studies mark our place by focusing on single states, such as Gray's Out in the Country: Youth, Media, and Queer Visibility in Rural America, which concentrates on Kentucky; Stewart Van Cleve's Land of 10,000 Loves: A History of Queer Minnesota; and, from Kansas's near-neighbor to the southeast, Brock Thompson's The Un-Natural State: Arkansas and the Queer South.

Kansas's neighbor to the northeast, Iowa, gets journalistic rather than scholarly coverage in Tom Witosky and Marc Hansen's Equal Before the Law: How Iowa Led Americans to Marriage Equality, an essential record—and reminder—of that midwestern state's crucial role in the long legal battle. When the Iowa Supreme Court legalized same-sex marriage in 2009, it became only the third state to do so, after Massachusetts and Connecticut, adding territory to an inconsistent legal landscape for LGBT citizens that would widen in the years ahead. Gary Martens and Larry Bunker of Salina, Kansas, experienced this firsthand when they celebrated their nineteenth anniversary in February 2013 with a trip to Des Moines to get married. Driving home after the wedding, Bunker remembered, "We hit the state line and realized, okay, we're not married anymore."[19]

Showing how the legal landscape ultimately evened out is Debbie Cenziper and Jim Obergefell's *Love Wins: The Lovers and Lawyers Who Fought the Landmark Case for Marriage Equality* (in which someone, presumably a Westboro member, makes an appearance as plaintiff Obergefell arrives for his climactic legal argument: "Protestors had already gathered in front of the Supreme Court when Jim tumbled out of his car in a new tan blazer and raced toward the building, past the young man whipping a Bible above his head, past the old man shouting 'God hates fags'"[20]). Obergefell's story is set in Ohio, where Cincinnati's antiabortion and anti-LGBT battles predated those that played out in Kansas, particularly when Cincinnatians passed an ordinance protecting gay people from discrimination in 1992, only to see it repealed by voters the next year.

It is perhaps appropriate that the full account of middle America's contribution to the nation's far-from-finished LGBT equality movement is arriving state by state, written by individuals who saw stories or fields of study and simply went to work presenting the material to their particular audiences, whether the writer was a journalist or a scholar—or a mother, as in the case of Judy Shepard, whose *The Meaning of Matthew: My Son's Murder in Laramie, and a World Transformed* was a bestseller in 2009. Though this approach has resulted in uneven intellectual terrain, some of it deeply mined by academics, some of it simply plowed by journalists—I'm clearly in the latter camp—our self-directed, localized efforts mirror the state-level work of activists, particularly here in the Midwest, where our legal and legislative battles are typically fought without help from the national LGBT organizations and our results are also uneven. Out here, the hard work of changing hearts and minds falls to individuals who carry it out family member to family member, neighbor to neighbor, coworker to coworker.

The ongoing need for documentation of this work is crucial. *The Gay Revolution: The Story of the Struggle*, by Lillian Faderman—one of our movement's preeminent historians—surveys the gay rights movement in America from the 1940s through the book's publication in 2015, providing an invaluable wide-angle view that, due to its scope, cannot focus too long or too narrowly on middle America. Nowhere is the need for *No Place Like Home* more obvious than at the end of Linda Hirshman's prematurely titled *Victory: The Triumphant Gay Revolution*, a 2012 primer on gay political history weighted toward the East and West Coasts. In her epilogue, while championing New York's legalization of gay marriage, Hirshman jokes: "Of course, New York is not Kansas, but the New York vote may be the turning point for this last, hardest-fought issue."[21]

Clearly, somebody needed to tell the story of Kansas.

This project began on June 26, 2013, a Wednesday. In Washington, DC, that morning, hundreds of people were waiting outside the Supreme Court Building when Justice Anthony Kennedy announced historic rulings in *United States v. Windsor* and *Hollingsworth v. Perry*. The first decision, named after its charming elderly lesbian widow plaintiff, Edie Windsor, had overturned the Defense of Marriage Act, giving equal treatment under federal law to same-sex couples who'd been married in the states where such marriages were legal. The *Perry* decision had overturned California's Proposition 8, a ban on same-sex marriage in that state. The crowd's jubilation was so loud it floated through marble: "A muffled cheer pierced the quiet in the Supreme Court chamber," Dana Milbank wrote in the *Washington Post*.[22] The euphoria rippled three thousand miles to the west, where it was 7 a.m. and people had been waiting in front of San Francisco's city hall, hallowed ground for the gay rights movement. Later, on Castro Street, music and dancing would go on all night.[23]

Here in Kansas City, it was different. After work that day, a couple hundred people gathered at a small park in front of the federal courthouse downtown. I saw a few people I'd known for years: The university professor, beloved by all of his students, with whom I had volunteered in the local chapter of the Gay and Lesbian Alliance Against Defamation in the nineties. The retired TV news producer with whom I had served on the contest committee for the Kansas City Press Club's annual Heart of America Journalism Awards. The comedy performer who had been part of the Kansas City Coalition against Censorship in the Tipper Gore days, now the host of a weekly music program on the community radio station. An ex-girlfriend who'd survived breast cancer.

But the fact that I didn't know more of the people around me was a consequence of my settled-down, middle-aged life with a partner of ten years. Clearly, many of the kids on the lawn that day had no experience of life before AIDS, or before the Supreme Court's *Bowers v. Hardwick* decision, which, as late as 1986, said it was constitutionally legal for the state of Georgia to arrest a man, in his own bedroom, for having consensual oral sex with another man. Back in 1987 and 1993 I had marched on Washington with hundreds of thousands of my gay brothers and sisters, and in those days gay marriage was not on the list of things we cared about.

As I listened to the speeches that day, the strangeness of the moment hit me: We were celebrating Supreme Court rulings that legally changed nothing for gays and lesbians here or in many other states—*Perry* applied only to California, and *Windsor* bestowed federal benefits to same-sex couples who were legally married, which could only happen in twenty-one states. None of us could have anticipated how quickly marriage equality would be legal everywhere; instead, I figured we were in for a long slog. And I wondered what had become of the Kansans who had fought the marriage amendment battle here a decade earlier.

Kansas had started its constitutional amendment push in 2004, but here the inevitable dragged out for two years. In the Kansas legislature, the two-session struggle to send an amendment to voters would be one of the last internecine battles between vanishing moderate and ascendant conservative Republicans. Prominent megachurches seized the antigay territory held by the Westboro Baptist Church. And gay people, blindsided, weren't in any kind of organizational shape to fight.

Those are the sad events I recount in the first section of this book. Titled "The Defeat," this section's three chapters visit distinctly different parts of the state, connecting key individuals who live with lasting consequences of their activism. In Topeka, Tiffany Muller found herself at the center of a battle against not only the Phelps family but the entire state legislature. In rural Trego County, having returned from Austin to her family's farm, Sandra Stenzel was one of the only openly gay people in the western part of the state; she spoke up against the amendment and lost her job. And in the liberal haven of Lawrence, Diane Silver and Bruce Ney clashed over strategy with Christopher Renner, an activist from the rival college town of Manhattan. Theirs was ultimately a futile battle to stop the Kansas legislature from finally sending the marriage amendment to a statewide ballot in April 2005.

But I knew that since the defeat, LGBT people had made quiet and sometimes surprising progress in Kansas. I suspected that Kansas was the perfect place to tell a story of America at a turning point. That story is, in one sense, a rejoinder to *What's the Matter with Kansas?* Frank depicted a political future, one that is still playing out nationally and might (or might not) have climaxed with the 2016 election of President Donald Trump. But Frank's argument left off in 2004. That is where *No Place Like Home* picks up, showing how LGBT activists have countered his portrayal of a ruined place. Here, well below the national media's radar (except for those occasions when news out of Kansas made for a good joke on *The Daily Show* or CNN needed to interview someone straight out of a central casting call for "politician from Kansas") and worlds away from the national gay rights organizations that threw big money behind high-profile legal battles, were a few disorganized and politically naïve citizens who, realizing they were unfairly under attack, rolled up their sleeves, went looking for fights, and ended up making friends in one of the country's most inhospitable states.

That story unfolds throughout subsequent sections. Part two, "The Dustoff," visits first the state's biggest city of Wichita and then its western high plains, where Dodge City is not a movie set but a real town and an unlikely place for LGBT advocacy. Connecting these two places are the activists who formed the Kansas Equality Coalition, a statewide LGBT rights organization (they later simplified the group's name to Equality Kansas, which is the term I use throughout the book for consistency and clarity). From his home base in Wichita, an introverted but newly enraged computer consultant named Tom Witt became a statewide political leader, cajoling a rural psychologist named Anne Mitchell and a transgender farm laborer named LuAnn Kahl, among others, to establish an outpost and raise LGBT visibility in the rural southwestern part of the state, earning allies in the process.

Part three, "The Comeback," profiles activists in Manhattan, Salina, and Hutchinson, showing LGBT citizens and their allies in those cities moving beyond the failed marriage issue to seek basic protections from discrimination in employment, housing, and public accommodations. In these efforts, from 2010 to 2012, hard-fought successes were inevitably followed by depressing reversals. Despite their exhaustion, however, activists began to see evidence that even when they lost at ballot boxes, they were winning in other ways. In Manhattan this included more transgender-friendly policies and the establishment of a full-time LGBT student resource center at Kansas State University, the state's land-grant university. In Salina it meant the city's first LGBT pride celebrations, where attendance exceeded expectations, solidifying the existence of a new and supportive community. And in Hutchinson it involved not only political challenges to Democratic Representative Jan Pauls, the longtime promoter of anti-LGBT state policies, but also the formation of a gay-straight alliance at Hutchinson High School. The final chapter of part three, titled "All Points Bulletins," follows the rapid events of 2014 and 2015 as ten years of activism by LGBT Kansans and their allies throughout the state began to pay off.

Their work moved the state in unexpected ways, as becomes clear in part four, "The Transformation," which profiles transgender activists who made headlines here years before Caitlyn Jenner's *Vanity Fair*– and Hollywood-chronicled transition in 2015. The experiences of women such as Sandra Meade in Kansas City and Stephanie Mott in Topeka, along with others elsewhere, suggest how the rest of the country will ultimately accept a gender-nonbinary future that it is only beginning to recognize.

Over three years of road trips around Kansas, on highways and stretches of interstate I'd never seen—not as a kid in the back of my parents' station wagon or as an adult driving up and down I-35 to family visits in Oklahoma—I came to know people with deep roots in Kansas who loved their state profoundly. Some of their experiences are newly documented every month in the *Liberty Press*, a glossy-covered newsprint magazine published for decades now by Kristi Parker in Wichita, its four thousand copies distributed throughout the state (sometimes, still, via regular mail in plain manila envelopes). The *Liberty Press* wasn't just an important source of information during my reporting; it had been a lifeline for some of the people I met.

Other key stories have become part of the historical record thanks to University of Kansas librarian Tami Albin's invaluable *Under the Rainbow: Oral Histories of Gay, Lesbian, Transgender, Intersex and Queer People in Kansas.* It is there, for example, that a man named Gilbert Baker recounts his childhood in Kansas. Born in Chanute in 1951, Baker remembers growing up "in a very sort of 1950s black and white way."[24] After a "horrible" time as a gay kid in high school, he went to college for a year, was drafted and served two years in Vietnam, then moved to San Francisco, where he would create the antithesis of that black-and-white childhood: Baker was the designer of the LGBT movement's iconic rainbow flag. "I'm just this guy from Kansas that had the stroke of luck to be the one to make the flag, and . . . sort of pulled the sword from a stone," Baker told Albin in June 2008, when he was in Lawrence briefly for a speaking engagement. By then he had settled in New York and was a man of the world. When Albin asked if he ever came back to Kansas, Baker said, "Never," then amended, guessing it had been twenty-five or thirty-five years since he'd been here. But even during this quick visit, he could see the place had changed. "When I lived here I was alone," he said. "Now there's a community, so that's wonderful."

No Place Like Home shows some of that community still under construction, while much of the state remains unfriendly. "Many young people, if they have the resources to get out of Kansas, they do," notes Equality Kansas's Tom Witt. "They don't stay in Wichita, Dodge City, or Hutchinson. They'll go to Denver, Chicago, or Houston."[25]

Here are the stories of some who have remained, staking their rightful claim to the Kansas lifestyle.

PART ONE

THE DEFEAT

Gay marriage started beeping faintly on the nation's political radar in the early 1990s, after three couples in Hawaii sued their state for marriage licenses and the Hawaii Supreme Court, in 1993, ruled that the state law limiting marriage to opposite-sex couples was unconstitutional. In 1998 voters in Hawaii and Alaska amended their constitutions to eliminate the threat. But in 2000 Vermont started allowing civil unions—all the rights of marriage without the vaunted brand name. And in 2004 Massachusetts unsettled the rest of the country by allowing full-on same-sex marriage.

Despite these gains, marriage equality had not been the LGBT movement's number-one priority. We had spent more than twenty years fighting for our lives and dignity since the beginning of the AIDS epidemic, and in general were more focused on protecting ourselves from discrimination in employment, housing, and public accommodations. It was not until 2003, after all, that the US Supreme Court's *Lawrence v. Texas* decision made it legal for us to have sex in the privacy of our own bedrooms. And as opposition to gay marriage became a rallying cause for the Republican Party's base, it was obvious we were going to get bludgeoned with it.

(Which is one reason I went on record, in a November 2004 *Pitch* column, as saying, "Gay marriage is the dumbest idea I've ever heard."[1]) Democrats were clearly going to be of no help. Since LGBT people had become a recognizable voting bloc in the post-Stonewall, post–Harvey Milk days, Democrats had always counted on us, seeking the endorsements of gay Democratic clubs, cashing our campaign checks, and giving speeches at our pride festivals. We had helped elect Bill Clinton on his promise to end the military's ban on gay service members, only to feel the burn of betrayal when he compromised with "Don't Ask, Don't Tell" and, in 1996, signed the Defense of Marriage Act. Heading into the November 2004 elections, George W. Bush was all for amending the US Constitution to ban gay marriage while John Kerry, in typically flaccid Democratic form, said he opposed same-sex marriage but didn't think the country needed to go so far as a constitutional amendment.[2]

Missouri was still considered a swing state, so Republicans pushed for a statewide constitutional amendment to go on the November ballot, where a big turnout of anti-gay-marriage voters could help Republicans straight up the ticket to Bush. Missouri's attorney general was a Democrat, Jay Nixon (he would be elected governor in 2008), whose job that summer was to get the marriage amendment onto the ballot in August, when it wouldn't harm Kerry (that was a lost cause; Missouri went for Bush by 53 percent to Kerry's 46). "If people are in favor of banning gay marriages, we ought to get to the task of doing it," Nixon argued in May 2004. "People are walking down the front steps of churches and city halls in Massachusetts because Massachusetts did not have a constitutional amendment banning gay marriages."[3] The Missouri Supreme Court sided with Nixon, and gay marriage went to voters in August.

Their vehemence surprised everyone. "After an overwhelming vote to ban gay marriage in Missouri on Tuesday," the *Washington Post* reported, "an issue that has gained little traction in Congress appears to be resonating with the American people and could play a growing role in this year's congressional and presidential elections."[4] The turnout was stunning. "In state records kept since 1980, there had never been comparable participation in an August primary," the *New York Times* reported. "Nearly 1.5 million people voted, a fact that Vicky Hartzler, spokeswoman for the

Coalition to Protect Marriage in Missouri, attributed to grassroots efforts, including notes in church bulletins, neighbors holding up signs along busy thoroughfares and preachers talking to their congregations."[5] (Hartzler would go on to become a US congresswoman, defeating long-term moderate Democrat Ike Skelton in the Tea Party rebellion of 2010.)

Supporters of the amendment to ban gay marriage had spent just $19,000. Opponents, including national gay rights organizations: $450,000. "Even though we were outspent and we had a national political machine descend on our state to try and defeat this," Hartzler told the *Times*, "people got out and worked and called neighbors and said a lot of prayers."

Four months later, while they were reelecting George W. Bush, voters in eleven more states—Arkansas, Georgia, Kentucky, Michigan, Mississippi, Montana, North Dakota, Ohio, Oklahoma, Oregon, and Utah—passed constitutional amendments banning same-sex marriage. In Kansas, however, even though the fight had started at the same time as Missouri's, it dragged on for two years. Ground zero was Topeka, a city that had made one proud contribution to the nation's civil rights history but had also incubated one especially ignominious brand of antigay activity—all of which made the challenge for activists uniquely toxic.

I

On a forlorn block a mile south of the Kansas State Capitol, across the street from a scraggly lawn and an empty white-rock parking lot, sits the former Monroe Elementary School. Opened in 1927, its two stories built of sturdy brick and limestone, it closed in the 1970s and is now a national historic site, officially memorializing the US Supreme Court's decision to desegregate the nation's schools. *Brown v. Board of Education* consolidated five lawsuits from around the country—besides Kansas, they originated in Delaware, South Carolina, Virginia, and Washington, DC—but Topeka carries the legacy of its name, for plaintiff Oliver Leon Brown and twelve mothers whose children attended the city's segregated schools.

I paid a respectful visit on a hot summer Saturday. A middle-aged white couple walked in just behind me, and we were greeted by an overeager National Park Service volunteer. "Do you know about *Brown v. the Board of Education?*" The question struck us as odd. Why else would we be there? It's sad, but I wasn't surprised to learn that the historic old school doesn't get many visitors. "It's a hidden gem," said the volunteer. "Not too many people find us."

Michelle Obama found the place in May 2014, when she came to town to give a speech for the Topeka School District's high school graduation events. White House photographer Chuck Kennedy took a picture of the First Lady in the entryway where I stood. In the image, which was either perfectly staged or poignantly captured, Obama listens intently to Stephanie Kyriazis, the site's head of interpretation and education. Hanging from the ceiling above Kyriazis, a stark sign reads "White." Above the First Lady: "Colored."[1] Anticipating the sixtieth anniversary of the Brown decision, school district leaders and National Park Service staffers had contacted the White House with invitations to speak. They had a connection: Kristen Jarvis, the grandniece of Brown's first plaintiff Lucinda Todd, worked for Obama in a role the First Lady described as her "right-hand woman in the White House."[2]

On Senior Recognition Day at the Topeka Expo Center, Obama challenged eight hundred graduating high schoolers to continue the Brown legacy. "For so many years, you all have studied together in the same classrooms, you've played on the same teams, attended the same parties—hope you behaved yourselves at those parties," she said. The most important parts of their education, Obama told them, had come not just from their classes but from their classmates. "And ultimately, that was the hope and dream of Brown. That's why we're celebrating here tonight, because the fact is that your experience here in Topeka would have been unimaginable back in 1954, when Brown v. Board of Education first went to the Supreme Court."

Topeka likes to think its place in history is secured by its role in the lawsuit that desegregated America's schools. But at the end of the Brown century, the national legacy of Kansas's capital city seemed more destined to belong to another family whose cause also went to the US Supreme Court.

In a working-class neighborhood three miles west of Monroe Elementary School, the Westboro Baptist Church's white stucco and timber-frame styling might look vaguely Bavarian but for the banner stretched across the front that reads, in three-foot letters, "GODHATESFAGS.COM." Established by the notorious Fred Phelps and consisting mainly of his children and grandchildren, Westboro claims a few dozen of Topeka's 125,000 citizens. Near the church entrance, a display case sign warns that "FAG MARRIAGE DOOMS NATIONS" while another banner explains: "Sodom gave itself to fornication & homosexuality & is an example, suffering the vengeance of eternal fire. Jude 7." Surrounding the front lawn is a tall wooden fence. Black-and-orange signs, the type sold at hardware stores, notify passerby that the area is monitored by security cameras, warning them not to trespass.

Across the street is a small ranch home now known as Equality House, where a man named Aaron Jackson runs a nonprofit called Planting Peace. Jackson earned national media attention in March 2013 when he painted the home in rainbow colors and announced an antibullying campaign. Equality House soon became a destination for anti-Phelps pilgrims fond of sharing pictures of themselves in front of the colorful backdrop. And in June 2016, Jackson's organization painted the adjacent house, which is also part of its property, in the light blue, pink, and white stripes that now represent the transgender movement.

Except for these garishly competing street corners, the neighborhood of World War II–vintage homes is unremarkable and quiet, still solid but looking as if it's seen better days, much like the rest of Topeka. The Phelps compound is within walking distance of Gage Park, which is home to a zoo, a mini-train and carousel, an elaborate water park, a theater, a rose garden, a science center for kids, and more than a hundred acres of green space. This was where Fred Phelps's obsession with gay men first went public.

Westboro's pickets, in which the cultish family members, some of them young children, carry neon-painted signs reading "God Hates Fags," "USA = Fag Nation," and "Pray for More Dead Soldiers," would eventually gain worldwide derision. But before the Phelpses picketed the funerals of countless men who'd died of AIDS; before they picketed the funeral of Bill Clinton's mother in 1994; before they picketed the funeral of murdered Wyoming college student Matthew Shepard in 1998; before they determined they would get more of the attention they craved by picketing the funerals of soldiers who had died in Iraq and Afghanistan, leading state legislatures and ultimately Congress to pass laws limiting the areas in which a few dozen Kansans could carry disgusting signs; before Westboro challenged those laws all the way to the US Supreme Court, which in March 2011 deemed such pickets to be constitutionally protected free speech; before December 2012, when the church announced its plans (eventually nixed) to picket the funerals of children killed at Sandy Hook

Elementary School, prompting more than 367,000 people to sign a petition at the White House's "We the People" website calling for Westboro to be designated a hate group;[3] before Fred Phelps's lengthy obituary in the March 20, 2014, *New York Times* described him as "a much-loathed figure at the fringe of the American religious scene"[4]—before all of that was a siege of Topeka that Phelps called the "Great Gage Park Decency Drive."

It started in 1991, when Phelps homed in on gay men who were cruising Gage Park. "It wasn't hard to pick out who the gay people were," remembered Pedro Irigonegaray, a well-known civil rights attorney.[5] Irigonegaray said Phelps would go to the park, watch, and then advertise the names of men he saw. Kansas had (and still has, though it's technically unenforceable) a sodomy law that criminalized gay sex, so, Irigonegaray said, "The police became involved, and consequently many individuals were horribly hurt."

Irigonegaray has watched the Phelps family for decades. His mother, a pharmacist, fled Cuba when Irigonegaray was a boy; she found a job at a state-run residential home for developmentally disabled adults in Topeka and settled her family there in the 1960s. As a teenager, Irigonegaray would open the door to knocks from Phelps family kids selling candy, a Westboro source of income in the late sixties and early seventies. "These kids were often out in miserable weather conditions," he remembered.

Irigonegaray went on to law school at Washburn University, a small public college that has anchored the neighborhood two miles south of the Kansas statehouse since the days of the Civil War. The law school's most infamous alumnus: Fred Phelps, who graduated in 1964 and proceeded to humiliate the profession. After Phelps was disbarred in 1979, he turned his attention to Gage Park. Irigonegaray was friends with one of the men Phelps targeted. "He killed himself because he could not imagine living with the stigma that Fred Phelps was going to create for him," Irigonegaray said.

Irigonegaray earned a reputation as the state's most prominent civil rights attorney. That's not a particularly large cohort, but Irigonegaray embraced the challenge. He represented Planned Parenthood in its years-long battle against the state's antiabortion-crusading attorney general, Phill Kline; he was one of the attorneys for George Tiller; and, in a role that earned him national headlines, Irigonegaray defended evolution (yes, he defended a scientific concept) in 2005 hearings involving the state's public school science standards. His work on LGBT issues began with a gay friend at Washburn and, Irigonegaray said, continued "in what has been a forty-two-year experience."

After a decade of the Phelpses' pickets at Gage Park's high-traffic entrance, Irigonegaray and a few civic leaders decided to try to do something about the local embarrassment. Co-leading their group, which called itself Concerned Citizens of Topeka, was psychiatrist Roy Menninger, whose father had been one of the founders of the Menninger Clinic, a famous psychiatry school and mental health treatment center that for nearly eighty years was one of Topeka's most-esteemed institutions (it moved to Houston in 2003).

In July 2002 Irigonegaray wrote an ordinance prohibiting discrimination based on sexual orientation and gender identity, adding those categories to existing municipal codes preventing discrimination based on race, religion, disability, gender, and other statuses. Along with the proposed ordinance, Topeka's mayor and city council members received a package of letters from local businessmen. "Topeka has remained silent too long. We must speak out against the hate which has tarnished the image of our city," wrote Harry Craig, the head of Martin Tractor Company, a dealership that had been in Topeka since 1928.[6] Echoing Craig's sentiments were others including John Fish, publisher of the *Topeka Capital-Journal*, and John McKelvey, president and CEO of the Menninger Foundation. "Failing to oppose hate is to endorse it," they argued.[7] Looking back on his effort to get citywide LGBT protections passed, Irigonegaray said, "We had a hell of a team."

"I kind of liked Topeka," said Tiffany Muller, who had arrived in December 1999.[8] Small and smart, Muller had always considered herself a troublemaker, to the extent that was possible growing up in Amoret, Missouri, a town an hour and a half south of Kansas City, with fewer than two hundred people. Muller also had a record of getting things done, having graduated from high school a year early. She began to wonder whether she might be gay during the spring of her junior year, after a woman made a pass at her. When Muller rejected her advance, the woman said she had assumed Muller was gay. At first Muller couldn't understand why anyone would have thought that—yet she was intrigued. She began to remember how she had sneaked out of her childhood bedroom at naptime to watch Susan Lucci on *All My Children*. She realized that her first crush had been on the high school cheerleader who had been her kindergarten babysitter. Now she understood that the close feelings she had had for some of her high school friends were probably more like what those girls felt for their boyfriends.

After she headed for Central Missouri State University in Warrensburg, Muller decided she needed to have a conversation with her stepmother, who, relieved that Muller wasn't quitting school and wasn't pregnant, said she had figured Muller was gay since she had met her at fourteen. Muller's father supported his daughter despite his initial discomfort; he was a little sad, she said, because he figured he would never have grandkids. Muller did quit school, for a while, taking a break from Central Missouri and heading to Lawrence, Kansas, where she went to work for the local domestic violence shelter. There, she said, "I met a lot of other amazing lesbian women doing feminist activist women's movement work."

She also met a woman named Erin Norris, and the two began dating. Muller had decided it was time to finish her degree and enrolled at Washburn, and she had a job at a women's alcohol and drug treatment center in Topeka, while Norris was working in Kansas City.[9] In October 1999 the two were married in a ceremony—it could only be ceremonial, after all—involving 150 friends and family members at a former barbecue joint that had been converted to a banquet hall in suburban Kansas City. (Years later, after Massachusetts legalized same-sex marriage, they would make it official.)

At Washburn, Muller majored in human services, studying with a professor named Rick Ellis. He remembers Muller as one of his better students. "Being able to grasp the responsibility to a larger cause—I've never had anybody grasp that as quickly as Tiffany," he said.[10] Most importantly, though, Muller was skilled at bringing in allies. "She was a really high-quality leader. But never a glory hound."

For her honors project, Muller helped conduct a major survey of discrimination in the city. She, Ellis, and other students sent questionnaires to thousands of Topekans and convened focus groups in each of the nine city council districts. The conversations were surprising. "People not only wanted to talk about LGBT discrimination but also the fact that they were still feeling discriminated against as African Americans and Hispanics," Ellis said. "It was really clear there was still a problem with discrimination across the board in this city." (He would publish the research in a July 2006 *Journal of Black Studies* paper titled "Debunking the Myth That All Is Well in the Home of *Brown v. Topeka Board of Education*.") Race and gender, however, were already covered under Topeka's human relations ordinance.

Muller's survey fueled Concerned Citizens' push to add LGBT protections to city statutes. After Irigonegaray proposed the ordinance, the city council agreed to consider it—and set a vote for just a few weeks later. Muller and a handful of others scrambled to recruit people to call council members, write letters of support, and show up for the hearing as average citizens to reinforce the business leaders' argument.

Also showing up were ministers unaffiliated with Westboro. "Roy Menninger and I were called names that to this day I find obscene," Irigonegaray said. "Telling us we would burn in hell—I'm an atheist so to me that doesn't mean a thing, but to hear the hateful way in which these people spoke, to hear the anger in their voice when all we were talking about was equality was quite an amazing experience."

Council members voted down the ordinance, 5–4. Menninger, Irigonegaray, Muller, and others met in a Washburn classroom to debrief. "We lost, but we didn't feel like we'd completely lost," Muller said. The group decided they would lobby the council to reintroduce the ordinance and then work to generate more public support. They also knew they would need to influence the next city election, which was coming up in 2003. Brainstorming on a blackboard, they decided to call themselves the Equal Justice Coalition. As Muller remembered it, "Roy Menninger looked around the room and said, 'Tiffany's going to lead this.' I'd gone into the meeting figuring I'd be a helper, but that's how I became director."

Norris would serve on the group's board of directors, along with some of Topeka's gay business owners who vacationed on New York's Fire Island, where they had met some leaders of the National Gay and Lesbian

Task Force. They sent Muller to a week of activist training with the task force, and the task force sent organizers to Topeka. Strategy in hand, members of the new Equal Justice Coalition started going door to door to register voters and made endorsements in every council race. Their candidates lost, but they had built an organization. There was, however, another problem. "We weren't paying any attention to the Kansas legislature," Muller said.

With its majestic Greek architecture and copper dome, the Kansas State Capitol might be the most distinctive feature of Topeka's skyline, if a handful of blocky beige office buildings could be called a skyline. Muller and the other members of the Equal Justice Coalition weren't thinking about the 40 senators and 125 representatives who arrive from points all across the state for a few acrimonious months at the beginning of each year. The anti-gay-marriage amendment of 2004 had passed out of a committee and arrived on the House floor for a vote before LGBT activists had even met to figure out how to respond. "We were totally taken off guard," Muller said. "I think most of the country was."

The Equal Justice Coalition had already been working with a few other groups—primarily a small nonprofit called the Kansas Unity and Pride Alliance, and Parents and Friends of Lesbians and Gays (PFLAG)—trying to lay the educational groundwork that would someday result in more protections from discrimination in Topeka. The Kansas Unity and Pride Alliance had a small budget it could put toward a lobbyist at the capitol, so Muller signed on for the job. She started showing up at the statehouse as soon as its doors opened in the morning and staying until sundown.

In between meetings with legislators, Muller began to find allies. Supporters fed her information during furtive exchanges in the marble hallways. "Lobbyists who wouldn't publicly oppose the amendment would come up to me and say, 'I just talked to so-and-so, you need to go talk to them'—and we'd secure a vote." Though Governor Kathleen Sebelius was publicly quiet, Muller started getting covert advice from members of her administration. "The one thing I was good at," she said, "was building connections and relationships."

Muller felt respected even by those who disagreed with her. "In Kansas, there is an appreciation for hard work, and I think that helped. And most of my interactions were very genuine." How could they not be? Muller was lobbying for a cause that couldn't have been more personal. "This was my life. Me, my friends. I felt great responsibility to carry the message for all of those who wouldn't be there day in and day out and whose voices needed to be heard."

The marriage ban passed easily in the conservative-controlled House, but something surprising happened in the senate, which was still held by moderate Republicans. In March, on the day the senate was scheduled to vote on whether to put the amendment up for statewide election, a Republican named David Adkins, who represented the wealthy Kansas City suburb of Leawood, started talking. In the beginning, his remarks went over the Lincoln-Douglas debates, going into some detail about the legislative concept of popular sovereignty and, Adkins noted, its immoral argument that the will of the people justified slavery.[11] He then considered whether the same concept justified banning gay marriage.

"I realize that the whims of popularity are in favor of discriminating against homosexuals, just as they are in junior highs and high schools all across this state and this country," Adkins said. "If you're an effeminate man, you're called a fag. The bullies pick on you mercilessly. Far too many of our young people who are bullied in such a way find suicide as their only way out. Others grow up with the permanent scars of that discrimination. Some, like Matthew Shepard, find themselves taken out, tied to a fence and left for dead." He talked about the Kansas legislature's fondness for defending property rights, its desire in cases of eminent domain "to protect the few from the many, the weak from the rich. And yet, when it comes to those who are by nature homosexual it seems to be a free pass for us to say, 'You're different, the rights and benefits that this government confers on to some class of citizens aren't available to you.'"

Adkins said what no other Republican—or Democrat—had the courage to say.

If you're asking me if I support gay marriage, yes I do. Because homosexual marriage does not threaten my marriage, my life, my wedding vows, and I don't know why we would believe that it threatens yours or anybody else's. But we are engaged in a culture war in this country, and we are polarized more than we've ever been polarized, with the exception perhaps of the Civil War. And that polarity is fueled by a politics that is ugly, that is driven by fear, and driven by hate. And we can either stand up to the bully, and say, "Not in Kansas, not in a place with a tradition of populism and acceptance, and a prairie mentality that said if you came here and carved your future out of this prairie, it was yours." Well, too many of us, because of our fear of popular sovereignty—of not being returned to this body—are simply not willing to stand in the door and say, "Not today, bully." We somehow all believe that being back here next year is more important than doing the right thing.

Adkins went on like this for hours. Occasionally he proposed amendments in a parliamentary tactic—LGBT advocates would later remember it as "magic"—that ultimately allowed his fellow senators to vote on the bill without having their names recorded. Some of his proposals involved weakening the bill so that it would be sent back to committee and redebated; more brazenly, he also proposed that divorce be made illegal. Adkins won the day. Instead of putting the issue on the ballot, senators sent it back to the House in drastically altered form, with language suggesting that gays might be allowed to have civil unions.

Far-right Republicans were furious. Senator Susan Wagle, a Republican from Wichita, called it "an absolutely shameful day" in the senate.[12] Larry Salmans of Hanston, a town with 211 people in the state's southwestern no-man's land, read from the Bible. Though there was no record of how each senator voted, Salmans said, "I can guarantee you, it is recorded"— in Heaven, he implied—"and someday we'll be held accountable."[13]

Conservatives won the next battle. After negotiators from the House and senate met to reconcile the proposed amendment's language, it would ban marriages, civil unions, and other legal benefits for same-sex couples. The final bill went back to the House, where putting a constitutional amendment up for a statewide vote required a two-thirds majority approval.

While all of that was happening, Muller's core group of ten or twenty people had grown to hundreds, including more moderate Republicans in elected office and in the business community. They saw an opportunity to change the minds of a few House Republicans who had been in favor of the gay marriage ban a couple of months earlier. One of her confidants told Muller she should go visit John Ballou, who represented the conservative Kansas City suburbs. "I thought, I don't need to go see him—he's as right-wing as they get." But she went anyway. "He's this whiskey-drinkin', gun-totin', flannel-wearin' redneck. He points to the Constitution and says, 'Show me where we have amended this to deny someone rights.' I said, 'Sir, I can't do that.' He says, 'Damn it, I thought you'd say that.'"

All these years later, Ballou told me, "I've tried to figure it all out and I still can't, but when you look at the Federalist Papers and read about the Constitution, everything you read about is granting people rights. It doesn't take away rights from one people or another. You can't do that. It's not to be used to discriminate against one group or another."[14]

"We started looking at who we needed to flip," Muller said. "There were eight or nine moderate Republicans and one or two Democrats." Muller and Ballou met with everyone on the list. "He would talk with them, and I'd put grassroots pressure on them," she remembered. "I promised them there were people who would walk for them and knock on doors and do whatever they could to help them win reelection. I had no idea if I could back that up. We did, but when I was making those promises I had no idea. We flipped the votes that we needed."

"What really switched the votes," Ballou said, "is we would say, 'Look at Fred Phelps and the Phelps family.' When you started talking about him and what they do, people were like, 'I can't be associated with someone like him.'"

When it came time for the final vote, ten House members—some Republicans and some Democrats—who had voted yes in March voted no in May. A constitutional amendment to ban gay marriage would not go to Kansas voters. "We were one of the very few states in the country to defeat it that year," Muller said. "We were the only state that just outright killed it in the legislature that year."

The House members who had changed their minds over the course of the spring knew they had put targets on their backs. "This will be a very unpopular vote in my district," said Bill Kassebaum, from the unincorporated community of Burdick.[15] He told the Associated Press he had changed his vote "because he sensed that too much emotion—and even hatred—marked the public debate over the amendment." Another Republican, Ray Cox of the Kansas City suburb of Bonner Springs, said his earlier vote in favor of the amendment had "nagged at him."[16] Cox said he couldn't help but think about the Westboro Baptist Church: "I had voted to put Fred Phelps and his 'God Hates Fags' placard in the constitution." After his "no" vote, Cox said, "I am completely at ease with the situation."

Absolutely not at ease with the situation were three megachurch ministers who had been steering the ban-gay-marriage bandwagon for months. Jerry Johnston, who ministered to three thousand members of First Family Church in the sprawling Kansas City suburb of Overland Park, along with Terry Fox of the six-thousand-member Immanuel Baptist Church and Joe Wright of the eight-thousand-member Central Christian Church, both in Wichita, promised they would spend the next two months registering a hundred thousand new voters, mustering God's army to unseat recalcitrant Republicans in the August primary.[17]

That summer, 150 ministers from around the state gathered at Johnston's church. On an oversized video screen, he projected mug shots of Kansas legislators with their voting records on abortion and the gay marriage ban. Theoretically, such politicizing should have put First Family Church's tax-exempt status at risk. But Johnston and his followers had the state's highest law enforcer on their side—up at the podium was Kansas Attorney General Phill Kline. "We have a culture going the wrong direction in the silence of the church," Kline told the assembly. "We need you to rise up."[18] A few weeks later Kline hosted his own seminar with Kansas US Attorney Eric Melgren, where about a hundred people, many of them ministers, learned how nonprofits could legally participate in politics.[19] (Kline's behavior as attorney general was so egregious that the Kansas Supreme Court would eventually strip him of his law license.

Conspicuously absent from the ministers organizing get-out-the-vote efforts over the summer of 2004: Fred Phelps. Thanks to Phelps, ministers like Johnston, Fox, and Wright could masquerade as mainstream—as long as they weren't carrying signs that said "God Hates Fags." Johnston said watching the legislature defeat the marriage amendment bill had awakened him. "I don't want this to be perceived as an arrogant statement," he said, but, "I really believe God is raising me up to help marshal the clergy."[20]

In August, Ballou, Kassebaum, and two other Republican incumbents lost their primary challenges. Four politicians losing their seats might not sound like many, but it would be enough. In January 2005, having made their point, the ministers would be rewarded with swift and decisive action as soon as the legislature convened for its new session: it took less than a month for the Kansas House of Representatives to send the question to a statewide vote to be held on April 5, 2005.

Tiffany Muller still remembers the day one of the papers ran a front-page picture of her crying. It was after the marriage amendment bill made it out of a committee, perhaps in the senate, and Muller felt crushed that day. It wasn't her picture in the paper that bothered her most, however. It was that Joe Wright and Terry Fox had been standing nearby and had seen her cry. "I could not grant them that satisfaction and, more importantly, let people think we were defeated," she said. "It was showing a weakness I didn't want people to see."

Muller had never been in this type of spotlight, and the feeling was surreal. "I'd always been an emotional activist. I suddenly realized I had this huge responsibility to carry, to be the face and voice that somebody could be proud of. It was an incredible amount of pressure." Muller had just turned twenty-six. Today she calls that front-page photo one of the defining moments of her life. Her picture would soon show up in other papers, including the *New York Times*.

While Muller's supporters in the state legislature were losing their seats in the primary purge, a member of the Topeka City Council resigned, creating an open seat in the Ninth District—the district where Muller lived. The council would choose a replacement, and the member who was leaving suggested that Muller put in her name for consideration. Muller and her fellow activists laughed at the idea that the council might choose her. "But I thought, 'Sure, I'll apply. Just to show that LGBTs have a voice and want to be taken seriously.'" Applicants would have a public interview in front of the council, whose members would then vote on candidates until someone secured five of the council's eight votes. Muller had a few friends on the council who said they would vote for her; another said he would vote for her if she made it to the third elimination round.

"I was assuming it never would happen," Muller said, "but I went door to door in the district, talked to people, asked what their concerns were." The public interview went well, and on the day of the council vote, it only took two rounds before Muller won the seat. "I was in shock," she said. Her new colleagues handed her some bulky binders. "They said, 'Here's the budget, all these plans. You have a work session on Tuesdays before the meeting. You're going to be on this committee. See you next week.'" Suddenly Muller was the only openly gay public official in Kansas. Her district included the Westboro compound.

The Phelpses picketed the council chambers every week. "Someone told me I had the record for the number of signs they had that used my name," Muller said. The family serenaded her with their alternative versions of songs like "America the Beautiful," one of which was "Oh Wicked Land of Sodomites," as she entered the building; a fellow council member always accompanied her.

The *Topeka Capital-Journal*'s editorial page weighed in with a cautious endorsement of Muller's ascension. "Tiffany Muller—Yes, but Wait," the headline read.[21] "The first reaction of a lot of Topekans to the appointment of Tiffany Muller to the Topeka City Council was, 'They appointed a lesbian!' It was an unusual and surprising move, but it's easy to make more of that than it deserves," the editorial read. The paper allowed that Muller had "showed during the interview process she is up to the job, in more ways than one" and was "not a single-issue person." Muller's intention to reintroduce the nondiscrimination ordinance, "but not right away," was good, the editorial said. "Not because it isn't an issue that needs to be addressed, but because it would create great divisiveness and controversy at a time when we need some calmer waters to address some other important issues." The city was changing from a strong-mayor to a city-manager form of government, and mayoral and council elections were coming up in the spring. Besides, the editorial said, Muller needed time to learn "a lot of little technical matters" at city hall. "Things like the difference between a revenue bond and general obligation bond, the workings of the long-range capital improvements plan, etc."

The *Capital-Journal* needn't have worried. "My favorite part of it was the dorky stuff: infrastructure, funding, zoning plans, how we were going to help Topeka reinvigorate downtown development," Muller said. But she also knew the council now had the five votes it needed to pass the ordinance. "I don't know if it was the smartest thing in the world, but we went ahead and introduced an expanded ordinance that would have protected people from discrimination in housing, public accommodations, and employment, based on sexual orientation and gender identity."

By then, Topeka's Equal Justice Coalition had been up and running for two years, and had a full-time executive director. The coalition's members and volunteers had raised money, made endorsements, and walked door to door for twenty-seven candidates—most of them Republicans running for the state House or senate—and had won 83 percent of those races, Muller said. With around sixty people willing to canvass neighborhoods, she said, "It was a pretty massive operation." The group collected thousands of letters of support from voters and lined up one hundred people to speak at the hearing. That night, hundreds of people marched from the capitol to a rally at city hall, where they stood out front cheering and singing civil rights songs. Inside, seventy people would testify before the night was over.

The first twenty speakers were mostly from Westboro. Steve Drain, one of the church's only members not related to the Phelpses by blood or marriage, was led away from the podium by police after Mayor James McClinton cut him off for violating the rules of testimony.[22] Phelpsian sentiments weren't limited to Westboro speakers. "The Rev. Stan Johnson used the term 'sodomites' to describe homosexuals, while acknowledging others often are uncomfortable with that term," the *Capital-Journal* reported. "Johnson echoed the comments of others who said homosexual behavior is morally wrong, then took that one step further by saying homosexual behavior is unwelcome in Topeka."[23]

During a break in the testimony, another council member pulled Muller aside with bad news: one of their colleagues was waffling. Muller thought his support had been solid—she and others had helped him get elected. Now the only way he would support the ordinance was if they removed the parts that applied to private employers. Then another council member made a motion to strip out gender identity, so the ordinance would only cover sexual orientation. "I do not know how I sat there and managed to project a face of being somewhat calm," Muller said. Rather than vote against the stripped-down ordinance, she decided to vote for the incremental progress and keep fighting later. "The vote was really, really painful. There were lots of people who thought I sold out, that I shouldn't have taken whatever win we could get at that point, that I should have walked away and made a big public statement. That was probably when I began experiencing both sides of being a leader."

Muller was also experiencing life in the Phelpses' neighborhood. She loved Gage Park. "It was one of my favorite places in the city, and I'd always wanted to live there," she said. Muller and Norris had bought a Kansas-meets-Cape-Cod-style, one-and-a-half-story house with sage-green siding on Anderson Terrace half a block from the park—and five blocks from the Westboro compound. "I don't think it dawned on me and Erin how close it was to them," Muller said. Seeing the Phelpses at predictable protests or at city hall was different from shopping at the same supermarket. Buying groceries turned grotesquely awkward as Phelps family members followed her through the frozen food section of Dillon's, yelling at her about going to hell.

Soon it was time for Muller to decide whether to actually run for the seat to which she had been appointed. There would be a primary in March before the general election in April. Looking back, she confesses: "I didn't want to run. I felt like I had given it a good go, but it was a lot of pressure and by that point I couldn't go out of my house without being screamed at." But Muller felt as if she owed it to the LGBT community. "It was basically out of a sense of that it wasn't about me, but about a bigger message."

That message got even bigger the second week in January, when the legislature reconvened for its 2005 session and immediately reintroduced the anti-gay-marriage amendment. Muller, still the primary lobbyist for the Kansas Unity and Pride Alliance, would soon be reliving the battle from the previous year's legislative session, only without key allies since those four moderate Republicans had lost their primaries.

Once again in a Washburn classroom, a handful of people from around the state met to organize a campaign to fight the amendment. Meanwhile, in Topeka, the Phelpses had been busy collecting enough signatures to force a citywide vote on whether to repeal the watered-down nondiscrimination ordinance that Muller and her fellow city council members had just passed.

Muller was facing a brutal four months. Her city council primary was in March; on that same ballot would be the Phelps-led question of whether to repeal the Topeka nondiscrimination ordinance. If she made it past that primary, her name would be on the April 5 ballot for city council—the same ballot as the statewide marriage amendment. Then came a layer of absurdity: a twenty-year-old nursing student—Jael Phelps, granddaughter of Fred—filed to run for Muller's city council seat. "It became this powder keg," Muller said.

"The [race] has become as much as anything a debate over Mr. Phelps, whose incessant daily pickets and hate-filled faxes have plagued Topeka for fourteen years, yet whose opposition to the antidiscrimination ordinance is shared by many residents of this church-laden, Republican-leaning city of 125,000," observed the *New York Times*.[24]

> The Phelpses' tactics have turned some evangelical ministers and conservative businessmen into unlikely crusaders for gay rights, backing measures like the antidiscrimination ordinance, if only as an antidote to the family's message. And with an amendment to the State Constitution to ban same-sex marriage on the ballot in April, many other religious and civic leaders are trying mightily to stop the Phelpses from hijacking what they see as a signature issue.

Muller's father, who was on the city council in his small town of Cleveland, Missouri, brought her stepmother and joined Muller for a day of door-to-door campaigning. Because father and daughter had city council service in common, Muller said, "he thought it would be so neat." But he was canvassing in a town where citizens had spent decades steeping in the Phelpses' toxins. "People would yell at him and scream at him: 'She's going to hell! How could you raise her to be like that? Get the hell off my porch! You're going to hell!' Other times people would say, 'Come in, you're our hero, I baked you lemon bars.'"

Tiffany Muller, on a radio program with Jael Phelps in the background, as they were pictured in the New York Times on March 1, 2005. Credit: Kenneth Dickerman/New York Times/ Redux

One night a neighbor who had asked Muller for a yard sign several weeks earlier showed up at her house. "She had a bloody lip and her face was messed up—you could tell she was going to have a black eye. I was like, 'Oh my god, come in, what happened?'" The woman told Muller she had left her house to go to the store, and some people nearby said, "Why do you have that fuckin' dyke's sign in your yard? Are you a dyke?" The woman said, "Yeah, so what?"—Muller had no idea her neighbor was gay—and they followed her to the store and beat her up in the parking lot. Horrified, Muller was preparing to call the police and take her neighbor to the hospital, but that wasn't why the woman had knocked on her door. "She says, 'No, no, no, don't call the police. They stole my yard sign and I want another yard sign.'"

Muller made it through the primary, finishing second—just like every other incumbent. She would move on to face Richard Harmon in April (Jael Phelps secured 203 out of 4,177 total votes cast for the district's four candidates). Most important for Muller, however, was that Topekans had rejected, with 53 percent of the vote, the Phelps-led effort to repeal the city's newly passed antidiscrimination ordinance. Muller enjoyed that night's party while she could. The chances of winning her council seat looked slim, and everyone knew they would lose on the marriage amendment.

In April, as she watched those inevitable election results at the Ramada Inn, Muller took some consolation in the fact that although all of the incumbents lost, she had received more votes and a higher percentage than the others. "I had a lot of support, amazing support," she said. In her concession speech, Muller emphasized how she had been humbled by all of that support, and how the marriage amendment had mobilized the community. "One of my reporter friends walked in about halfway through, and afterward he said congratulations—listening to the speech, he thought I had won," Muller said. "But I was like, 'No, I lost.'" Muller remembered that her speech was "optimistic and full of hope, but I still have no idea what I said." The next day, "it was back to being Joe Schmoe citizen."

Muller got jobs with the Sebelius reelection campaign and with the Kansas Democratic Party. But emotional shrapnel remained in her system. "I worked a ton, did a lot of Equal Justice Coalition stuff, and not much else. I didn't hang out with friends any more, didn't go out in town. I remember Erin saying, 'This is crazy. You need to go out.'"

"You don't understand," Muller would tell her. "Every time I go out I have to answer these questions. People say, 'You're that girl.'"

One night after a couple of years, Norris convinced her enough time had passed. "So we go out in March 2007 to a friend's going-away party. And we're at a restaurant, and the waiter says, 'You look really familiar— oh wait, you're that girl, you were on city council.' In the middle of dinner. Two years later."

Muller had thrown herself onto the front lines of a political fight at a cost only the most dedicated activists understand. "Those years were the most intense, all-encompassing, wonderful-awful years of my life. I was doing so much gay work it defined who I was. Every moment was about this fight, whether we were going to be treated with dignity and respect. We just wanted to create a place where we could live our lives and be in peace. It just didn't make for the healthiest life."

Muller and Norris left Kansas for Florida, where Muller got a job at a polling firm and worked on gubernatorial, senatorial, and congressional races all over the country. But her marriage to Norris would not last. Eventually Muller moved to Washington, DC, and started her own firm. A decade after her work against the gay marriage amendment in Kansas, Muller would be serving as chief of staff for a US congressman. "I wanted to know if my life could be more than just gay rights," she said. "I easily proved that."

By the time he died in March 2014, Fred Phelps hadn't been the face of his church for years. Some said he had actually rallied the nation in favor of gay rights. But Topekans would still be struggling to prove that Westboro didn't speak for all of them. Evidence of progress came in small steps. The school board added sexual orientation and gender identity to its antidiscrimination and harassment policies for students and staff in 2011. In 2013 the city council voted to include sexual orientation and gender identity in the Human Relations Commission's educational programs intended to prevent discrimination. And in 2014, the city approved a same-sex domestic partner registry and added gender identity to the watered-down city employment protections Muller had secured a decade earlier.

Veterans of the marriage amendment battle in Kansas still remember Muller. She was a "force of nature," said Sandra Stenzel, from rural Trego County in the western part of the state. "I would have marched into hell and back for, and with, Tiffany."[25] For Stenzel, that's exactly what happened.

2

Sandra Stenzel's grandfather homesteaded five hundred acres of scrubby flatland, planting his family in a patch of raw Trego County dirt in 1915. Volga Germans who knew their priorities, they built the granary and the barn first. Only after the barn was finished did they build the two-bedroom house where two generations of Stenzels would grow up.

Working the land meant also working the weather. Wheat was ready for harvest in June and done by the Fourth of July unless it was a late year. The Stenzels spent the rest of the summer doing heavy field work, plowing, discing, and undercutting from the dark of morning to the dark of night, until the wheat planting began again in September. Later in the fall they would harvest livestock feed and milo. Then in the winter they would bring cattle in from the pastures, feed them, and make sure their water didn't freeze each day, delivering their calves in February, sometimes in the middle of the night during a blizzard, because that's when cows seemed to love giving birth. While waiting for the spring thaw, they would fix fences so those cattle could get back out to pasture by mid-April, then plant the corn, milo, and feed for the fall harvest.

Stenzel and her family lived a mile from their nearest neighbor, ten miles from the nearest paved road, twenty miles from the nearest town. Her first community was the handful of kids who went to the one-room South Downer

Creek schoolhouse. She would hunt and fish on Downer Creek, and in the evenings she and her father, August, would ride horses out to the pastures. Their task was to make sure all of the cattle were accounted for, but really it was their time for talking. Sandra, an only child, idolized her father.

On Saturdays the family drove to WaKeeney, an agricultural town of about 2,800 people. Downtown was a two-block stretch lined by storefronts, its wide Main Street paved with red bricks. The Stenzels' first stop was Rudy's Produce, where they unloaded wooden crates of twelve dozen eggs each and sold their cream, likely destined for a distant milk or cheese processing plant. Cash now in hand, they moved on to the Dietz brothers' or Hinshaw's grocery store to stock up on whatever they needed for the week ahead. Sandra trailed her father to her favorite destination, the hardware store, where Mike Dreiling earned her lifelong affection by greeting the two of them with: "Here comes August—and Little August!" After dropping her nickel in a red-and-chrome dispenser in return for peanuts, she would stand mesmerized in front of the display of pocketknives, knowing they weren't for little girls but wanting one anyway. Instead of knives, she and August would leave with ropes for her 4-H steers. As she got older, Sandra came to think of local business owners as extended family, giving kids jobs, making donations to school fundraisers, celebrating Trego Eagle victories, keeping the local news flowing.

The summer between her junior and senior years of high school, some friends invited her and a guy named Gene along on a double date to the drive-in with the requisite case of iced-down beer. The two continued seeing each other even after they graduated, when Gene went to the vocational-technical school and Stenzel went to Fort Hays State University, thirty miles east of WaKeeney in Hays.

Stenzel was smart and articulate and carried a strong sense of justice. She had learned leadership and citizenship skills early on through the rural youth development activities in 4-H, and by the time she moved into her dorm room at Fort Hays State she had also logged miles going to high school debate tournaments. Intending to go to law school, she started out majoring in political science, but after she got elected student body president and repeatedly lost arguments in student senate meetings because she didn't understand budgets, she switched her major to finance. Once she understood it, it turned out she had a talent for it.

Living on the same floor of her dorm was a girl from Russell. Stenzel had known her from debate tournaments, and about halfway through their freshman year, the girl went to a feminist conference in Wichita. "She came back roaring excited because she'd met a bunch of lesbians," Stenzel remembered. "She couldn't wait to tell me. She said, 'This is what I am too!' I was listening, thinking, 'Fuck, that's what I am too.' It was the first time I had the realization, but I didn't tell anyone."

Stenzel was already engaged to Gene, and like so many gays and lesbians of her generation who did what they thought they were supposed to do, she got married. It was 1976, and they were both twenty. Not surprisingly, it wasn't a particularly happy union, despite the weekends when everyone in the county seemed to end up at the Stenzel farm for raucous keg-and-weed-fueled parties that turned into sleepovers—a hippie version of the older tradition in which country families entertained themselves by "visiting" each other on Saturday nights.

Stenzel's community was expanding in other ways. In the spring of 1979, a woman named Vera Metcalf was running for mayor of WaKeeney. "I really liked her, and being a major feminist I was like, 'I gotta help this woman.' She didn't really know how to run a campaign, so I coached her through that and she won by a landslide." Stenzel's work caught the attention of some older friends who were mainstays of the Trego County Democratic Party. "They said, 'We need young blood in the party—why don't you come help us out?' I'm thinking, 'Cool!' I was willing and honored, as only someone young and dumb could be." She ended up chairing the county organization, making sure the central committee had a vice chair, treasurer, secretary, and a man and a woman representing each precinct; hosting booths at the county fair and fundraising dinners; and running advertising on behalf of the Democratic ticket in county races.

Stenzel guesses that when she was chair, Democrats still made up 60 percent of Trego County's voters, thanks to its population of European immigrants historically loyal to the party. But things were clearly changing. A turning point was the 1974 race in which a Democratic congressman named Bill Roy challenged Bob Dole for his Senate seat and almost won. *Roe v. Wade* was fresh, and the Roy-Dole race was, Stenzel said, "the first time I remember somebody [Dole] using the antichoice hammer. Bill Roy would have won that race if he had not been a physician who had performed perfectly legal abortions. We lost the Volga German Catholics at that point—they started leaving the Democratic Party." President Carter's embargo on wheat to the Soviet Union, which (along with the boycott of the Moscow Olympics) was meant to punish the USSR for invading Afghanistan, didn't help the Democrats' cause in rural America either. "Also during the Carter administration, interest rates went to 18 and 21 percent on farm loans," Stenzel remembered. "When those loans had started out at 10 percent, it doesn't take a finance major to figure there would be bankruptcies. That was last straw for the Democratic Party in rural America."

By Ronald Reagan's second term, Stenzel was divorced. She had graduated and started working, first at a bank, then as an accountant at an agricultural manufacturing plant, then as a writer at the local newspaper, and finally helping with economic development at the regional planning commission, trying to bring businesses to the back half of Kansas. "One day the boss walked in and threw a brochure on my desk. It was the middle of the military buildup during the Reagan recession, and the Department of Defense had allocated several million dollars for economic development organizations to help small businesses sell their goods and services to the federal government," she explained. Stenzel made a trip to one of these "procurement assistance centers" in Beaumont, Texas, to learn more about how to set them up. "While I was there, the director announced she was leaving and they offered me the job."

Stenzel said she was perfectly happy living as a single woman in western Kansas, but she recognized the opportunity of a lifetime and took it. In Beaumont, her agency secured more than $20 million in federal, state, and municipal contracts for five hundred small-business clients. Soon she was flying all over the country teaching small business owners how they, too, could get government contracts. That led her to a job in Austin, where she circulated among powerful women highly placed in Texas state government—many of whom lived together, she would finally learn, after she figured out the subterfuge of two separate phone lines running to the same house. And after one particularly debaucherous weekend with a married woman in San Antonio, Stenzel was officially a lesbian. She was thirty-two. "Austin is a great place to come out," Stenzel said. "However, it can give you a skewed perspective on how the rest of the world is."

Stenzel had a big career, and Austin was heaven. But back home on Downer Creek, August Stenzel had died and Freda Stenzel was getting older. Having just finished a major consulting project, Sandra felt the pull of home. "You can take the girl off the farm, but you can't take the farm out of the girl. I'd always dreamed of coming back and living on the farm. There was never going to be a good time, so I just picked a time."

It was April 2001. She had been gone for sixteen years. "When I left in 1985, I thought Kansas was a pretty wonderful place where people were judged on what they did," she said. "You weren't judged so much by skin color, and sexual orientation wasn't even an issue." But now Kansas was a very different place. Throughout the 1990s state politics had taken a hard right turn. A moderate Republican named Bill Graves was governor, but the state's march toward theocracy was gaining momentum. Still, Stenzel made no secret of her sexual orientation. She had left a girlfriend in Austin who occasionally came to visit. "Everybody in town knew," she said, "and nobody seemed to mind."

She hadn't been home long when a job as director of Economic Development, an office operated jointly by Trego County and the City of WaKeeney, opened up. Stenzel landed the position. But clearly, she was not going to fit in with Trego County's esteemed civic leaders. The mayor of WaKeeney had a reputation for drinking and unlocking women from jail and taking them on afternoon drives in the country to fulfill their "community service." (In 2006 he would plead guilty to giving alcohol to a work-release prisoner under his supervision.[1]) In 2003 the Kansas Bureau of Investigation busted County Sheriff Curtis Bender for conspiring to distribute cocaine; the next year Bender would be convicted on federal drug trafficking and gun charges.[2] In 2006 another former county sheriff, James Ryan Bloom, would be convicted of raping and taking indecent liberties with a twelve-year-old girl.[3] Several years later, the school board president, John Alan Reeder, would plead guilty to marijuana distribution and methamphetamine possession.[4]

As far as Stenzel was concerned, the man who actually ran things in Trego County was David J. Harding, a lawyer who was simultaneously the attorney for the City of WaKeeney and for Trego County. The Kansas Supreme Court would eventually suspend Harding's law license temporarily and censure him for violating the Kansas Rules of Professional Conduct.[5] Among other things, Harding had a habit of disclosing privileged attorney-client information in letters to the editor of WaKeeney's newspaper, the *Western Kansas World*. The Kansas Supreme Court determined that Harding had knowingly violated his duties, acted on anger and selfish motives, engaged in a pattern of misconduct, and caused injury to a client, which in this case was the City of WaKeeney. The Supreme Court judges considered suspending Harding's law license for good, but took mercy because Harding, who had been practicing law for thirty-two years, had no other record of disciplinary problems and enjoyed "the respect of his peers," as evidenced by the letters they sent to the court in support of him.

What got Harding censured was a feud with the City of WaKeeney that started when a city councilwoman accused him of improperly accepting city contributions to the state's pension fund for public employees. In response, Harding accused the city councilwoman, the mayor, and the police chief of racking up extra charges on their city-issued cell phones; he also accused the police chief of using a city dump truck to deliver a $60 load of rock to his home. Petty investigations and pettier counterinvestigations ensued, many of them summarized in the Kansas Supreme Court's disciplinary decision. But that window into the level of civility with which WaKeeney conducted its politics would not open until 2010—nine years after Sandra Stenzel found herself in the middle of it, trying to be a professional director of economic development.

"I thought I could really help these people," Stenzel said, especially since the office had seemed sleepy at best, known primarily for putting on the annual parade and, with the Chamber of Commerce, the Christmas tree-lighting ceremony. Thinking that the people who had hired her actually wanted her to accomplish something, Stenzel got to work.

"She came in with experience, enthusiasm, ability, ideas, connections—it was quite a contrast to what we'd ever experienced in the community," remembered Jon Schmitt, who owned the funeral home and served as president of the Economic Development board of directors.[6] Stenzel secured a grant for streetscaping that would transform the industrial entrance to downtown, with its grain elevator and railroad tracks, into a park with sidewalks and native grasses. And instead of the unsightly lot where the public works department parked its heavy equipment, visitors coming into town now saw an attractive limestone wall adorned with "Welcome to WaKeeney."

But she had more than cosmetic changes in mind. Stenzel knew that if businesses were going to come to the city, workers would need places to live. WaKeeney was a pleasant-looking town with good housing stock, but many of the people who lived in those houses were elderly. Stenzel commissioned a study that confirmed what she already suspected: WaKeeney needed housing for senior citizens—twenty-four units, to be precise. So she got a $3.3 million grant to build it, which would free up homes for the influx of workers that she anticipated filling the new jobs she would create. By 2004, Stenzel said, Trego County led the eighteen-county region of northwest Kansas in population growth, though she was quick to put the accomplishment in perspective: "We added ten new people and nobody else did."

In retrospect, she shouldn't have been surprised when things began to grow tense with WaKeeney's movers and shakers. Stenzel said that Harding made a paperwork mistake that nearly cost her office the grant for the senior housing project; at a city council meeting, she said Harding hadn't done his due diligence. Soon, WaKeeney city council members began complaining in public meetings about Stenzel's supposedly foul language. "A couple of them were saying her language was terrible and she shouldn't be representing us," remembered Dave Schneider, general manager of Western Electric Cooperative, another member of the Economic Development board of directors.[7] "But the gal who was criticizing Sandra had said the F-word in city council!"

Stenzel figures she became a target because she was "not appropriately deferential." Stenzel, Schmitt, and Schneider said her agency's results had begun to embarrass the WaKeeney establishment. "They could have been having a lot more success all along," Stenzel said. "All of a sudden here comes this person, and we started having all that success. That didn't sit well with the good old boy network."

But there was something else about the hostilities, which began to intensify as soon as word got around WaKeeney about Stenzel's off-duty activities. When she had come back home from Austin, Stenzel had resumed her activities with the Trego County Democrats. Now she was chairing the county chapter and had a seat on the state Democratic Committee. There was an LGBT caucus, so naturally Stenzel joined—just in time for the marriage amendment.

"There were about five of us who regularly attended the LGBT caucus meetings," she remembered. Just before the party's annual Washington Days convention in Topeka, Stenzel said, "I got this phone call and they said, 'Hey, we got trouble. There was a vote held today in the House about this proposed constitutional amendment to ban gay marriage, and a Democrat of all people, Jan Pauls from Hutchinson, led the fight. The Democratic people in the House didn't even bother to tell us.'" One of the other members of the caucus said he'd been sitting in the office of the House minority leader, who hadn't said anything about it. "We got this list from Sebelius's office of Democrats who'd voted in favor, and we were supposed to give them a pass," Stenzel said. "It was a bunch of freshmen from conservative districts. We did not understand. We were hot and the Democratic Party was sheepish but unapologetic. It was as if they were patting us on the head saying, 'We know you're mad, but you'll get over it and surely you understand, we had no choice.'"

Thanks to her time in Austin, Stenzel believed it didn't have to be that way. "I remember thinking these were the most disempowered people I had ever met," she said of the LGBT caucus. "I thought, 'What's wrong with these people?' The caucus's strategy just seemed to be, 'Maybe if we're really quiet and ask for a few things we'll get 'em.' That wasn't my style at all."

But the problem was bigger than the caucus. The party she had worked for her whole life had abandoned her. The most forceful thing Sebelius said publicly about the amendment was: "I'd like folks to concentrate on issues that we really need to deal with. I think this has been adequately dealt with."[8]

It seemed as if a few Republicans in the House and senate were the only ones who had the guts to oppose the amendment. And gay people willing to stand up against it were scarce, so when Stenzel heard that a woman named Tiffany Muller was trying to find people to testify, she decided she should head to Topeka. "Since I was about the only person in the western half of the state who was out," Stenzel said, not really exaggerating, "I felt it was important for me to testify. The legislature needed to hear this wasn't something that only applied to Johnson County and Wichita—that it was truly a statewide issue."

Smart enough not to mix politics and work, Stenzel had been careful to take vacation time and pay her own expenses when she went to the capital city. "I went to testify in full business drag. Suit, silk shirt, briefcase, the whole thing." Stenzel arrived at the hearing room first, and was sitting there waiting when Muller walked in. "Tiffany and I had never met in person. She thought I looked like a good Jesus-y woman testifying for the other side, so she didn't speak with me." It wasn't until another member of the LGBT caucus arrived and introduced them that Stenzel and Muller realized they were there for the same reason.

Stenzel was not there to testify on behalf of the Trego County Economic Development office. But when she stepped to the microphone, she made an economic development argument.

I talked to them about Fortune 500 companies, how many of them offered domestic partner benefits. I reminded them that recruiting a talented workforce in Kansas is not always the easiest thing in the world to do. Would the highly valued employees of these Fortune 500 companies want to move to Kansas? It was insane to try to recruit people and businesses here while saying the entire population is not welcome. I closed by saying, "As director of Economic Development it's my job to bring people to western Kansas. Don't make my job any harder than it already is."

It was a powerful statement. She and her fellow amendment fighters thought they had made a valiant effort. "We shook hands, slapped backs, had drinks, and went home."

When she woke up the next morning, Stenzel had made headlines all across the state. The Associated Press called Stenzel's testimony "a new argument."[9] "I don't know what the hell I was thinking," Stenzel said. "I thought I could slink down there and testify and nobody would notice."

Soon the WaKeeney City Council summoned the Economic Development board of directors to a meeting. "They wanted to talk about whether we'd authorized Sandra to go to Topeka to testify," said Jon Schmitt. He said one councilman told him, "I don't think a lesbian should be representing Economic Development in Trego County." The city council didn't have the authority to fire her, so they tried to talk Stenzel's board members into doing it. "They told us if we didn't fire her, they would zero out our budget," Schmitt said.

When Stenzel's board refused to fire her, the city council called a public meeting in August to discuss eliminating the Economic Development budget. There, they were overwhelmed by a show of support for Stenzel. "WaKeeney City Council members were outnumbered by a 20:1 ratio Tuesday night as more than 100 people crammed into every nook and cranny of the group's meeting room—and even more stood outside the city building," reported the *Hays Daily News*.[10] The council had allotted thirty minutes for comments, but the meeting stretched on for two hours. Jerry Millard, the editor of the *Western Kansas World*, "read letter after letter from state and area officials who have worked with Stenzel and support her."[11]

Stymied by the unexpected results, the council convened another meeting. This one would be a joint meeting of the WaKeeney City Council, the Trego County Commission, and the Economic Development board. They reserved the biggest room in WaKeeney: the aluminum-sided Commercial Building at the county fairgrounds. Once again, the hall was packed with Stenzel supporters.

One group of women had grown so disgusted by the condescending behavior of their elected officials that they formed the Trego Women's Alliance, fifty or so women of all ages and classes and political persuasions, whose presence at meetings seemed to infuriate politicians who were used to conducting business out of public view. "We dogged them. We went to every city council, hospital board, fair board, you name it. We sat at meetings and took minutes, and they'd shoot daggers at us," said

Gwen Schmitt, laughing at the memory of one woman bringing a tape recorder.[12]

Ignoring the obvious opinion of citizens, the city council met again and voted to eliminate funding for Economic Development. The response? "Residents cried foul and threatened a recall," reported the *Hays Daily News*.[13] In addition to Stenzel supporters who had shown up to previous meetings, the paper reported, "some new faces approached the microphone too, including a woman who questioned if the city council members even listened to what their constituents were saying. 'Does our showing up and caring mean nothing to you people?'"

Council members had erased the city's half of Economic Development's budget—a grand total of $27,500. But county commissioners decided they would find a way to fund the office anyway. They proposed a countywide sales tax, which voters passed overwhelmingly. "We decided we weren't going to take it lying down," Stenzel said. "Small towns are like sharks—they're either moving forward or backwards, but if you stand still you're going to die. We were doing too much work to have it halted by bigotry or jealousy or whatever human emotion."

But the fight got harder after elections in November, when two new members decidedly less supportive of Stenzel won seats on the Trego County Commission. And as 2004 headed toward 2005, Stenzel, along with Muller and the handful of activists who had fought the anti-gay-marriage amendment all year, braced for another round when the legislature reconvened in January. Stenzel knew her fellow Democrats would be no help. "We just all did the best we could but we were screwed walking in the door. We were fighting the legislature, fighting the Sebelius administration, fighting the religious organizations. Just this small group of people."

She was also fighting for her career. In February 2005 the Trego County Commission voted to disband Economic Development. As of March 1, Stenzel was out of her job. Her supporters made one last stand, at a town hall meeting convened by *Western Kansas World* editor Millard. Once again, the Commercial Building at the fairgrounds was packed with 150 people who showed up and angrily signed petitions to change the structure of the Trego County Commission. It was a loud but futile effort. The new commissioners went on with their plans.[14] "I had so much grassroots support. For every dollar they spent on my office I returned twenty-four dollars to the community. But I could not fight the bigotry with the elected officials and neither could anybody else," Stenzel said.

Two weeks later, the *Hays Daily News* ran a front-page story headlined "Sexual Politics?" It questioned Stenzel's claim that she had been fired because she is a lesbian. "That's absolutely not true," said one county commissioner. "That topic has never been discussed in any open meeting or closed meeting of this board. A person's sexual orientation is not our business." The chair of the county commission told the paper he was "shocked" by the suggestion that Stenzel's firing was due to her sexual orientation. Commissioners knew she was gay, but the subject, he said, "was never brought up. Never ever."[15]

Stenzel knew it didn't have to be brought up. Given the success of Economic Development, the city council's hostility toward the office made no logical sense. "I'm a country boy. I can tell there's something starting to smell in the barn," said former board president Schmitt. "It had nothing to do with Sandra's professionalism. It was all personal attacks. They couldn't differentiate. They couldn't see the talent and what she'd brought to the community. They had an agenda, and they couldn't see what it cost the community." He paused. "There are things in the world that just aren't right, and what they did just wasn't right."

Harding denied that Stenzel's trouble had anything to do with her testimony at the legislature, and had no comment on whether she ended up on his wrong side as director of Economic Development. "There's no point in me discussing any of that at all," he said. "It would be confidential. I'm not interested."[16]

"Sandra was sharp, smarter than any of them," said former board member Dave Schneider. "That was intimidating to a lot of them, which bothered them. Plus the gay thing." When I spoke to them, Schneider and his wife, Sandy, were sitting in a sunny nook off the kitchen in their newly built house in Hays, where they moved after Dave retired as general manager of the utility company. With its twenty thousand people, Hays felt to the Schneiders like a whole different world. "People are just much nicer, friendly," said Sandy. "People visit."[17]

"Even the megamillionaire who donates to the college will talk to you," Dave marveled. "In WaKeeney, it was just jealousy," Sandy said. "It's just a sad town." Decorating the coffee table in front of the Schneiders, making a loud and clear statement, was an enormous Bible.

The Schneiders both knew Stenzel was gay. "I knew who she was, but I didn't really know her until I worked with her on Economic Development," Dave said. "I knew her parents better." Both families lived on farmland south of WaKeeney, and Stenzel's parents were customers of Schneider's utility company. "I didn't think it was any big deal," he said of Stenzel's sexual orientation. "They just used it against her on Economic Development."

"I knew, but as long as she didn't push it off on anybody, it didn't bother me," said Sandy. "She was just so smart. People said she was promoting gay rights in Trego, but the only thing I ever heard Sandra promote was her town."

Even if the subject of Stenzel's sexual orientation wasn't part of official meeting agendas, it was clearly a topic of conversation in WaKeeney. "One lady in the community was circulating a flier at the school saying 'watch your girls,'" said Dave. "It was totally uncalled for." Sandy remembered an argument with one of the men who worked in the grocery store. "It was after one of the town meetings. I was at the meat counter and we started talking. I said, 'I can't believe those guys are being so nasty.' He said, 'My religion doesn't teach that.' I said, 'Well, that's yours.'" Ten years later, Sandy said she had recently found out the man's son is gay. "He's a nice kid, but you can just tell," she said, suggesting but unwilling to say outright that there is something stereotypical about the son's mannerisms. The one thing she would say: "He had a male friend who died. He's buried out at the VA cemetery, and the son is out there all the time."

"WaKeeney could be so much better now if they would have stayed out of it and let Sandra do her thing," Dave said. "They ruined a life there," added Sandy. "Why? What did they get out of it?"

After the county commission shuttered her agency, Stenzel hunkered down on her farm, stunned and humiliated. She stopped going into WaKeeney for groceries, instead driving forty miles south to Ness City because she didn't want to see anyone from Trego County. She quit the

Democratic Party. Her mother died in 2006 at the Lutheran nursing home, and Sandra is grateful that Freda Stenzel spent her final years not particularly aware that her daughter was in the news.

Figuring no one would hire her, Stenzel went to work on her lifelong dream of being a farmer. "I planted an acre garden. I got a bunch of chickens, went to four or five farmers' markets a week and sold produce, chickens, and eggs privately. I was able to support myself doing that. I had cattle. But I have to say, being fifty years old and fixing fences is not the romantic thing I had envisioned."

The farm needed more maintenance than she could keep up with. Eventually, Stenzel rented out her land to a farmer with a much larger operation who would grow his own wheat and milo and run cattle on her five hundred acres, while she stayed in the two-bedroom house built by her grandparents a hundred years ago. It needs siding, the paint long ago blasted away by Kansas wind and rain, its wooden boards now the color of pencil lead. But the home is solid and warm and clean inside, with Carter-administration shag carpet and hanging lamp décor that might be fashionably vintage in some big city.

Well known for her chicken-frying skills and her mastery of other classic farm food, Stenzel tried opening a weekend-only restaurant in a former convent in Collyer, population 109, fifteen miles west of WaKeeney. But the operating margins were too fragile for the business to survive beyond one especially brutal blizzard that spoiled an entire delivery of perishable food she had unloaded into four refrigerators and three freezers just before the power went out for ten days.

After getting fired as director of Economic Development, Stenzel would never again hold a full-time job with benefits. Over the years, she gained weight, got a diabetes diagnosis, and now has a leaking heart valve probably caused by stress-related high blood pressure. But she managed to piece together a living writing and selling advertising for the newspaper in Ellsworth and made a few attempts to rebuild her consulting business, which she could do online from the security of her living room. "I just wanted to come back to the farm," she said. "I came back here because I love this place. I had faith in it. I didn't want to see it go to hell." Despite her dreams and best efforts, everything around her went to hell anyway.

Sandra Stenzel on the steps of the Trego County home built by her grandparents. Credit: C. J. Janovy

One day in March 2014, Stenzel drove the dirt roads of Trego County. Every mile or two there was an abandoned farmstead with a hundred-year-old house and barn falling in on itself or slowly being overtaken by brush. Around these family settlements, cottonwoods that had once shaded farmyards were brittle after seven years of drought, and fallen chunks of rotted-out limbs littered the dead ground. Drought and farm crises contributed to this desolation, but what really emptied out Trego County's countryside was rural school consolidation in the 1960s. One-room buildings like the one where Stenzel went to grade school closed, and country kids got bused into town where they suffered the indignities of being outsiders. Parents who wanted to stay close to their kids bought homes in town; even if they kept working their farms, they had no use for the old frame houses, so they left them, sometimes empty, sometimes still full of furniture and books. In now-overgrown groves where farmsteaders decided they would build houses, raise families, and make lives, hand-raised buildings are now sinking back into the earth. No one is coming back.

That early in the spring the land was still dormant, pastures covered with a short carpet of faded tan grass except for where the summer wheat had just begun to rise. "That wheat looks terrible," Stenzel said, passing a field of dirt with scattered patches of green. "That wheat looks good," she said half a mile down the road, where a spit of rain might have fallen a little harder as its lonesome cloud passed over the county.

A few months ago she put the farm up for sale. It was the hardest decision she has ever made.

Stenzel can picture a dystopian future for western Kansas, based on "Big Ag" business models and rural population patterns. Already, combines are so enormous that they use GPS systems to navigate the fields, which can be monitored by drones. Her prediction: "There will be an Airstream trailer every hundred miles, with one guy living in it, who drives the biggest farm implement you can imagine. They'll helicopter supplies in to him." She's not sure how long it will take, but someday there will be just six communities in western Kansas. She wanted WaKeeney to be one of those communities. "I told people: You have ten years. If we don't do something in ten years, we won't be one of the six." Now, almost a decade after she lost her job, "there's one grocery store in WaKeeney when we used to have two. There's one less farm-implement dealership in the county. Half of downtown is empty." WaKeeney has lost a thousand people since Stenzel's childhood trips to town. At the 1960 census, about 2,800 people lived there. In 2010 the number was down to around 1,800.

Stenzel still sees beauty in the dried-out, faded amber pastures, and it reminds her of a Robert Frost poem titled "Nothing Gold Can Stay." It's about nature's promise of the inevitable. As a new leaf eventually turns into a dying leaf, Frost writes, "So Eden sank to grief."

While Stenzel was losing her farmland idyll, other activists were learning their own painful lessons four hours to the east, in the Kansas town that most resembled her other utopian one-time home of Austin.

3

For Diane Silver, meeting Patty Doria was like standing in front of a fireplace after coming in from a blizzard. The two of them were part of a lively community of lesbians that flourished in the relative safety of college-town Lawrence, less than thirty miles east of—but a world away from—Topeka.

When Silver moved from East Lansing, Michigan, to take a job as a journalist covering the Kansas legislature for the *Wichita Eagle* in the mid-1980s, she arrived too late to experience what she heard was a golden age for Lawrence lesbians, when there was a restaurant (Sister Kettle Café was billed as "A Vegetarian Delight") and a newsletter ("The Monthly Cycle"). But Lawrence still had a lesbian-feminist bookstore, called Spinsters, up on the second floor of a storefront along Massachusetts Street, the main drag of shops, restaurants, and bars supporting a fermenting ecosystem of professors, university employees, students, and hangers-on.

It was no accident that Lawrence's main street was named after Massachusetts. The town's founders were abolitionist members of the New England Emigrant Aid Company who had settled there in the 1850s; they proceeded to name streets east of Massachusetts in honor of the original thirteen states and, to the west, after states in the order in which they joined the Union. Today, heading westward from Mass Street, the midwestern Victorian-farmhouse architecture of Vermont, Kentucky, and Tennessee streets gradually gives way to the ranch homes of Iowa. High above it all, atop a thousand-foot rise known as Mount Oread, is the University of Kansas, its historic limestone buildings overlooking an isle of Kansas liberalism.

Doria was a social worker who had been there since the 1970s. Silver met her at a potluck. "She was not what you'd call your classic beauty," Silver said.[1] "She was very round, but the warmest, most interesting person I'd met." Their conversation was brief, but they encountered each other again a few weeks later at the farm of a woman who hosted an annual Labor Day barbecue (inevitably followed by skinny dipping in the pond). Silver learned that Doria was six months pregnant, having conceived via the classic lesbian method: a turkey baster, with sperm from a donor located through her network of women. Silver and Doria started seeing each other, and though Silver was in the not-yet-committed phase of the relationship as Doria's due date neared, her feelings changed on the night in November when she drove Doria to the hospital and Doria gave birth to a son, Tony.

"The viewing room filled up with lesbians," Silver remembered. "Oh, my god, they were standing on chairs and taking pictures." Soon Silver moved into a hundred-year-old, two-story house Doria had bought. Five months after moving to Kansas for a job, Silver said, "I had a honey, a house, a chain-link fence, a mortgage, and a baby." It took her a while to get over the shock. "But I was deeply in love, and it was a joy to have a family."

That family extended far into the community. An earth-mother type by nature, Doria would sit for hours on the front porch listening to people who showed up to share their problems. And she had healthy ways of dealing with her own issues. "She was a hefty woman," Silver said, "so to make herself feel better about her body she would go model for life drawings for the art students up on campus. There used to be a lot of pictures of her naked around town."

The two of them did their own kind of modeling, serving as a visible example of a lesbian family. "We were just out," Silver said. They did presentations at the University of Kansas (KU) and at other colleges around the area. "We'd hand out pictures of Tony, and we'd talk about our family. That was our activism."

Their efforts intensified after the National March on Washington in October 1987. Silver and Doria didn't go, but other people from Lawrence were amid the hundreds of thousands of gays and lesbians on the mall, righteously furious over the Reagan administration's criminal lack of response to the AIDS crisis and the US Supreme Court's 1986 *Bowers v. Hardwick* decision. "People came back all fired up, and they got everybody else all fired up," Silver remembered.

For all of Lawrence's supposed progressivism, city ordinances didn't prohibit discrimination against gay people. A social welfare professor at the university named Ben Zimmerman formed an organization called the Freedom Coalition, and the newly energized Lawrencians decided they would try to get the city commission to pass an ordinance prohibiting discrimination based on sexual orientation. City commissioners decided there wasn't enough evidence of discrimination to change city codes, but they did proclaim five days in April 1988 to be "Gay and Lesbian Awareness Week." Disappointed but determined, the members of the Freedom Coalition began building an organization to fit their name. "We had teas and coffees at people's houses on Sunday afternoons," Silver remembered, "asking everybody, 'What do you need? What kind of organization do you want?'"

Following up on the city commission hearings, the *Lawrence Journal-World* published a package of stories headlined "GAY: Homosexuals Say Lawrence Isn't San Francisco, but It's a Place They Can Call Home."[2] Reporter Nancy Smith interviewed twelve people, identifying most by their first names only. Not Doria. "As a non-traditional family, we are very aware that our current sense of security here could be shattered at any time," Doria told Smith. Though Silver was not named in the story, Doria described their commitment to each other, and told Smith that Tony "believes he has two mothers, rather than a mother and a father." Smith noted that the couple owned their house, "and both of their employers are aware of their lesbianism, Patty said. 'We are very fortunate to have the safety of being fairly out lesbians,' Patty said. 'Tony's day care is very supportive and his pediatrician is too.' One concern, though, is how to ensure Tony would stay with her partner should anything happen to Patty, whose family is not very accepting of her lesbianism."

That last sentence proved prophetic. Silver and Doria would not be among the activists pushing the human rights ordinance through to its passage in 1995 (it would be another sixteen years before the city added gender identity). They were fighting other battles.

In 1990, Doria was diagnosed with breast cancer. After chemotherapy and a double mastectomy, they thought she was in the clear. But a year later, doctors discovered that the cancer was in her brain and in the bones of her back. As they had at Tony's birth, lesbians from all over town embraced the family. At first, Silver, who had quit her job at the *Eagle* to be a freelance writer before Doria's diagnosis, was taking care of Doria at home with the help of a visiting nurse (also a lesbian) who convinced Silver she needed more help. After one especially bad night, Silver called friends, who called friends, who called friends. "It was the most wonderful, loving thing," she said. Their volunteer list grew to more than a hundred, and Silver put them down for three-hour shifts while she took care of important business before Doria died: she had to go through the process of adopting Tony, even though she had been his parent since the night of his birth.

Doria died in their big house on a Saturday in early February 1993. She was forty-five. Her obituary in the *Lawrence Journal-World* described her as "a leader in the Lawrence lesbian community," before listing her many social service roles. First among her survivors was Silver, "her companion."[3]

Three hundred people showed up to her funeral. Besides most of Lawrence's lesbian and gay community, there were people Doria worked with and people from Tony's school. Musicians played and friends went up to the microphone and told stories. Silver remembers laughing a lot. While she was waiting to get in a car for the drive to the cemetery, a friend came rushing up. "You will not believe what I just heard in the bathroom," the friend said. She had overheard two women, obviously not part of their lesbian circles. "One woman said to the other, 'Wow, that was an amazing service. I didn't know they could love each other that much.'"

Doria might have been opening hearts and minds even in death, but that didn't help Silver, who in her grief was facing the indignities of an officially unrecognized relationship. She got no survivor benefits from Social Security. They had put the house in Silver's name, but not soon enough to avoid the state's one-year requirement for avoiding inheritance tax, so Silver paid tax on the house she had been living in, and on half of the money in her joint bank account. "That really made me mad. You're grieving and you need money more than ever and you lose several thousand dollars," Silver said.

There was an argument with a clerk at the state health department who doubted whether Silver had the authority to order copies of Doria's death certificate so she could settle other business; an insurance company representative accused Silver of trying to bilk the estate. "They said our life together was a 'housekeeper situation,' where a person comes in as the housekeeper for a dying soul and gets the patient to sign their will and everything they own over to the housekeeper. The thing that saved us was that Patty and I had been in the paper and on the news." That's how Silver was able to convince the insurance company that she was not a housekeeper. "But if we hadn't been in the news," Silver said, "there was no way I could have proved that." Silver was also on her own with a first-grader to raise. For years, Silver did not have the time or energy for activism. But when the marriage amendment came up for debate at the legislature in 2004, Tony was graduating from high school. She could no longer sit on the sidelines.

Once again, a small band of Lawrence activists, including a few members of the old Freedom Coalition, gathered in people's kitchens. Silver's group was mostly Democrats (she would later learn that supportive Republicans were having meetings across town in another kitchen). One of the people who showed up was Tiffany Muller. "The first time I met her, I thought she was incredibly sharp," Silver said. "She really knew what she was doing. I liked her approach, her ability, her warmth. If I'd have been a few years younger, I might have made a pass. But, my god, she looked like she was fifteen."

After the marriage amendment died that session, while the Reverends Johnston, Fox, and Wright were rallying to unseat recalcitrant legislators, Silver and Muller decided to form a political action committee to counter the far-right conservatives. Silver drove over to Muller's house in Topeka, where she got a dose of her own prejudices.

Bruce Ney didn't just look like a corporate lawyer—he was one. Ney lived in Lawrence but made the drive to Topeka every day to handle legislative and regulatory affairs for what was then SBC Communications (later AT&T). "A gay Republican?" Silver had to fight the impulse to leave. "I thought Republicans were evil people who drip venom off their fangs," Silver said. "But then I also believed in the Golden Rule." Now, that meant "be nice to Republicans." Besides, the handsome, clean-cut Ney was so warm and friendly. He wasn't a contradiction. Like many other Kansans, Ney was a legacy Republican, and one with extra cachet: He had grown up in Bob Dole's home town of Russell.

Ney had grown up on a 230-acre farm along the Smoky Hill River Valley, raising steers, feeding chickens, driving the tractor, showing cattle and hogs in 4-H, joining Future Farmers of America. The oldest of four brothers, he was raised a good Catholic. "Out there you're born a Republican," Ney said.[4] "Whether good or bad, that's just the way it was." (Ney's experience differed from Sandra Stenzel's Democratic upbringing in Trego County, about an hour west of Russell.) "You always had famous people coming through," Ney said. "President Ford came to Russell. I met Barbara Walters in Russell. I remember meeting Elizabeth Dole, right after she and Bob got married, at the funeral home after Bob's dad died." Ney's father managed the co-op where Dole's father had worked, and Ney's great-grandmother spent her later years in a duplex across the street from Dole's parents. It was impossible not to be interested in politics. "It was very cool at that point, in the late seventies, early eighties, to be out there."

What was not cool, though, was being gay. Ney had known he was different since he was twelve, when the girls at school taped *Tiger Beat* pictures of boys on their lockers and the pictures caught Ney's attention, as did the older boys his dad hired to help bale hay. There was no one Ney could talk to about his feelings. He had a night job near a church that was always unlocked, so after his shift he would stop there, light a candle, and pray to not be gay. It never worked.

Ney graduated from high school in 1982. Rather than fleeing to Lawrence and KU, however, he drove two hours east to Manhattan and enrolled at Kansas State University. With about fifty thousand people, Manhattan was ten times the size of Russell. It felt big, but K-State is an agriculture school, filled with people who had also been in 4-H and Future Farmers of America. "There were a lot of people like me," Ney said.

Set back in a tallgrass floodplain where the Kansas and Big Blue Rivers meet in a shady fold of the Flint Hills, the town had, like Lawrence, been founded in the 1850s by abolitionist settlers from the New England Emigrant Aid Company. But the rival college towns, just an hour's drive apart, each embraced their differences from the other. In a proud celebration of K-State's rural identity, for example, Manhattan's raucous district of bars, restaurants, and shops near campus is called Aggieville.

Ney majored in agricultural journalism, and he took an agriculture law class from an attorney then in private practice in Manhattan: future governor Sam Brownback. "He was well spoken, energetic, a kid from Parker, Kansas—a role model at the time. He was a great orator, and I admired that," said Ney, who pledged Phi Delta Theta and then joined the College Republicans because it was one of the school's biggest organizations and all of his fraternity brothers were members. Eventually Ney ran for, and won, the chairmanship of the state organization, beating out a pugnacious KU law student named Phill Kline. "I always joke that I was one of the few people in Kansas who ever beat Phill Kline in an election," Ney said of the later-disbarred attorney general.

But he was also starting to encounter people who weren't like him. During two terms in the student senate, Ney met some arts and sciences students who were gay. And he was on the finance committee when a gay students' organization requested funding for an HIV-prevention pamphlet. "People thought it was so graphic," he remembered. Though he agreed that the content could have been toned down a bit—were the fisting references really necessary?—Ney was surprised by the committee's reaction. "It didn't get funded," he said. "That was my first encounter with a deliberative body. It was also the first time I heard of HIV."

Ney was turning into a social moderate, and after college he put his ag-journalism degree to work doing communications for Republican campaigns, ultimately getting a job as deputy press secretary for Governor Mike Hayden in the late 1980s. When he was twenty-five, Ney decided to go to law school.

He was beginning to build a successful career, but his personal life was less fulfilling. "I didn't have boyfriends, but there were encounters," he said. "There was some emotional pain because you're lying to everybody." That began to ease after Ney went to work for the politically connected, and politically diverse, Morris Laing law firm in Wichita. Its roster included big-name Democrat Tom Docking, who had been lieutenant governor in the mid-eighties and was the son of a former governor. Living in the state's biggest city, Ney made gay friends and found his first boyfriend. His sexual orientation was an open secret and Ney's coworkers were warm and accepting, but Ney waited until he became partner before officially coming out.

During those years, Ney chaired the Sedgwick County campaign for Carla Stovall, a tough cookie who was the state's first (and so far only) female attorney general, and who looked on track to win the Republican nomination for governor in 2002 until she quit the race to get married. Stovall knew he was gay, and she was "very fun about it," Ney said. "That's when I figured out: When people get to know you, their opinions change and they're pretty good about it."

That revelation was what motivated Ney to get involved in fighting the marriage amendment campaign. By 2004 he had taken the job with SBC, gone to work covering legislative affairs in Topeka, and moved to Lawrence. There, he and a few other men had started a group they called NetworQ. "It was purely a social organization," Ney said. "There was nowhere for guys who weren't college students to get to know each other and network. There was a corresponding group for women that met once a month and had a giant potluck" (the long-running "First Friday" potlucks started by Silver and Doria). "We wanted the same thing for guys, so we started a Thanksgiving dinner." Growing to about 120 members, NetworQ turned out to be a good way to organize people. The *Lawrence Journal-World* ran a story about the group, quoting Ney saying that Lawrence "was an island of blue in a sea of red."[5] But, reporter Joel Mathis noted, "As the Kansas legislature moves closer to letting voters weigh in on a state constitutional amendment banning gay marriage, the gay and lesbian community in Lawrence is feeling less comfortable."

Ney was thankful that SBC valued diversity, and the company had gone so far as to offer domestic partnership benefits for employees. So, early in 2004, Ney went to the statehouse to offer personal testimony against the amendment. "As long as I took vacation time and didn't testify on behalf of the company, it was fine," he said. He testified in front of the Federal and State Affairs Committee in both the House and the senate. "I watched the bill come and go," he said, "and I saw what Senator Adkins did." He also saw what a Democratic representative from Leavenworth did: the representative had been one of Ney's close friends in law school and knew he was gay, but she voted for the bill anyway. "I was devastated," Ney said. "I wrote her, and when the bill came back she voted against it. So there was hope that people, when they understood what it was, would vote against it."

Tiffany Muller knew those powers of persuasion would be crucial if they had any hope of stopping the amendment when it came up the next year, which is why she recruited Ney to help form a political action committee. And Diane Silver quickly warmed to her charming Republican compatriot. Calling their PAC the Kansans for Justice and Equality Project, the trio spent the early summer of 2004 trying to protect moderate Republicans who had stood with them against the marriage amendment. After losing four key seats in the August primary, they concentrated on helping Democrats hold off their opponents. By the end of election season they'd worked on about thirty-six races. "We organized thousands of volunteer hours sending people door to door for our candidates, we built a massive volunteer database and listserv, we raised money and cut PAC checks for our candidates," Muller remembered.

But they could not stop the inevitable.

When the legislature reconvened in January and set an April date for the amendment vote, Muller sent word around the state, calling everyone to a meeting at Washburn University. When Silver arrived that Saturday afternoon in February, she was stunned to find herself surrounded by people she had never seen. "I just looked around and thought, wow. We had no idea we existed." Everybody was angry. "We were scared," Silver recalled, "but I felt power in that room for the first time." They had seven weeks before the vote. "We had no money, we had no organization," Silver said. "Someone said, 'If we're going to fight this thing, let's put up or shut up. Everyone write a check.' People wrote checks."

The next order of business was naming a campaign chair. "Everybody kind of looked at Bruce," Silver remembered. "He's a photogenic, well-spoken guy." He had been involved in politics, worked on campaigns. And he was a corporate lawyer. "Somehow I came out of there as the chairman of that organization," Ney said.

They called themselves Kansans for Fairness—nothing L, G, B, or T about the name, in recognition of their straight allies. They divided up other duties. Silver said that everyone turned to her and said, "You keep opening your mouth. Why don't you do communications?" Sitting behind her was a woman she had never met named Cyd Slayton. "We realized we both had communications backgrounds, so I said: 'You're in this with me, lady.'"

"I went home in a daze," remembered Slayton, who actually had a bit more than a "communications background": she was director of communications at H&R Block, headquartered in Kansas City. The previous November, after the marriage amendment had passed in Missouri and came close to going on the ballot in Kansas, an acquaintance had called Slayton and asked her to join the local board of the national Human Rights Campaign. Slayton knew the business community was growing more supportive of LGBT equality, but she wasn't particularly out at work, although she had begun to take her partner, Madeleine, to company events. She had also never been politically active, but she did come from a political family: her abolitionist ancestors had helped settle Kansas in the 1850s; her great-great-grandfather, J. H. Cunningham, had served in the state legislature from 1878 to 1880; and her parents had worked so intensely on fair housing, anticorruption, and other local issues that she couldn't remember a childhood summer when there wasn't some sort of campaign activity at her house. "I grew up with maps in our kitchen of where the precincts were, where the swing voters were," she said.[6]

Now, Slayton cranked up a war room at her home in the tony Johnson County suburb of Mission Hills. "Just as my mother had done fifty years earlier," she said, "I put up maps on the wall. I didn't know much about anything west of Lawrence. Even though I had relatives in places like Garnett, Independence, Hutchinson, and Wichita, I never considered Kansas a very friendly place to go. So I studied the maps, and we created media lists and tried to understand who might be willing to talk with us. Really, hardly anyone wanted to talk about it."

As the face of the campaign, Ney set out to speak at fundraisers and Rotary Club meetings wherever Kansans for Fairness could get on the agenda, in big towns like Wichita and small towns like Pittsburg. He debated Terry Fox on the Wichita public television station and Jerry Johnston on the Kansas City public television station.

In a vain attempt to counter religious-right arguments, Kansans for Fairness lined up almost 140 ministers who signed a letter opposing the amendment and sent it to their local newspapers. "In our considered view, this proposal threatens to dignify discrimination and undermine religious liberty," they wrote. "Furthermore, we feel that it violates a basic tenet of all our faiths: That all people should be treated equally, with respect and love." On the Sunday before the election, one of the ministers who had been most vocal against the amendment, Rev. John Tamilio, hosted a service at his Colonial Church.

For Slayton, that service was the high point of the campaign. More than four hundred people filled the red-brick church in Prairie Village, one of Johnson County's older, shady suburbs. People sat in the aisles, crowded into the lobby and the library, spilled out onto the sidewalk. "All these people stood up and talked about how much they supported us," Slayton said, "and I even saw a couple of relatives in the audience."

Ney had a unique perspective on other developments. Brownback, who was by then a US senator, had moved so far to the right that his former student no longer recognized him. "I'd always respected him until this whole issue came up," Ney said. "I knew members of his staff at the time who were gay."

All of which might have made Kansas a poster state for the equality battle nationwide, but the Kansans got little help from national gay rights organizations. Eventually the Human Rights Campaign came through with $15,000 and the National Gay and Lesbian Task Force sent $10,000—chump change compared to the more than $235,000 spent promoting the marriage ban by a national organization calling itself DOMA, Inc., and the Knights of Columbus in Kansas City, Kansas.[7] The national gay organizations, Ney said, "didn't think Kansas was really worth spending any money on. Realistically that made sense—you could see where the vote was going to go."

But regular Kansans donated money as if there really was hope. "It was very moving," Ney said. "Money would just come in from all over. People we'd never met, never knew, would just send checks to our mailbox in Topeka. That kept me going on days when it was really rough." Roughest of all, it turned out, wasn't the opposition; it was the group's own infighting.

Christopher Renner of Manhattan was dubious about the cause. He thought there were more important, basic things to fight for: equality in employment, public accommodations, and housing, for starters. What good would it do for a couple in Manhattan, Kansas, to get married if they could still lose their jobs for being gay? The whole marriage equality effort, he thought, was an ill-conceived ploy by some in the wider LGBT movement to make themselves acceptable to heterosexuals. "I've always found that annoying in the least," Renner said.[8] "I'm acceptable as I am. I don't need to be in a marriage."

Still, the amendment needed to be fought, so Renner and an activist named Tammy Hawk had also driven from Manhattan to Washburn. They left the meeting disillusioned, having deemed Kansans for Fairness to be "a group of wealthy and Republican people" from Lawrence, Johnson County, and Topeka. *They're going to accomplish nothing*, Renner thought.

The product of an intensely Catholic upbringing in Beattie, a town of a few hundred people near the Nebraska border, Renner had left Kansas in 1976 with no intention of returning. He was a lover of art, music, and photography who had always known he was "different from the others." In a 2008 interview with University of Kansas librarian Tami Albin, recorded for KU's *Under the Rainbow: Oral Histories of Gay, Lesbian, Transgender, Intersex and Queer People in Kansas*, Renner recounted how he logged a couple of years at a junior college, left to work for missionaries in Appalachia, went on to finish school at a Catholic college in Ohio, then worked on youth programs for a diocese in Oklahoma.[9] By the summer of 1980 he was in New York City getting ready for graduate school at Saint John's University. On his first weekend free to explore the city, Renner remembered, "I come up out of the Christopher Street exit of the subway and there's this huge parade going by"—the gay pride march. His immersion in gay culture was sudden and complete: gay literature, gay bookstores, gay artists. When his work for

Catholic youth programs took him to Chesapeake, Virginia, he searched the (pre-internet) Gay Yellow Pages, looking for Dignity, the gay Catholic organization. "I found this very supporting group of gay Catholic men who I really got close to," Renner said, "but also within a year I was totally gone from the church and I have never returned." He worked at a record store and waited tables at a gay disco in Norfolk, joined a gym, and bulked up his body while he expanded his mind with different spiritual ideas.

But at the end of the seventies, even the East Coast felt too restrictive. Renner would become what he called "a political refugee from Ronald Reagan." Through friends, he made his way to Naples, Italy, where over the next seventeen years he taught English while becoming thoroughly and incontrovertibly Europeanized and academic, publishing textbooks on English as a foreign language and earning tenure as a professor at the University of Naples.

Most of the men who had become Renner's friends after he left Kansas died of AIDS in the 1980s. Renner sewed some panels for the Names Project AIDS Memorial Quilt and traveled back to the United States in October 1987 for the March on Washington, which he called "glorious." Renner had signed up to volunteer, and organizers assigned him to the corner of 17th and Pennsylvania, where the route turned in front of the White House. One of his tasks was to count the marchers. "It was just phenomenal the amount of people who were at that march. I just couldn't believe the *New York Times* got the numbers so wrong." (The *Times* went with the US Park Police's official estimate of 200,000 marchers, giving gay activists a lesson in the insult of undercounting.[10] Those of us who were there might never have seen so many gay people in one place, but we could tell it was at least twice as many as what went into the official record.) "We lost count at over three hundred thousand," Renner said. "Today they say it was probably between five and seven hundred thousand."

Renner returned to Europe angry and radicalized—and questioning where he fit. "That's one thing about living abroad. You really weren't part of that culture and you really weren't part of this culture anymore." He moved from Naples to a rural village two hours away and commuted to work by train. "I knew that if I was going to survive the AIDS crisis I had to get out of urban gay life." He lived on twelve acres with olive and fruit trees and a garden. "I grew my own food for the next ten years, was back to nature, an environmentalist, hippie-type person."

Renner's life as an expatriate ended in 1998, after his mother died and he moved back to Kansas to take care of his father. While struggling to adapt to the culture shock, he worked as an ESL/bilingual program consultant for the Kansas Department of Education, then taught graduate courses at Emporia State University and Kansas State University and dove into as many activist causes as he could. A small gay rights group called the Flint Hills Alliance had been active in the late 1990s, hosting monthly potlucks, putting on a Valentine's Dance, screening documentaries, and bringing speakers to town (the biggest name was Candace Gingrich, Newt's openly gay half-sibling; other speakers included a detective from the Riley County Police Department who spoke about personal safety and harassment). But the Flint Hills Alliance had faded by the time Renner returned, so he joined chapters of the NAACP and the League of Women Voters and headed up the Unitarian Universalist Church's effort to become a congregation that officially welcomed LGBT people.

"I was not happy taking up the battle for marriage," Renner told me.[11] He questioned why LGBT people wanted any part of heterosexuals' failure-prone institution, one that, he contends, historically kept women oppressed. But gay Kansans had no time for such philosophical discourse. The vote was in seven weeks. Having determined from the outset that Kansans for Fairness would accomplish nothing, Renner said, Tammy Hawk convinced him that the Manhattan contingent should not wait for the state organization to get its act together. "We said, 'We're going to do our own thing.' We set up a committee. We got big buy-in from the Unitarian Universalist Fellowship of Manhattan and the First Congregational United Church of Christ. We had lots of volunteers. People walked door to door. We put it to the local level."[12]

For Renner, "the local level" meant rural counties in the center of the state, where they hosted public forums and showed documentaries such as *Tying the Knot* (it includes the story of an Oklahoma rancher besieged by vulture-like relatives after the death of his partner of twenty-two years). They were countered by members of small-town churches armed with detailed information on the sexual behaviors of gay men. "Very few people would show up for these public gatherings," Renner said, "but there was a woman in Abilene who was so versed in gay male homosexual acts that she actually made me blush a couple of times, saying things I wouldn't say if I was drunk with a bunch of raunchy friends." Renner said he was "flabbergasted" over the woman's ability to "sit there and talk in mixed company and not even have a clue that they've gone beyond the line of common decency." But Renner wasn't too shocked to counter her argument. "I turned to her and said, 'You have no space to talk because of what your priests and nuns have been doing to children for hundreds of years.'"

While Renner and his allies were making their stand in the Flint Hills, Kansans for Fairness was doing its best to mount a statewide campaign. And the activists' disputes over strategy and tactics made an already-losing battle feel even bloodier. They fought over a campaign slogan. Diane Silver said, "We came up with the campaign message of 'This Hurts Kansans.' It wasn't a great slogan, but the point was that the amendment will hurt people." Renner recalled: "When we heard the state organization's motto, it was such a waste."[13] Predictably, they fought about money. While Renner was leading the effort in Manhattan, an aggressive but inexperienced newcomer named Tom Witt in Wichita had managed to round up so many volunteers he had trouble finding room for them all. "We had people sitting on each other—twenty or thirty people a day either making calls or out knocking on doors or both," Witt said. "We'd have a fundraiser in Wichita, and the Wichita people thought we should give them all the money instead of trying to do a statewide campaign," Ney said. "Same with Manhattan. Christopher didn't want us there."

Renner called the Kansans for Fairness effort "extremely inept."[14] "There was resistance to having a central organization to run the campaign," Ney said. Renner and Witt "were very effective at what they did," he allowed, "but they had a very different way of approaching the issue."

"It was so stressful," Silver said. "Tempers got heated. And yes, I did scream at one person very loud and very long. Actually, more than one. There were a lot of hurt feelings out of it."

And for what?

"Of course we were creamed," Silver said of the election results. "The poll we commissioned at the beginning of the campaign told us we were

Left to right: *Kansans for Fairness campaign workers Braidy O'Neal, Bruce Ney, Lynne Leifer, Kevin Hager, Tiffany Muller, Cyd Slayton, and Diane Silver on election night, April 5, 2005.* Credit: Nick Krug, Topeka Capital-Journal

going to lose 70 percent to 30 percent, and that's what happened. You talk to anyone who's a political expert: Seven weeks for a campaign is absurd. Particularly for an organization that didn't exist before that."

"I don't know what kept us going because the outcome just seemed so dismal," said Cyd Slayton. "Except I think we were just fighting for our own respect."

Renner took solace in the margin of loss in his territory, noting that Riley County (home of Manhattan) came in second only to Douglas County (home of Lawrence; it was the only county where voters rejected the amendment). "We lost Riley County by six hundred votes," he told Albin. "If some Democrats would have got off their butts and voted we could have won Riley County. If I'd had some of the money that Kansans for Fairness blew out their butt, I could have won Riley County."[15]

"There was a lot of finger pointing about how it would have been different," Ney said. "But I don't think anybody could have done more than we did in trying to fundraise, getting people to go speak, getting diverse people together to try to make a difference." But, he said, "I was never so glad as when it was over. I had gotten burned pretty badly in those seven weeks."

Ney pulled out of politics. Others simply left. "Kansas hasn't felt quite right to me after all of that," said Slayton, who, newly politicized, would move up in the ranks of the national gay rights organizations. She spent a few years volunteering for the Human Rights Campaign's national committees, encouraging corporations to support nondiscrimination policies and laws. This activism frequently took her to Washington, and eventually the pull of the nation's capital became irresistible. She and Madeleine moved to DC, where Slayton would work on a doctorate at Georgetown University and serve on the national board of the Gay and Lesbian Victory Fund, trying to get LGBT people elected to city and statewide offices. She and Madeleine still own their house in Mission Hills, and spend about half their year in Kansas City. Her family's roots predated Kansas statehood, but after the amendment passed, she said, "I felt like it wasn't my homeland."

Ney is still a registered Republican, though he hasn't voted a straight ticket in a long time. "I still hold those core beliefs of moderate Republicanism that I grew up with. I understand Republican issues on the business side—less government interference and business regulation. I draw the line on interference in our private lives, whether you're a man or a woman. That's how I was raised. Back on the farm, your life was your life." Government's role wasn't about social issues, he said. It was about farm subsidies and agriculture programs. "I was raised on the story of Bob Dole supporting the idea of food stamps and taking care of elderly women and children and veterans. You heard about how Bob Dole had to sign the welfare checks for people he knew and for his family and not being opposed to that." In the Republican county where he grew up, Ney said, "we had amazing schools and people thought highly of public school teachers. So, that's what my idea of the Republican philosophy was and still is today: that you can have those kinds of programs within a strong-defense, business-friendly environment."

Ney avoided political activism but he still worked in Topeka, handling legislative affairs for AT&T, so he monitored the mood of the state, paying particularly close attention to one set of data. "The Office of Vital Statistics publishes a survey of the prior year's records," he said. Over the decade when Kansans had supposedly "protected" heterosexual marriage, the number of those marriages continued to decline. "Divorce rates have not changed," he noted. Despite all of the opponents' campaign rhetoric, Ney commented, "everything they said has been false." In the years ahead, as others took over for the veterans of the marriage amendment battle and continued the fight for equality, more Kansans would come to the same conclusion.

PART TWO

THE DUSTOFF
BATTERED ACTIVISTS ORGANIZE

During February and March of 2004, while Kansas lawmakers were making a first futile attempt to ban gay marriage, Mayor Gavin Newsom out in San Francisco was making national headlines by greenlighting marriage licenses. It was illegal and the California Supreme Court put a stop to it, but not before nearly four thousand couples—some of whom had traveled from other states—had their licenses. The court then invalidated these, but only for the four years it took for justices to decide that the state's law prohibiting same-sex marriage was unconstitutional. That was in June 2008, but voters' response was fast and punitive: in November they passed Proposition 8, banning gay marriage statewide (and setting up the 2013 US Supreme Court's *Perry* decision).

Marriage-equality supporters shattered by the Prop 8 vote took some solace in another outcome on November 4, 2008: America elected its first black president. Although the Bush era ended with the rise of another Democratic president who had said he didn't believe in gay marriage (despite saying that he favored it on a questionnaire during his 1996 run for the Illinois state senate), we knew Barack Obama would be friendlier to our causes.

And regardless of whatever was happening on the coasts, something monumental shifted when the Iowa Supreme Court legalized same-sex marriage in April 2009. Unlike courts in Massachusetts, California, and Connecticut, where the rulings had been 4–3, the Iowa decision was unanimous. Journalists Tom Witosky and Marc Hansen would later liken it to a famous ruling from Kansas, writing that it set "an unmistakable tone of necessity and inevitability reminiscent of the 1954 school desegregation decision, *Brown v. Board of Education*," and suggesting it was a harbinger of "now-snowballing acceptance."[1] The feeling of inevitability escalated that same year when legislatures passed marriage equality bills in New Hampshire and Vermont (where lawmakers also overrode the governor's veto) and Washington, DC. But that sense of momentum was tempered when voters in Maine repealed a marriage equality law that the legislature had passed.

Such pushing and shoving on marriage equality would continue for five years. Among the casualties were three Iowa Supreme Court justices, removed from office by voters in the state's regularly scheduled judicial retention elections of 2010. Angry Iowa voters had plenty of encouragement from out of state, with the National Organization for Marriage, the Family Research Council, the American Family Association, and the Citizens United Political Victory Fund spending nearly a million dollars on the campaign to send the trio packing.[2] Former Arkansas governor Mike Huckabee, who had won the Iowa caucuses in 2008 and by 2010 had his own syndicated radio show and was a Fox News personality, weighed in on a robocall to 250,000 Iowans, saying, "The last thing this country and especially Iowans need are activist judges who put their own self-interests ahead of the common good. Most Iowans and really a majority of Americans agree that marriage is a sacred vow between one man and one woman."[3]

Escalation of the marriage battle tended to overshadow other evidence of our progress, such as the fact that twenty states had laws prohibiting various forms of discrimination based on sexual orientation. And by the end of 2010, Obama had put an end to Bill Clinton's compromise, repealing "Don't Ask, Don't Tell," a policy under which seventeen thousand members of the military had been discharged.[4] "No longer will our country be denied the service of thousands of patriotic Americans who were forced to leave the military, regardless of their skills, no matter their bravery or their zeal, no matter their years of exemplary performance, because they happen to be gay," Obama said at the signing ceremony. "No longer will tens of thousands of Americans in uniform be asked to live a lie, or look over their shoulder, in order to serve the country that they love."[5]

On the other side of the country, in Seattle, the gay syndicated advice columnist Dan Savage, distressed by reports of LGBT kids being tormented and committing suicide, sat down in a coffee shop with his partner Terry Miller and recorded a video for YouTube. In an effort to simply convince kids to stay alive through their worst years, the handsome, muscular couple, then parents to a thirteen-year-old son they had adopted at birth, spent eight minutes talking about how awful their early years had been and how wonderful their lives became as soon as they were out of high school. "If my adult self could talk to my fourteen-year-old self and tell him anything," Savage said, "I'd tell him to really believe the lyrics to 'Somewhere,' from *West Side Story*. There really is a place for us. There really is a place for you. And one day you will have friends who love and support you. You will find love, you will find a community, and life gets better."[6] It was the first video in what would become the massive antibullying It Gets Better Project. At the organization's last count, more than fifty thousand people (including Barack Obama, Hillary Clinton, Ellen DeGeneres, and stars of Broadway shows) had submitted videos that had been seen more than fifty million times.[7]

Progress in Kansas during these years, meanwhile, was quintessentially midwestern: hardworking, quiet, and determined, as a small but effective network of individuals throughout the state proceeded to win hearts and minds in surprising places. Before they could do that, however, they had to figure out how to recover from defeat.

4

Every morning at his breakfast table, Tom Witt stewed as he read the newspaper. He lived in a quiet Wichita neighborhood, sharing a modest buff-brick ranch-style home with a man named Michael and their daughter. One day the paper printed a list of Wichita politicians who had voted to put the marriage ban on the ballot. Witt blasted a furious letter to his state representative, a Democrat, who was on the list. (He suspects many of her constituents did the same thing, because she was one of the House members who later changed her vote.) That might have made him feel better for a day, but each morning he seethed all over again.

One *Wichita Eagle* story quoted Mike Farmer, the director of the Kansas Catholic Conference, who said, "The state has the obligation to uphold the family."[1] On another day, the *Eagle* published editorials from student newspapers around the state. "Gay marriage, and the chaos it entails, will lead to married parenthood becoming a minority phenomenon," wrote Kansas State University student Grant Reichert. "Once a minority, marriage as a means to raise children will lose its power as a socially normative force . . . with disastrous effects for the youth of tomorrow."[2] For weeks, Witt read the arguments about how homosexuals shouldn't be allowed around children. One day he looked up at Michael and his daughter. "This is fucking horseshit," he said.

"They were coming after my family," Witt said, a decade later, "and I was not going to sit there and let it happen." Witt had worked hard for the settled life he was now enjoying. The son of military parents, he had known he was gay since he was thirteen; though he doesn't discuss his childhood, he has the bearing of a man who scrapped his way into adulthood. Now in his early forties, when Witt let loose it involved feasts of exquisitely smoked meats, Irish whiskey, and Pink Floyd. Mostly, though, he was focused on two things in life: his job as a computer contractor and his family.

He had always wanted to be a father. "Gay men don't get pregnant very easily, especially in the 1980s, when my daughter was born," Witt said. He moved to Wichita from Oregon in the 1990s to raise his daughter with Michael but will say little else about the two of them, protecting those details with the fierceness of a man whose own privacy has long since been annihilated. The reasons for his move from the Northwest to the middle of Kansas matter only because they underscore the strong feelings he had every morning while reading the *Wichita Eagle* in early 2004.

Witt was far from an activist. He didn't go out to the bars. He was an atheist, so he didn't go to one of Wichita's liberal, gay-welcoming churches. His job with a California-based computer consulting business didn't get him out of the house much except for work-related travel to other cities, but after living in Wichita for a little over a decade, he had recently found a group of atheists who hung out in a bohemian coffee shop called the Riverside Perk. A few of them had been getting together to write letters to their representatives, but Witt knew that wasn't enough.

It would take a while before Witt engineered a string of unlikely legislative victories, and before Witt told gay couples all over Kansas to go get married and some of them followed his instructions. First, trying to channel his fury into action, Witt went looking for a gay rights organization to join. He found none.

It had been a long time since Wichita played a key if barely remembered role in the gathering gay liberation movement of the late 1970s, the one that ultimately pitted Florida orange-juice queen Anita Bryant against San Francisco icon Harvey Milk. In what now seems like a fluky blip of history but was actually the result of a few Kansans being exactly in sync with the spirit of their times, the Wichita City Council passed an ordinance protecting gays and lesbians from discrimination in 1978, making it one of the first cities in the country to do so. Wichita's ordinance was similar to one that had been passed in Miami-Dade County, Florida, so Kansas's biggest city was the second stop on Bryant's California-bound "Save Our Children" campaign.

Bruce McKinney remembers those days. He had moved to town from Coffeyville in 1974 to attend Wichita State University, where he founded Wichita State's Student Homophile Alliance. His motivation was not political. "I wanted to get laid," McKinney said. Underage and unable to get into the bars, he didn't know of anywhere to meet men. "I was looking for a group," he said. "There wasn't one. I formed one."[3]

That earned him an unpleasant trip to the dean's office, where he was informed that he would not be receiving recommendations. McKinney dropped out of college and went to work for Coleman, the camping supply company headquartered in Wichita. After work, he turned his attention to city politics. Calling themselves the Homophile Alliance of Sedgwick County, McKinney and a handful of others campaigned for a couple of city council candidates who had promised to work for a gay rights law. Their candidates won, and McKinney's group asked the city council to pass an ordinance protecting gays and lesbians from discrimination.

The *Wichita Eagle* chronicled the tempestuous months that followed, as the council considered legal opinions and ministers staged rallies that drew five hundred people and packed the council chambers with opponents.[4] But the commission passed the ordinance. Response was predictable: the city's Concerned Citizens for Community Standards, and its leader, Rev. Ron Adrian, gathered forty thousand signatures on a petition to repeal. Bryant flew in for a concert where she warned the crowd that if Wichita's ordinance stood, "next you will have thieves, prostitutes, and people who have relations with St. Bernards asking for the same rights."[5] Voters reversed the ordinance by a five-to-one margin in May 1978.

Afterward, McKinney said, he was evicted from his apartment and felt unwelcome in gay bars, where all the attention had lured vandals who smashed windshields on customers' cars parked in the nearby alleys.

He thought about leaving town, but he stayed. "It always boiled down to: I love my community. I've seen this community beaten up, dragged through the mud, vilified, and they hold their head up and they reach out to each other, take care of each other."

That certainly was the case after the heady seventies ended, when a Wichita doctor named Donna Sweet was one of country's early experts on AIDS. Sweet began treating patients with the disease at her clinic in the early 1980s, and would end up devoting her career to the cause, ultimately becoming known as "the AIDS doctor" of Kansas.[6]

As the state's biggest city, Wichita was a natural destination for LGBT Kansans who wanted to get out of smaller towns. "Wichita was big enough to have a gay community, but still close to home and small enough," said Pat Munz, who made the pilgrimage in 1985 when he was in his late twenties.[7] Munz had grown up in Hudson, a town of a couple hundred people; his route to Wichita had taken him through Great Bend (population 16,000) for a stop at a junior college and then to Topeka for an accounting degree at Washburn. He settled in Wichita and went to work for a company that builds enormous metal-cleaning systems and ships them around the world. He had been to Kansas City and Denver, but they weren't for him. "I'm not crazy about really big cities."

These days nearly four hundred thousand people live in Wichita, a sprawling metro surrounded by the flat Arkansas River valley, about fifty miles north of the Oklahoma border. Oil pumps work the surrounding prairie like massive mechanical praying mantises, but Wichita is mostly an airplane manufacturing town. Tens of thousands of people once worked here for Boeing, which auctioned off its last hangar bay remnants in 2014 after shipping its operations to Oklahoma City, San Antonio, and Seattle; Beechcraft, Cessna, and Bombardier continue to crank out parts and planes. It's also a Big Ag town, where, from its headquarters, Cargill Beef oversees eight North American meat-processing operations that reduce millions of cattle into billions of steaks, burgers, and byproducts each year.[8] The city's legacy may ultimately be tied to Koch Industries, whose founding family has not forgotten its hometown: the Wichita State University basketball and volleyball teams play in the Charles Koch Arena; local primates enjoy the accommodations at the Koch Orangutan and

Chimpanzee Habitat at the Sedgwick County Zoo; and each year at the Wichita River Festival, tens of thousands of Wichitans get a free concert sponsored by Koch Industries. But the city's cultural life isn't limited to Koch-sponsored entertainment. The Wichita Art Museum has eight thousand pieces in its collection,[9] and like many midwestern cities, Wichita has rehabilitated a neighborhood of brick warehouses dating back to its frontier days into a trendy district of restaurants and art galleries.

When he first moved to town in the 1980s, Munz said, there were enough gay bars—Fantasy, the R&R Brass Rail, Jack's Lounge, a few others—that each one could have its own clientele and the regulars at one would rarely mix with the regulars at another. The Kansas Gay Rodeo Association was up and running, and gay men who enjoyed all things leather had a group called Pegasus. In addition to Donna Sweet's clinic, the Wichita AIDS Task Force was responding to the national health crisis. There was an organization called WGLA—the Wichita Gay and Lesbian Alliance.

But despite its rich LGBT history, Munz said, Wichita has always been "kind of a fractured community." He could see that in the cliquishness of the city's bar scene, for example. That began to change a little, and in 1990 the city held its first gay pride parade. A few hundred people gathered for the procession, which started at the Sedgwick County Courthouse and headed a mile or so south and cut over to a park near the city's performing arts and convention centers on the banks of the Arkansas River. "It was just our day to walk down Main Street and say, 'Here we are,'" Munz remembered. "It was a big deal. Every person who had the guts to actually come out and stand and proudly proclaim who they were was there. It was picketed by Fred Phelps, of course."

Leading that parade was a contingent from the gay Metropolitan Community Church. That's where Munz, the son of German evangelicals, had found a spiritual home and met his partner, Mark, in 1985. In those days the church had a membership of about sixty people, but after a new pastor moved to Wichita from Washington, DC, the church's membership more than doubled. The gay congregation even bought its own building, an old brick synagogue on a residential street. The MCC was "the big thing happening in town," Munz remembered. "Mark and I were carrying the church banner leading the parade down the street in front of the TV cameras. That was the day I really came out."

Over the next few years, Wichita's gay community grew and contracted in spurts. The pride activities continued, old organizations dissolved, a few LGBT newspapers came and went and, crucially, Kristi Parker started the *Liberty Press*, stacking it in racks in bars and friendly restaurants and places like Barnes & Noble and eventually distributing it throughout the state. Since the Anita Bryant–fueled defeat of 1978, however, nobody had been interested in fighting to get another nondiscrimination ordinance passed at city hall. "We were not organized politically, and I don't think anybody really felt we could get anything through the city council," Munz said.

So that was the complacent, stagnant political landscape that Tom Witt—the non-bar-going atheist who lived a quiet family life—discovered in Wichita in early 2004, when his blood heated up as he read the *Wichita Eagle* and he went looking for a gay rights group to join.

Munz remembers meeting Witt at a rally against the marriage amendment on a cold March day in front of the Sedgwick County Courthouse. McKinney introduced the two men. "All I wanted to do was go home and get warm," said Munz, who by then had spent two terms on the Metropolitan Community Church board and thought he was finished with nonprofit service. Other than attending a rally in miserable spring weather, and sometimes giving a little money to causes, Munz wasn't inclined to get involved in politics. Witt, however, was just getting started. If nobody else was doing anything, Witt figured, he would. In the years ahead, Munz would witness what he describes as Witt's remarkable political evolution. "The last thing you want to do is have Tom pissed off at you," Munz said, "because he can be a rather formidable opponent."

Witt knew exactly enough about organizing to own a small business, which is what he had done back in Oregon, where he and his seven employees wrote custom software and installed and maintained networks in industrial facilities. "At my core I'm that backroom computer nerd that nobody ever talks to," Witt said. "I had experience organizing for a purpose, but not politically."

In 2004 Witt watched Tiffany Muller stop the marriage ban from going to a statewide vote. "With no experience as a lobbyist, no money, and up

Tom Witt, executive director of Equality Kansas, in his office at the Center of Wichita. Credit: C. J. Janovy

against every odd imaginable," he said, "she was successful." But after that legislative session, with megachurch ministers infuriated and promising revenge, Witt knew that the lawmakers who had supported LGBT causes needed all the help they could get. He started with the people who had been coming to the letter-writing meetings at Riverside Perk. By June of 2004 they had incorporated and elected a board. They called themselves Equality Kansas, a nod to one of Wichita's many previous but now defunct gay rights organizations.

Their first project was voter registration. Over the summer, Witt and half a dozen or so volunteers registered more than seven hundred voters in the gay bars. Equality Kansas endorsed candidates who were running for state representative. "And then we did a big turnout operation," Witt said, "with direct mail and phone calls right before the election to get people to go out and vote."

That election, November 2004, reupped George W. Bush on the supposed wave of "values voters" and, in Kansas, anointed conservative

Republican legislators who had beaten moderate gay rights supporters in the August primaries. "The results of the November election were really bad," said Witt. He spent the next few weeks looking at the numbers. "I did a lot of studying on: How does the Kansas legislature work? Who are the yes voters? Who are the no voters?" Going over the lists, he knew that if the marriage ban were reintroduced in the coming session, LGBT Kansans would lose.

Which is what happened, of course. Activists with much more experience than Witt had predicted that the legislature would wait until the end of the 2005 session and use the marriage ban to bargain on other bills. Witt understood the logic, but living in Wichita had given him an up-close view of the legislative tactics being used by abortion opponents since the 1991 Summer of Mercy. He also remembered the tactics in Oregon back in the 1980s and early 1990s, when a born-again Christian named Lon Mabon, trading on his ex-hippie, Vietnam vet status, formed the Oregon Citizens Alliance and lured a national spotlight to one Reagan-era hot spot of antigay activity. "When they had a victory, they would capitalize on that by immediately going on a new offensive," Witt remembered. "I just looked at it and thought, 'They're going to come after us.' Sure enough, the legislature went into session the second Monday in January. On Tuesday, the marriage ban was introduced in the senate. It was passed out of the senate on Thursday the first week of the session with no hearings."

Opponents protested loudly enough to at least force hearings in the House. While Muller was scrambling to get volunteers from around the state to Topeka to testify, Witt was making trips to the capitol on behalf of Equality Kansas. "I didn't even own a suit. I had a tie and a nice windbreaker. And I didn't know shit about lobbying. I knew the textbook legislative process, but I didn't know how it really worked," he said. "Boy, did I get an education."

One thing he learned quickly: "In the Kansas legislature, the easiest thing in the world is to walk into that building and get a meeting with a legislator. That was a surprise to me. I figured people would be buried behind layers of protective bureaucracy—but you just walk in and start talking. That was an eye-opener." But that supposed openness had another side. "The other thing I learned was the lying and duplicity," Witt said. Legislators would talk publicly about how much they supported equal rights, but behind the scenes they were working to put the marriage ban on the statewide ballot. "If anybody wasn't a cynic before going up to Topeka, they certainly would have been after."

The first time he encountered that duplicity was in early January, when the senate voted to approve the ballot amendment and send it on to the House. "We lost it by two votes. And it was two people who had promised Tiffany that they would vote against it." Adding insult to the injury, Muller and her grassroots group had helped elect one of those senators. The other vote they lost was from Witt's senator in Wichita, who had also promised Muller she would vote against it. "Then she voted for it, because senate leaders told her if she voted no, she wouldn't be chair of the education committee anymore," Witt said. "Her committee chairmanship was more important to her than the civil rights of thousands of Kansans."

Witt, Muller, and others still had hope for the House, where, by their calculations, they had managed to earn exactly enough votes to stop the amendment from advancing to the statewide ballot. "And then we lost three of them," Witt said. "We were lied to."

Witt said he and Muller had spent three hours meeting with the House minority whip. "He told us to our faces that he was going to vote against it. The next morning, he went down to the House floor and voted for it. You can watch the board, who is voting one way or the other. When his 'yes' vote went up, we saw two of ours that had been 'no' votes turn to 'yes' votes right in front of us," Witt remembered. "That was the worst feeling in my life."

At the beginning of the session, Witt had thought the vote wouldn't even be close. Working so hard and believing that a win was within reach and then seeing it evaporate—that made the loss sting even harder. On February 2, 2005, the minority whip and eighty-six other members of the House voted to put the amendment on the April 5 ballot. Witt and his allies knew they weren't going to stop Kansas voters from passing it. But that didn't mean they weren't going to fight. "The question was, how are we going to make a dent in this at the ballot box?"

That was when word went out around the state to meet at Washburn University and the disastrous seven-week campaign against the marriage amendment commenced. Muller fought her two-fronted battle with Westboro Baptist Church and the Kansas legislature in Topeka, Silver and her Lawrence colleagues worked the media, Ney went to Rotary Clubs and debated megachurch ministers on public television stations, and Renner hit small towns where he encountered proper church ladies with odd fixations on gay men's sexual behaviors. In Wichita, Witt and his volunteers manned phone banks and knocked on doors. Before the election, hundreds of people rallied at the statehouse. And on April 5 they lost, just as they knew they would.

Bruises were still tender in mid-May when Witt sent another call around the state, hoping to work through the differences that had surfaced during the campaign. "I said, 'Everybody needs to be in the same room at the same time and we have to hash this out,'" he remembered. He booked an auditorium at the Topeka Public Library and more than fifty people showed up—the LGBT leaders, their allies in PFLAG, the church groups, the League of Women Voters. "It was a contentious meeting," Witt said. "It lasted almost four hours."

They argued over political strategy. "We felt like we had been blindsided by the amendment," Silver remembered, "so we wanted to make sure there was someone in the capitol paying attention all the time." But others rejected the idea of letting a lobbyist take the lead, she said. "Some very experienced organizers felt that we just needed to organize locally." But they kept talking. "Emotionally, we couldn't not do it," Silver said. "We were too wounded. We knew we had to do something, create a statewide organization that would be permanent, that would outlast any individual person."

Every third weekend in the summer of 2005 was consumed by hours-long meetings. Witt characterized the conversations as "merger talks" between almost a dozen organizations that had worked on the campaign. Trying to overcome the dynamics that had derailed previous organizations—volunteers burning out, egos clashing, groups disintegrating over irreconcilable differences, people leaving for jobs in other states—they pounded out the details of a statewide organization that could work. Chapters in different cities would be independent, but everyone would use the same bylaws and report to a state board of directors. And the board wouldn't be "self-selecting"—when board members' terms expired, the remaining directors wouldn't just get to choose their friends to replace them; instead, each chapter would appoint two delegates to the state board. Every month, they would meet in a different city hosted by a different chapter to exchange information, talk about the projects they were working on, and set direction for the chapters.

By October 2005, five of the six groups that started the merger talks— Equality Kansas of Wichita, the Flint Hills Human Rights Project of Manhattan, the Equal Justice Coalition from Topeka, the unorganized remnants of the Freedom Coalition in Lawrence, and the Kansas Justice and Equality Project PAC—agreed to dissolve and reincorporate themselves as chapters of a new organization they called the Kansas Equality Coalition (later called Equality Kansas). Witt would be the chair, and Silver would serve two years as vice chair.

Throughout the marriage amendment fight, Silver had learned a few things about Kansas. "I thought we had no support. I thought we were going to face baseball bats. We didn't. Maybe that's because Kansans try to be polite, but we found support everywhere. What people didn't realize is the attack brought us together."

Nine years after the marriage amendment defeat, on a warm, sunny Sunday, a dozen teenagers wearing T-shirts and cutoffs stood in a formation rising up the stone steps of Wichita's old Sedgwick County Courthouse, a relic of prairie Renaissance architecture circa 1888. Each teenager held a tall flag—a rainbow flag, a blue flag with the yellow equality sign, a flag with American Indian symbols, a "We Support Our Troops" flag with logos for branches of the service, a Kansas state flag, other flags. On the sidewalk in front of them, and spread out under shady trees, several hundred people had gathered for the annual gay pride rally.

It wasn't just gay pride day; this Sunday capped ten days of pride events in the state's biggest city. There was a bowling tournament (sponsored by AARP); a local version of New York City's Wigstock drag hairstyle contest; a Friday night bar crawl with a bus that made stops at six drinking establishments; a roller skating party at the Skate South rink; the Third Annual

Family Picnic at Watson Park (sponsored by Cargill); and a Saturday night block party with entertainment by a roster of drag queens, local karaoke stars, the Heart of America Men's Chorus, and a trio of lady folk singers called Women without Purses who had once opened for Janice Ian.

Welcoming the crowd was a board member from the new Gay and Lesbian Center of Wichita, which had opened a meeting space nearby at the corner of Market and Murdock—in the same utilitarian brick building where Tom Witt now had an office as the full-time executive director of Equality Kansas.

Next up to the microphone was Rev. Jackie Carter, pastor to a few hundred LGBT members of the Metropolitan Community Church. A strong-looking woman with short dark hair, Carter bestowed aggressive blessings in a salt-of-the-earth southern drawl. "God loves you just the way you are! You are created in God's image and I am gonna preach that word until the day I die and probably from the grave!" Over the crowd's wild applause, her voice rose even louder. "You are perfect in God's eyes just the way you were created! And I'm not gonna let somebody tell you somethin' differ'nt without *me* gettin' in their *face!*"

Contrasting Carter's fired-up delivery was Stephanie Mott, leader of the Kansas Statewide Transgender Education Project. Short, gentle, and soft-spoken, Mott had become a well-known figure at these kinds of events, telling anyone who would listen her story of drug addiction, jail, suicidal contemplation, and redemption upon embracing her true identity. "It's always an honor to speak about what it's like to be transgender. It wasn't all that long ago it was something I wouldn't share with anybody," Mott said in a calm, gritty, but soothing voice. "I am very proud of who I am." The crowd showered her with applause. "Things are changing," she promised. "Things are changing."

Everyone knew Mott, but no one in the crowd had ever seen the person to whom she passed the microphone. "Hi. My name is Sandra Stenzel. I drove four hours today from western Kansas to be here." Over the past few months, Stenzel had begun a creaky reemergence from her post-marriage-amendment decade of depression and isolation in Trego County, and people clapped when she told them how far she had driven to be with them. "Because it's important that we have community," she said, holding the microphone but not speechifying, just talking, as if these people were sitting at the kitchen table of her farmhouse on Downer Creek. "Don't forget the people you left behind," she told them. "There are so many of us here today who grew up in a small town, grew up in a rural area, and we blew that pop stand and we never looked back." This earned cheers from people who had done exactly that. "But there's work for us to do in the rural areas. If nothing else, it's just to reach back because there's some kid like you out there. There's some single farm woman out there who needs company. And there's someone who's willing to drive four hours just to be with other gay people. Just to not be alone." Stenzel reminded everyone that they were part of a long tradition and that the struggle didn't begin with the marriage amendment. "The biggest problem we had keeping it off the ballot was we couldn't find other gay people to work against it. We didn't know how to reach each other. I look out here today, ten years later"—finally, she yelled: "You are magnificent!"

Amid a huge cheer, Witt's voice boomed out. "Does anybody here know where Trego County, Kansas, is?" It was obvious this big-city crowd didn't know its western Kansas geography. "Fort Downer? Anybody from Fort Downer?" (He was referring to some rocks in a clearing near Stenzel's property, the only remnants of a military outpost once used by Custer and abandoned in 1868.) "Fort Downer in the house, everybody! Give Sandra a hand! I tell everybody it's in the middle of nowhere, but I lie—you gotta go another twenty miles after that."

Witt reminded the crowd that this was the tenth pride rally since organizers restarted the event in 2005. He gave a quick history lesson, going over the marriage amendment disaster. "We got our asses handed to us," he yelled. "It was bad. But we are working to undo the damage, and we are making progress. Three years ago, shortly after Sam Brownback got elected"—he paused for the boos to subside—

we went to have a rally at the state capitol with these flags, and Sam Brownback's people told us that these were dangerous weapons! And that we were going to be arrested if we carried these dangerous weapons and stood with them on the capitol grounds. Flags! American flags! Kansas flags! Community flags! These are dangerous weapons.

The only danger in these weapons is the danger of the ideals that they stand for. They stand for freedom, and community and the struggle that we have all gone through for the past several decades.

Soon, Witt predicted, the Supreme Court would settle the marriage issue. "It's almost over on marriage. But marriage isn't everything." He reminded everyone that they could be fired, evicted, denied services. "Sadly, Brownback and his minions are trying to further legalize discrimination. They're trying to put the right to discriminate against LGBT people into our state laws under the guise of what they call religious freedom." Witt hyped the elections coming up in November, yelling out the names of a few candidates who supported LGBT rights. He implored everyone to register and vote. "We are on the road to equality and there is no turning back! And we will continue to carry our dangerous weapons high and proud, and nobody is going to tell us anymore that we are second-class citizens! This is a first-class group and a first-class city and I am damn proud to be one of you. Thank you!" Then the teenagers who had been standing behind him lifted their flagpoles as Witt gave marching orders. "Our color guard is going to head out," Witt yelled. "We're going to let the flag crew go first."

The ensuing parade was short on spectacle and long on baby strollers, though the senior citizens in Wichita Prime Timers had a place of honor near the front, where Joe Mueller and Gary Ricketts, in their straw hats, shorts, Hawaiian shirts, and white socks, carried a hand-drawn sign: "Forty years together forever." A pickup truck hauled a trailer with disco DJs and loudspeakers and men dancing; Miss Gay Wichita perched on the back of a black Mercedes convertible; banner carriers represented a handful of churches. Mostly, though, it was a procession that had grown to two thousand people in bright clothing just walking west on Central Avenue as the wide thoroughfare wound away from the edge of downtown and became a park-like boulevard bridging the Little Arkansas River. Few spectators were out on this Sunday morning (and only two held signs imploring the marchers to "turn from sin"), but the mood grew more festive as everyone turned onto the grounds of the Mid-America All-Indian Center, a museum with a big hall and lawn to rent out for events like this one. For the next several hours, LGBT Wichitans—and people who had driven hours to be around other gay people—shopped the vendor tables and listened to music and ate Mexican food and watched drag shows and folk singers on the outdoor stage.

Witt spent the afternoon registering voters at the Equality Kansas table and nursing a plastic cup of cheap whiskey from the bar tent. He was red-eyed, exhausted. Besides his job as executive director of Equality Kansas, Witt was also by this time a political consultant; that season he was running campaigns for three people who had promised to support LGBT causes—two candidates for the Kansas House of Representatives (one from up in the Kansas City suburb of Olathe and the other from Hutchinson) and a former mayor of Manhattan who was taking a long shot at Republican Congressman Tim Huelskamp, an entrenched and hostile Tea Partier. With the election just five weeks away, polls were looking surprisingly good for Paul Davis, the Democratic state representative from Lawrence who was challenging Brownback for governor. Democrats thought they might actually rack up some wins.

They didn't. Come November, they would get their asses handed to them once again. Witt likely already knew this, and was just putting up a good front with his get-out-the-vote cheerleading at the noon rally. Over the previous ten years, as he grew from an angry newspaper reader to the director of a statewide organization, Witt earned the battle scars that serve as a diploma in Kansas politics.

Pat Munz, equipped with a walkie-talkie, stopped by the voter registration table. After he met Witt at that marriage amendment rally on a cold, wet spring day a decade ago at the same courthouse where they began that day's march, Munz took on duties as the treasurer for Wichita Pride. He might have thought his thirteen years on the board of directors for Metropolitan Community Church was enough nonprofit service for one lifetime, but, drawn into Witt's orbit, Munz was now also the treasurer for Equality Kansas.

"I've gone up and lobbied the legislature, gone to several protest rallies, thrown money at it to keep Tom as a lobbyist so we could have somebody standing up there and looking at the legislature and reminding them we exist and are not going to go away quietly," Munz said. "We have managed to kill, bury, and stop a number of pieces of bad legislation." First, however, Equality Kansas headed out to, as Witt put it in a rare moment of understatement, "start a conversation on LGBT rights with people who'd rather pretend we don't exist."

5

Leonard Kahl was a strapping farmhand whose marriage had gone sour. Kahl was forty. He had lived his whole life in Malvern, Iowa, a town of about a thousand people, driving a tractor since he was seven and struggling with something else for almost that long. During his annual physical before eighth grade, Kahl mentioned his feelings of being a girl to his family doctor. "He says, 'Oh, you grow up, get married, have kids, and they'll go away.' That SOB. I'd like to find him and kick his butt, because the feelings never go away."[1]

Kahl followed the doctor's instructions, getting married right out of high school, having a son and then a daughter. The feelings persisted, so Kahl visited libraries and learned more about them. On rainy days when he couldn't do farm work, he would drive up to thrift stores in Omaha, Nebraska, or Council Bluffs, Iowa, and buy women's clothes, which he would hide at home to wear whenever he could. His wife always found his stash. He would throw it all out and vow it wouldn't happen again, but that lasted only a few months. "I tried and I tried. I was married for twenty-three years. I saw my son grow up and move on. My daughter was fifteen. I was unhappy as hell."

One day, it was Kahl's daughter who discovered the lingerie. "The crap kinda hit the fan," said Kahl, who confided in his sister, who had a former college roommate in Kansas who was going through a divorce and looking for someone to run the family farm. "I opened up to her quite a bit," Kahl said of this family friend. "She joked, like, 'You're not going to go into the local co-op in a dress and heels, are you?' I told her, 'Oh, hell, no. I have things to work out, but I can take care of your farm.' I packed what I could get in the back of the truck and moved." Destination: the fortuitously named Haven, population 1,200. Leonard left for Kansas to become LuAnn.

The boss lady lived ninety miles away, in El Dorado, so Kahl had an old five-bedroom farmhouse to herself. The farm was a mess, but after a year, Kahl had it straightened out. Then she needed to pay more attention to herself. She had read enough to understand she could "change from the guy on the outside to what's in my heart and mind and soul," but she was scared to death. One night she drove to Wichita and looked for an adult bookstore. "I was hoping I could find a gay and lesbian group or a support group or something to help me start finding resources."

What Kahl found was a copy of the *Liberty Press*. Seeing an ad for a doctor named Mila Means, Kahl made an appointment. (A decade later, Means would make national headlines for planning to fill Kansas's need for an abortion provider after the murder of George Tiller; the *Los Angeles Times* would describe Means as "a solo family practitioner with neon red hair and a neo-hippie style."[2]) Means had helped another woman transition and said she would help Kahl. By spring 2003 Kahl was taking female hormones.

She let her blonde hair grow out and wore it in a ponytail. "I really wasn't paying a whole lot of attention to the fact that I was developing boobs until one day, it was hot as hell, and the center pivot irrigation motor broke down." With the heat threatening to burn the crops, Kahl drove twenty miles to Hutchinson in a hurry. "I walked into this parts store and the fella says, 'Can I help you, ma'am?'" Kahl was dumbfounded. "I stood there and stammered for a minute. I had on this sweaty T-shirt and the girls were showing through plenty. I thought, 'maybe I should work on this transition thing better.' I went to Walmart the next day and bought some bras that fit properly." If getting called *ma'am* was a shock, it was also a morale booster. "When I made runs to town," Kahl said, "I tried to start looking a little more feminine."

After a while the irrigation system needed more repairs. The boss came over from El Dorado to meet with Kahl at the dealership. Now Kahl was wearing a tight T-shirt and jeans that showed her feminine figure, and she was trying to work on her voice, which was deep enough to match her six-foot frame. The boss introduced her to the irrigation salesman as Leonard. "Afterwards she says, 'We have to talk.'" Kahl reminded her that she had been honest when she had taken the job. "She says, 'I thought you were more of a cross-dresser. But you want to become a woman.' I says, 'Yeah.' She says, 'I would love for you to stay, but I'm worried about what people would say.'" There was another problem: post-divorce, the owner wasn't making enough money to keep the farm.

Kahl had been thinking it was time to move on anyway. She had been in Kansas for four years, and despite living alone outside a tiny town, she had made connections. Dr. Means had written to tell her about a gay man who farmed about ninety miles away in Great Bend and was looking for new friends, so Kahl met him and his acquaintances from all over the state. One was a trans man named Charlie who lived in Newton, about thirty miles northeast of Haven. "Charlie'd already had a double mastectomy and was on male hormones, with a full beard and everything. When I told Charlie I was looking for a job, he says, 'You need to apply for a new job as LuAnn instead of Leonard.'" But even though Kahl was now getting called *ma'am* fairly often, she couldn't do it. "I wasn't comfortable enough. It still felt like too much too soon."

Kahl put an ad in Dodge City's *High Plains Journal*. "Experienced farm help looking for a job," was all it said. She got calls from all over, and was hired on with a father and son in the unincorporated community of Kalvesta, just a grain elevator and a handful of houses thirty-two miles from any town with a grocery store. "They questioned me about the long hair, but other than that, I think they were hard up for help they could trust."

Reading the *Liberty Press* as she prepared to move out of Haven, Kahl learned about an upcoming meeting of LGBT people in Dodge City. Hoping she could find friends close to her new place in what felt like the middle of nowhere, Kahl got dressed and drove a couple of hours west. The woman who had called the meeting was named Anne Mitchell. She had moved to Kansas from Berkeley—yes, that Berkeley. Mitchell was working as a legal secretary in downtown San Francisco in the late 1980s when she and a college friend decided it would be fun to meet in Kansas City and drive out to visit another college friend who was managing cattle in the Flint Hills. They had ended up at a ranch called the Prairie Women's Adventure Retreat. "Women could come learn about ranching or just get away," Mitchell said. "It was mostly lesbians. It was so beautiful and exquisite. And it was so much fun. I shot a rifle for the first time."[3]

One day there was a party at the bunkhouse and Mitchell met a woman who owned a ranch in Comanche County along the stark Oklahoma border. To make a long story short, Mitchell moved to Kansas in February 1993. She fell in love not only with the woman but also with the landscape. Mitchell went to graduate school at the University of Kansas in Lawrence and earned a degree in clinical social work. Then, from the ranch, she would drive to various counseling jobs in sparsely populated counties. "You work as a case manager, do crisis work at all these little mental health facilities, go out and screen suicidal cowboys." She sat with good Christian parents who had made their daughters get abortions, or people who could cope with their ostensibly idyllic small-town lives only with massive amounts of Xanax. "You hear what people say out in public," Mitchell said, "but you know the truth."

Mitchell ended up with a job in Dodge City, or Dodge, as most Kansans call it. The town celebrates its mythical status with a few downtown blocks of faux frontier architecture and a Hollywood set–type Front Street and Boot Hill Museum. But it could probably live without whatever cash it separates from tourists who venture down two-lane highways ninety miles from the nearest interstate; today's reality is that this town of twenty-seven thousand people, at the top of a hill in the arid High Plains just under 250 miles north of Amarillo, Texas, and 300 miles south of Denver, is a modern meatpacking town, its largest employers Cargill and National Beef. More than half of the city's population is Latino.

As a transplanted Californian, Mitchell found Kansas politics annoying, though she tried to keep a sense of humor about it. But she was devastated by the marriage amendment vote. "I realized: all our neighbors hate us. They might be very nice people and good Christians and smile at

Anne Mitchell, with her dog KJ, on the ranch where she lived in Comanche County. Credit:
Photo courtesy of Anne Mitchell

you and cook you dinner, but then vote against you." Mitchell wanted to respond, and because of her graduate school connections, she was among those who got the email about helping to organize Equality Kansas. She remembered driving hours to a meeting at a library with "a lot of egos sitting around the table." Asked if she would be willing to start a chapter, Mitchell was hesitant but agreed. In February 2006 Tom Witt drove out to make the southwest chapter of Equality Kansas official.

Mitchell called and emailed everyone she could think of who was slightly progressive, inviting them to supper at the western-themed Dodge House Restaurant on West Wyatt Earp Boulevard. Eighteen people showed up. Among them was Lindy Duree, a fifty-something reading teacher at Dodge City Middle School who had been troubled by other teachers' response when a student confessed to one of them that he was gay. "They kept saying, 'What are we going to do with this kid?' Everybody was shocked that I wasn't more shocked about him."[4] She had grown up an army brat and approached people with an open mind thanks to a childhood lesson from her mother: "You don't know when we're going to leave. You don't know when the people next door are going to leave. You don't have time to get to know them. They are your friends." Besides her own upbringing, Duree's husband, Warren, who had been born and raised in Dodge City, had grown up with "Aunt Barbara and Margaret." Lindy had known the two women since she started dating Warren. "We never talked about them being a couple, but my kids grew up with Aunt Barbara and Margaret."

When someone in the local Democratic Party forwarded Mitchell's email to her, Duree thought, "Maybe I need to meet some of these people and find out how to deal with stuff when it comes up at school, because I didn't handle it very well that day. I'm an old, white woman. There are a lot of things I don't know, but I'm willing to learn." Duree headed to the Dodge House. "I sat down at a table with two very nice ladies." Across the table, she recognized a former student. Then, Duree said, "I realize the two ladies I'm sitting with are not ladies. It was like, 'Oh my god, I have never been in this situation.' But these ladies were really nice. I thought, 'Okay, Lindy, get over this. If you're behind this kid [at school], be behind everybody.'" Afterward, Duree's former student came over. "He said, 'Mrs. Duree, I didn't know you were gay.' I said, 'I'm not, and I didn't know you were.' After that, I came home and said to my husband, 'You need to meet these people—they are fun.'"

Some of the people who went to that first meeting never came again. But Kahl was eager to get involved, she said. "I jumped in and told Anne I'd help her." Also joining was a chiropractor named Tanya Jantz, who drove the twenty miles to Dodge from Cimarron. The gregarious Jantz, whose family had been in western Kansas for generations, always fit in with everyone. She had grown up a tomboy, riding bikes and building forts, playing in the boys' baseball league and on the girls' basketball, tennis, and track teams. She had also been in the orchestra and the band and the choir and the science club. "Sometimes the jocks would say things that were inappropriate about the music group and I'd go, 'Hey, that's my people too. Don't be talking about them,'" Jantz told Tami Albin in an interview for KU's *Under the Rainbow* oral history project.[5] Woe to the schoolyard bullies when Jantz was around. "I was always on top of them, pigtails flying and carrying on, punching, kicking whatever boy might have been teasing somebody else."

She had known she was different from age seven or eight, but in the seventies in western Kansas there were no words to describe it. Jantz dated men after heading to Southwestern College, a tiny Methodist school in Winfield, south of Wichita, on a tennis scholarship. But she kept discovering that more of the girls on her teams were lesbians. Her dorm was filled with them. They invited her to their parties, which made her uncomfortable until she finally came out herself, fake IDing her way into Fantasy in Wichita in the mid-eighties. "It was awesome," she said of the bar. "You had the country [music] side and the rock side and the outside part with the volleyball nets. And it was just two hundred gay people every Friday and Saturday night. All the basketball players from Bethany and Bethel and Southwestern"—these were the Evangelical Lutheran–, Mennonite-, and Methodist-affiliated colleges in Lindsborg, Newton, and Winfield that competed against each other on Saturday nights, but on Friday nights "we'd be out there and hook up and talk and communicate in our little secret language, secret world."

Jantz moved to Kansas City for chiropractic school, and as her graduation drew near, in the early nineties, she planned on establishing a practice in Denver. "I thought, I need to go someplace and be gay, really, and not have to hide myself." But the chiropractor in Cimarron, Dr. Ellis, was ill with emphysema and cancer. Jantz had to do an internship anyway, so she figured she would spend a few weeks studying with him and visiting her family. People begged her to stay. "This is not someplace I want to live at all," Jantz thought. Unlike Denver, Cimarron was home to only about two thousand people. She liked mountains, but Cimarron was High Plains flat. She liked to ride jet skis, but Cimarron was an hour and a half from the nearest decent lake. She didn't like the heat, didn't like the constant wind or the omnipresent stench of feed yards. "People would say: 'That's the smell of money, Tanya.' Well, it's not my money. It's like, jeez, it stinks out here."

But the people were irresistible. "People in southwest Kansas, they're just very endearing, very loving, very giving." Sometimes for Jantz the smell of money was fresh bread or a casserole. "A Mennonite lady might come in with six kids and say, 'I need them worked on and I can't afford it.' Okay, sure, I'll take cookies and whatever you've got. So I did a lot of free care. I still do a lot of free care." When Jantz says "still," she's talking about more than twenty years.

Jantz buckled down, healing the aches and pains of Cimarron and spending time with her grandparents. Fearing she would lose her family if they found out she was gay, she hid that part of herself. Or thought she did. One day she went to pick up her seventy-six-year-old grandfather, who was being released from the hospital in Dodge. Listening to music on the drive home, he asked if she had any Melissa Etheridge. "I was like, 'Really?' He goes, 'Yeah, your aunt Linda listens to that 'Come to My Window' song all the time. Do you have that?'" Of course Jantz did. "So I popped in the CD and we're listening to it. And he goes, 'You know she's from Leavenworth, right? She's from Kansas?' I said, 'Well, yes, Grandpa, I do.' He says, 'Do you know she's a lesbian?' I about choked and wrecked the truck. I said, 'Yes I do.' And he goes, 'Well, you know that's just all right.' And that was all that was said." It was all that needed to be said. Jantz stayed with him every night for the next month, helping her grandmother take care of him until he died at home.

After a while, Jantz would have a partner, and her other grandmother would drive over from Wichita for their ceremonial wedding. The eventual breakup was painful enough that Jantz isn't much for talking about it, but the woman brought to the relationship an eight-year-old daughter, Alex, who became Jantz's daughter as well. "The community kind of had to accept us. We went to every parent-teacher conference. We went to every volleyball game as the parents that help bring the food and set up everything." Jantz coached and sponsored a girls' softball team, and never heard complaints from other parents.

When marriage amendment politics hit Kansas, some people in Cimarron asked Jantz how they should vote, because the ballot language was confusing. "Or they'd say, 'Did I vote right? Because it was worded funny.' I go, 'Yes you voted right, thank you for that.' And they're like, 'Hey, no problem.' These are farmers and feed-yard guys and truck drivers."

Jantz was among those who got Mitchell's email, and Alex heard about the Equality Kansas meeting from a bisexual kid she knew. "Alex was like,

'We've got to go get equal rights for gay people.'" And in August 2006, the southwest Kansas chapter of Equality Kansas ended up at the center of an only-in-Kansas manure storm.

J. R. and Robin Knight were a couple from California who had opened a bed-and-breakfast in tiny Meade, a sunbaked intersection of two desolate highways about forty miles south of Dodge. The inaccurately named Lakeway Hotel was a three-story brick building, built in 1926, that took up half a block and could have been the bar-and-brothel setting for some movie about the Dalton Gang, whose alleged hideout is Meade's sole tourist attraction. The Knights' twelve-year-old son, living with his grandparents in California, had sent his parents a rainbow flag because he liked the colors. The couple would later tell the *Hutchinson News* that they hadn't intended to fly it as a gay rights symbol. "It has pretty colors, it's bright, it's summery," Robin said.[6] But when they did fly it, someone cut it down and threw some bricks—one had "fag" written on it, the other said "get the fuck out of town"—shattering a window and some neon signs inside the building. The Knights ordered another flag and raised it.

Equality Kansas board members were planning to meet in western Kansas anyway, and figured they would show their support by staying at the Lakeway Hotel.

Fred Phelps and the Westboro crowd decided they would show up, too.

The standoff took place at high noon.

"Police chief Loren Borger, his colleagues, and sixteen troopers from the Kansas Highway Patrol kept an eye on protests," reported the Associated Press, adding that the locals had gathered on downtown corners to videotape the notorious Phelpses.[7] "I was interviewed on TV," Mitchell remembered. She had done some consulting at the nursing home in Meade, so she braced for trouble after being on the news. "I didn't get a lot of flak, but I heard through other people: 'So-and-so was asking about you, where you live.'" She was glad she lived on a ranch with a woman who had firearms.

The Meade incident blew over, and the southwest chapter moved on to less-sensational work. Mitchell would run ads in small-town newspapers for documentary screenings at libraries, and twenty or thirty people would show up. "I'd stand in front of the room and talk about Equality Kansas. I had to get my guts up each time—it was like coming out all over again." She was struck by how many straight people supported the cause, or just showed quiet signs of acceptance. "One of our neighbors at the ranch had a Premier party," Mitchell said, referring to the jewelry sold Tupperware-party-style at in-home gatherings. The neighbor invited Mitchell but not her girlfriend, then told Mitchell's girlfriend: "If Anne sees something she likes, I'll let you know.'"

Whenever anyone joined the chapter, Mitchell met them for coffee. "There was a woman in her eighties who wanted to keep up on what was going on. Her oldest son was diagnosed with AIDS and wanted to come home," Mitchell remembered. The woman had asked the local doctor to treat her son, but the doctor said he could not guarantee her son would get good care. "That was early on, so the son wasn't able to come home until the very end," Mitchell said. "You hear these stories all over Kansas.

She kept trying to keep her name out of the papers because her clients needed a therapist who didn't have a "big personality" in public. But being in the paper made her approachable. People would come up and say, "I've never met anyone like you—can I ask you questions?" In any case, over the next few years it would have been impossible for Mitchell to keep her name out of the *Garden City Telegram*.

Garden City is essentially Dodge's fraternal twin, fifty miles up the road: another meatpacking town—its top employer is Tyson Foods—about the same size as Dodge and with nearly identical demographics. First there was the incident at Garden City Community College, where school officials had invited Finney County Attorney John Wheeler to give a presentation on sex crimes. A college spokesman told the *Telegram* that the point of Wheeler's talk was "to educate college level students about the implications of interacting with minors, since people of various ages interact on the open campus."[8] That sounded reasonable enough, but it wasn't how Wheeler's talk felt to an old friend of Jantz's.

Kristie Stremel had grown up in Hays with Jantz's younger sister; she later moved to Kansas City and joined three women in a rock band called Frogpond, which signed with Sony's Tri-Star in the mid-nineties and played opening slots for R.E.M. and Everclear. After Frogpond broke up,

Stremel spent a few years fronting her own bands, releasing records, and touring. Now between bands and girlfriends, Stremel figured some time back in peaceful western Kansas would do her good. And going back to school wouldn't hurt, either, so Stremel enrolled at Garden City Community College—where she was stunned by Wheeler's January 2008 lecture to about a hundred students in the gym.

The fact was, even though the US Supreme Court's 2003 *Lawrence v. Texas* ruling made sodomy laws unconstitutional, Kansas hadn't taken its law off the books. Wheeler made sure his audience understood the definition of sodomy: "Oral contact or oral penetration of female genitalia or oral contact of the male genitalia; oral or anal sexual relations or sexual intercourse between a person and an animal. . . . Anal penetration, however slight, of a male or female by any body part or object is sodomy." His PowerPoint slide made use of bold-face type and all-caps. "Sodomy with a person of the same sex (or animal). PENALTY: $1,500.00 Fine/Six months jail."[9]

"I refuse to let Mr. Wheeler, or anyone else, make me into a criminal in front of a gym full of my classmates," Stremel wrote in a lengthy letter to college officials, pointing out her 3.6 GPA and demanding accurate education and sensitivity training.[10] And the *Telegram* quoted Mitchell reminding everyone that the law was unenforceable, regardless of whether it was still in statute. To which Wheeler agreed, telling the paper that he wouldn't prosecute even if it was the law: "Everyone is treated fairly in this office, and in my sixteen years as county attorney I have never filed a homosexual case and will not unless it is a nonconsensual forced sexual act on another person."[11]

The next spring semester was even more eventful at Garden City High School. Isaac Unruh, a senior, had come out to his Southern Baptist parents. The revelation had not gone well. Unruh had spent his childhood helping raise pinto beans, corn, milo, and wheat, and going to grade school with fifty-five other white kids from upper-middle-class farm families in tiny Holcomb (the site of *In Cold Blood*'s Clutter family murders). For high school, though, he traveled the six miles to Garden (as with Dodge, the "City" in the town's name isn't necessary), where the high school had two thousand students. "I'd never been around other cultures," Unruh said.[12] Excited to find activities besides sports, he joined the Latin Club, the chess team, and the Quiz Bowl team that traveled the state for tournaments testing students' knowledge of history, science, literature, fine arts, current events, sports, and pop culture. He had never known gay people existed, but by sophomore year he had his first crush on a boy. Nothing physical happened, but Unruh told some friends he was bisexual. No one at school had a problem with it. But at home, after his mother found out about Unruh's crush by looking at his MySpace page, it was a different story.

His parents took him to a meeting with their preacher, Unruh said. "He started reading scriptures and at one point ripped up the Bible in front of me, told me that's what I was doing to my religion." For the next year and a half, Unruh and his parents met with the preacher once a week. And each week, Unruh had a session with a Christian counselor. "I kept telling my parents she was crazy, but they didn't really believe me. Towards the end, she said she was out of options and the only thing left to do was an exorcism to get rid of the gay demon." This was too much even for his parents, who quit sending him to counseling.

School was what saved him from the hell at home. Unruh loved his friends and his classes. Everyone knew he was gay, he said, and everyone was nice to him, including his friend June, the straight daughter of liberal parents who knew about Equality Kansas. "The first meeting I went to was just shocking," Unruh said. "I had never met adults who were that set on making change or voicing their opinions so loudly in a room of other adults and people actually agreeing with them."

Since the end of counseling, Unruh and his parents had come to a tense understanding. Noting his father's prominence in the farming community, Unruh said, "My dad told me that as long as I didn't be open and proud in public and let other people know that I'm gay, then I could still live in their house." That ultimatum conflicted with what Unruh was hearing at Equality Kansas meetings: encouragement to start a gay-straight alliance at Garden City High School.

Unruh decided to go for it. Securing support from his closest teachers, he took the idea to the administration and was referred to an assistant principal. "He was pretty defensive at first and told me he didn't know if we could have a group like this at our high school because it would be too offensive to others. I bluffed and said Equality Kansas had talked to the ACLU, and he calmed down." The assistant principal told Unruh he would need signatures from fifty students and at least two teacher sponsors; by the next day, Unruh had one hundred students and five teachers.

Their efforts drew the interest of *Garden City Telegram* reporter Shajia Ahmad. Unruh told her about his precarious situation at home and said he was nervous to be named. "She enlightened me, and told me it would be less helpful to the cause if you're not able to stand up for it with your name." Unruh agreed, imagining a small story buried in the back of the paper. The next morning it was on the top of the front page: "Gay-Straight Alliance in Place at GCHS."[13] It quoted Unruh as the group's founder.

Unruh had already made arrangements to stay with June and her family if it came to that, which it did. His father called and told him he had ten minutes to get his stuff out of the house. "Mother was crying up a storm. I went straight to my friend's house with what I could grab." The next day at school, he said, "two kids I'd never met came up to me and said their parents said I could live with them if I needed to. Two teachers said I could stay with them." A couple of days later his mother called, saying his father wanted to talk. "He sits down and stares at me: 'As long as you promise not to live this lifestyle I'll allow you to live in this house. If you're going to stand up and think you're right, you can leave.'" Unruh would not speak to his father for another year and a half.

"When Isaac came out it just threw me for a loop," Sharon Unruh told me.[14] "I thought I was very open to the whole thing, but it's different when it's your own kid." She was all too aware of how others felt about gay people. "In my mind he was in for a lifetime of being judged, and I didn't want that for him." Roger Unruh had other fears. "My husband is a self-employed farmer," Sharon said. "He deals with a lot of people in the community, and he thought people would turn against him business-wise because of the article." Tensions between Sharon and Roger grew so intense that after he kicked Isaac out of the house two weeks before high school graduation, she thought about leaving the marriage. But she wanted Roger to pay for Isaac's college, so she stayed.

What her husband didn't realize, Sharon said, "was we had a lot of support from people he dealt with publicly—people letting me know what a wonderful article it was." Church, however, was another matter. "People would turn their backs and walk away from us. You could tell they were talking about us."

Isaac stayed at June's through the summer, then headed to Wichita State University in the fall. City life agreed with him. He majored in theater tech and design, made a small group of friends and, after a year of living in the dorms, moved in with three drag queens and went to his first gay bars.

Meanwhile, his parents began reconsidering their Southern Baptist affiliation. "The Old Testament says homosexuality is a sin, but so are a lot of other things," Sharon said. "We had people in our church who were abusing their wives, they were divorcing, cheating on their wives. Everybody was accepting of that but they couldn't accept that we had a gay son." Unable to find a church whose teachings didn't "preach hate against people like our son," they stopped going altogether. "I still believe in God, I still believe in Jesus and that I'm going to go to heaven," Sharon said. "I haven't lost my faith. I've lost faith in the church."

Up in Kalvesta, LuAnn Kahl was having her own struggles. "I could feel my transitioning sliding backwards because I was so buried in farm work there." Kahl's closest companions were 1,200 cattle. Her boss lived sixteen miles away in town, and his son lived fifty-six miles away in Cimarron. Kahl had taken the job with the understanding that they would help occasionally in the feed yard. But, she said, "as time went by they showed up less and less. If you're raising cattle, you have to take care of them seven days a week." Getting a weekend off, she said, "took an act of Congress, and I had to listen to them complain." That made it hard to manage her own life. By the time she finished work in the evening, the grocery store half an hour away in Ness City would be closed. That meant late-night runs to the Dodge City Walmart, which had an upside: "I would dress when I'd go to Dodge."

One downside to the Dodge City Walmart happened on a July night during the wheat harvest, around 10:30. "I'm going up and down the aisle, not paying much attention around me," Kahl remembered, "until I turn one aisle and something caught my eye that bugged me: this long-haired, grubby-looking guy in a duster" (the long, western-style trench coat). "He looked at me kind of funny. I thought about it and went on. Another two aisles down, here he is again. Then I got a weird feeling, got nervous. As I went to check out, he was there at the exit with another guy who was wearing a duster too. I thought, 'I'm not going out of this store alone.'" A couple was paying for their groceries and Kahl asked if she could walk out with them.

> They followed me out and those two guys were at the entrance. I could feel their eyes on me. I had a hunch they were looking for something— were they going to rob me? Take me out and abuse me or then rob me? Leave me for dead? I'm a six-foot-tall blonde. I'm well built, but if it's two-on-one there's no way I'm gonna win. That's when I realized the vulnerability a female feels.

But that was the only time Kahl really felt scared. "If I'd been in a more populated community, I probably would have feared for my safety more than I did," she said. "But it was not damned easy to find me. I do know how to shoot a gun and have one around."

Other evenings, Kahl passed the time reading about Dr. Marci Bowers, a surgeon in the small southern Colorado town of Trinidad. That one-time coal-mining town of fewer than ten thousand people had come to be known as "the sex-change capital of the world," thanks to a surgeon named Stanley Biber, who, by the time he died in 2006 at the age of eighty-two, had performed more than four thousand such operations. Biber was not media shy, and had been the subject of numerous newspaper articles and documentaries; after taking over when Biber retired in 2003, Bowers—a male-to-female beneficiary of his expertise—continued her mentor's dual practices of performing surgery and welcoming publicity. Eventually, administrators at Trinidad's only hospital, the twenty-four-bed Mount San Rafael, tired of all the cameras and changed their media policies, and Bowers moved her practice to San Mateo, California[15]—but not before Mount San Rafael was a location for six episodes of a 2007 reality TV show called *Sex Change Hospital*.

Kahl makes an appearance in episode 5. She had driven her old friend Charlie from Newton to Trinidad for surgery, and *Sex Change Hospital* followed his procedure. In the episode, Charlie, last name of Snook, age fifty-four, arrives for testicular implants, a vaginectomy, and clitoral release. He's a slight man with short dark hair, a little pasty from the prairie winter, with thick wire-framed glasses and the trace of a dark goatee.

"I was born in Dodge City, Kansas, home of Miss Kitty and Matt Dillon," Snook says in a deep, gravelly voice to an off-camera interviewer.[16] Old family photos show Snook growing up as a girl, while he explains how hard he tried to be feminine. As a teenager attracted to girls, he figured he must be a lesbian. "Coming out in the 1970s as gay in Kansas was a big thing," Snook says. "It was suggested that I move to a different area so I did not upset and embarrass my dad." It would be nearly thirty years before Snook finally understood he wasn't really a lesbian and decided to transition. "This time around my family was pretty easy. I called my mom and told her. Her true, true response was, 'Well, honey, I know how they take those things off but I don't know how they put 'em on.'"

Bowers does both. In the episode, Snook wakes up groggy and disturbed by the size of his new testicles. Bowers tells him they come in three sizes: small, medium, and large. Usually, she says, if guys have come this far, they want the larges. "You're a little more than most mortal men," she tells him. "You're gonna be ridin' high in the saddle, let's put it that way." By the end of the episode Snook's new testicles have fallen out and he's storing them in a plastic bag in the medicine cabinet of his small house in Newton while planning another trip to Trinidad to exchange them for smaller ones.

His complications didn't discourage Kahl, who beams in the background when Snook first meets Bowers. "The big thing about getting to bring Charlie to Trinidad was the chance to meet Dr. Bowers," Kahl tells the interviewer. Ruddy and ranch-tanned, her long hair like corn silk, Kahl is wearing a brightly striped turtleneck. She talks about living on a cattle ranch and being a farmhand: "I don't know anything else better to do than being outdoors and working with my hands and being busy."

But the Kalvesta bosses were keeping her too busy. One rainy Sunday morning coming back from a grocery run to Dodge, with her hair done and makeup on, "Who do you think I met on the lonely road? It was the boss and his wife. He's like, 'Um, what's going on?' I says, 'Well, I'm transitioning. That's the long hair I hem-hawed about during my job interview.'" The boss told her: "No matter what you do, in our eyes you're going to be Leonard."

That put things in perspective: It was time to make LuAnn official. Legally changing her name from Leonard to LuAnn would require public notice, which she published in the newspaper in Jetmore, the county seat, where nobody knew her. "It ran for three weeks, saying 'Leonard E. Kahl is seeking a name change.'" Anyone who objected had to contact the court before the hearing date. Her boss never mentioned it. "But the son, he's a little more open-minded. He was having a little fun with it, because people who had read the paper were questioning him. He was playing dumb: 'Hmm, I don't know what he's doing, beats me.'"

Nobody showed up to oppose her name change—but Mitchell made the two-and-a-half-hour drive from the ranch to be with her in court. Mitchell had connected her with a lawyer, who informed the judge that it was no longer appropriate for Kahl to be Leonard. The judge was calm and professional, Kahl said. "I had to swear I wasn't doing it for tax evasion purposes or to hoodwink somebody out of some money. So that was the end of that."

Mitchell followed Kahl to the Dodge City DMV, where they got her a new driver's license and went out to breakfast to celebrate. And Kahl gave the Kalvesta bosses notice. When she left the cattle ranch, Kahl headed ninety miles north to stay with a friend in Trego County: Sandra Stenzel. Kahl had heard about Stenzel through Tiffany Muller at Equality Kansas meetings, and the two farm girls hit it off.

Kahl put an ad in the WaKeeney paper. Once again it was "experienced farm hand looking for work," only this time it was LuAnn. The paper came out on a Wednesday morning and by that evening her phone was ringing. Kahl accepted an offer from Stenzel's neighbor a mile and a half down the road. If he suspected LuAnn might once have been a Leonard, he never let on. "His only comment was how I was so big and broad-shouldered," said Kahl, who figured that the only thing that mattered to him was that she was good at her job, and her personal life was her business.

LuAnn Kahl, on Sandra Stenzel's
property in April 2012.
Credit: Anne Mitchell

After a while with Stenzel, Kahl got her own place. There was an empty house on one of the farms she worked, so Kahl tracked down the woman in Hays who owned it. "She was tickled to death that someone was interested in trying to live in it," Kahl said. "I kind of had to take it away from the mice and bugs, but it was a nice house."

Kahl still owned her other house back in Iowa, the one where she had raised her family. She reasoned that if she could sell it she would have enough money to pay Dr. Bowers for bottom surgery. "A lot of the other girls, they all go for facial surgery and a boob job and all that. I knew I didn't have that kind of resources on what I made for farm labor, and would be totally, completely happy with the penis gone and having a vagina," Kahl said. She advertised the house a few times in Iowa but never got any bites. "I thought well, maybe someday," she said. Knowing she would have to book her surgery a year in advance, Kahl went ahead and reserved an appointment for March 2009. Around the same time, Kahl's stepgrandfather died and her parents auctioned off his eighty-acre farm.

When she went home for Thanksgiving, she had news from her parents. "Mom said, 'You can keep your surgery date. Dad and I have talked it over. We want you kids to use your inheritance now, when you need it, rather than later on. That's what you really want, and we know it'll make you happy.'" Kahl was overwhelmed. "Especially when I hear about so many transgenders whose families don't even want anything to do with them."

Lindy Duree's husband, Warren, accompanied Kahl to Trinidad in early March, barely ahead of spring planting. "I couldn't do anything physical for darn near six weeks," Kahl said. Her boss was getting antsy, but Kahl made it back onto the tractor in time. "I was still pretty tender when I started, but it wasn't too bad," she said. "I got to be a full-blown woman, or at least as close as I'll be."

Other big things changed that summer. Mitchell's relationship ended, and she moved off the ranch and into Pratt, a town of about seven thousand people, and rented a place in a trailer court behind a Walmart. She was determined to serve out her term as chair of Equality Kansas's southwest chapter. She estimates that the chapter got up to a hundred members, counting everyone who paid five dollars to join. It outgrew the rooms available at small-town libraries, so they met at people's houses. Kahl had even hosted a meeting at her Kalvesta farmhouse. "I made up some rainbow-colored signs and put them in the middle of nowhere, down on the main highway and up the road where I was. Everybody came up. I went up to the pizzeria in Ness City and got four big pizzas."

Kahl knows the southwest chapter wasn't as political as activists in Wichita, Topeka, and Lawrence might have wanted. But simply finding other LGBT people in western Kansas, let alone organizing them in any way, had been a project. "We wanted an outlet for LGBT people in western Kansas, somewhere we could go and be ourselves and be comfortable and not worry about people calling us names," she notes. After Mitchell's term as chair ended in 2010, Witt came out to try to get others to take on new roles, but the group started losing momentum.

Mitchell moved back to San Francisco in 2012. She said Kansas made her a better person. "Being a therapist, sitting in a room with people who are intensely religious Christians and trying to help them, I had to just be with them and not judge them. It's hard. I thought because I was liberal,

I was open-minded and accepting. No, not really. I used to think: 'I don't want them to judge me, so I can't judge them.'"

Kahl's work in Kansas was also done. By the summer of 2012 the western part of the state was in full-on drought, and her boss cut back on her hours after the harvest. Her mind was back in Iowa anyway, where six little kids "were wanting to see more of Grandma LuAnn." She contacted an agricultural career placement service and within a couple of weeks had a job on a place ten miles south of where she had grown up. She is now back in the house she couldn't sell, where she was living when she got divorced. It's a little strange, being surrounded by the memories of her former life, so it was good that she spent ten years away. "I can't imagine trying to transition in my hometown," Kahl said. "People around here still know me, and there's a few who don't have a word to say. Others come up and talk to me and have no problem calling me LuAnn and saying they are glad I'm back up here."

Even if it was simply showing a couple of Kalvesta ranchers that a trans woman could keep their cattle alive all by herself, each member of the southwest chapter had opened a mind or two—in a part of America where there just aren't that many people anyway.

Tanya Jantz knows some people snicker and call her "the lesbian doctor" in Cimarron. But rural America has a shortage of physicians, and for a while there weren't any medical doctors in town. "I was it as a chiropractor," Jantz told KU interviewer Albin. "I saw everything from skin lesions to 'What's wrong with my little pinky?' I was hoping by having a professional career out here for as long as I have and surviving and not being burned at the stake, so to speak, maybe people would listen and go, 'I've respected her all these years. I should really respect that sixteen-year-old that's walking around like that.'" She believes she's helped make life smoother for some kids. "Because there's been an enormous amount of kids come out of Cimarron that are gay," Jantz told Albin, and people's attitudes there had changed "big time" over the years.

At Dodge City Middle School, Duree sees evidence of progress not just in each new generation of seventh- and eighth-graders but also in her colleagues. One day during their regular planning meetings, some of the newer teachers were talking about a transgender person on the news and how wrong it was. Instead of all the other faculty joining in, the science teacher spoke up. "He said, 'I'm the science teacher, and you don't know what you're talking about. They were born that way.'"

After graduating from college in 2013, Isaac Unruh made a trip from Wichita home to Garden City. "That was the first time in a couple years that my husband hugged Isaac and told him he loved him," Sharon said. Roger had done research, she said, "and he just came to accept him." Later, when Isaac got a serious boyfriend, he said, "Dad said he wanted to meet him. I ended up taking him home for Christmas." Garden City is changing too, Sharon said. Her generation still isn't accepting, but younger generations are. For her part, she said, "I hold my head up high. It's not hard for me to say I have a gay son."

Diane Silver, who was vice chair of Equality Kansas in those days, remembers driving from Lawrence all the way out to a meeting in Mitchell's territory. "I have never been in a more isolated place in my life," Silver said. "I remember hearing stories about how they were actually putting up Xeroxed signs around town to announce the meeting, and someone came up and said, 'I want to help. I'm not an organizer, but can I make cookies?' When I heard that I just about cried. You would think they'd take their lives in their hands, putting signs up like that, and maybe they were."

LGBT people in college-town Lawrence, Silver realized, "lived in a lot of privilege" that she hadn't understood. "People in the more rural areas talked about the need to have Equality Kansas be a social organization as well as a political organization. Us folks from Douglas County thought, 'Well, okay, but isn't that a waste of time?' But we had other opportunities for socializing and they didn't." Silver realizes she was naïve. "I remember being surprised that we had any differences. I thought, 'We're all gay people. We all have the same fights.' Except we didn't all have the same fights."

But in the next couple of years, LGBTs in three different cities concentrated on starting the same fights.

PART THREE

THE COMEBACK

THREE CITIES, THREE LOSSES, AND A YEAR OF WINS

In Cincinnati, in the spring of 2011, John Arthur was diagnosed with amyotrophic lateral sclerosis. The effort to have Arthur's partner of nearly two decades, Jim Obergefell, listed as the surviving spouse on his death certificate resulted in an ambulance transporting Arthur on July 11, 2013—two weeks after *United States v. Windsor*—to a medically equipped plane for a flight to Baltimore/Washington International Thurgood Marshall Airport, where the plane stayed on the tarmac just long enough for Arthur's aunt, ordained to perform such duties, to marry them legally in Maryland before it turned around and flew home. Arthur died on October 22, 2013. When Ohio did not recognize their marriage, Obergefell sued.

The rest of the country, meanwhile, continued its remarkable turnaround not just on marriage equality but on LGBT acceptance in general. When New York legalized same-sex marriage in 2011 not by a state Supreme Court ruling but rather through a vote by state legislators, it seemed to signal an irreversible shift in public opinion. In 2012 Tammy Baldwin of Wisconsin became the first openly gay person to win election to the US Senate, while Maine, Minnesota, and

Washington legalized gay marriage by referenda—the opposite of voter behavior less than a decade earlier in other states.

An extraordinary assist came from the country's private employers. In 2016, approaching the one-year anniversary of *Obergefell v. Hodges*, the *Washington Post* reported that "corporate America's embrace of gay rights has reached a stunning tipping point."[1] The *Post* gave much credit to the Human Rights Campaign (HRC), which in 2002 had established its Corporate Equality Index, rating companies on LGBT equality in their workplaces. "An all-time record of 366 major businesses—spanning nearly every industry and geography—earned a top score of 100 percent and the coveted distinction of 'Best Places to Work for LGBT Equality,'" HRC noted in its 2015 report. "This designation reflects true inclusion of the transgender workforce, from nondiscrimination protections, to inclusive benefits and diversity practices, to respectful gender transition guidelines, allowing employees to self-identify based on gender identity, and engaging the broader transgender community. Wherever these 366 companies are doing business, transgender-inclusion is a priority." By HRC's count, 66 percent of the country's Fortune 500 companies include gender-identity protections.[2]

But these monumental changes did not sit well in certain quarters, and equality advocates faced a burgeoning backlash: HRC also logged more than one hundred anti-LGBT bills in twenty-nine states. "These bills, which are often under the guise of religious freedom," the organization explained in its 2015 annual report, "would allow people to be denied service or a hotel—or even medical treatment—because of their sexual orientation or gender identity."[3]

Battles in state legislatures were essentially just higher-level versions of fights that had been happening in cities and counties since the days of Anita Bryant, when gay people sought to be protected from discrimination in places like Miami-Dade County, Florida; Saint Paul, Minnesota; Eugene, Oregon; and Wichita. Diane Silver's hometown of East Lansing, Michigan, had passed sexual-orientation protections before the Bryant days, in 1972. (I remember the fight—a losing one—in my hometown of Lincoln, Nebraska, in 1982.) Kansas City, Missouri, passed protections in 1993. By the time of *Obergefell*, national LGBT organizations were counting around two hundred such protections all around the country and in twenty states. In the early days, most of these nondiscrimination efforts did not consider transgender people; some cities (like Lawrence) added gender-identity protections years after protecting lesbians, gays, and bisexuals, while in other places trans rights are still the final frontier. Some places passed full protections in employment, housing, and public accommodations, while others, for example, prohibited discrimination in public jobs but not in private employment.

These city-council-level efforts were carried out by small groups of LGBT people and their allies, some of their names making the local papers while behind-the-scenes work by many others has been lost to history. Often, these citizens knew they would lose, or that they might win at city hall but that their victory might be reversed by angry petitioners. But part of the point was to engage in a few months of debate that brought news coverage, forcing their friends and neighbors to think about things that had never occurred to most people in these communities.

This strategy, which predated, then paralleled, and now continues after the marriage equality movement, has been a crucial factor in America's dramatic shift toward LGBT acceptance. Three small cities in Kansas—Manhattan, Salina, and Hutchinson—were among those providing text-book examples of how this most grassroots of efforts worked.

6

Cora Holt didn't know whether the striking person who moved as gracefully as a ballerina through the coffee shop was a man or a woman, but Holt was mesmerized. Even in a college-town espresso bar like Radina's in Aggieville, Holt thought a gender nonconformist such as the one she was observing would have looked afraid, or at least nervous. But this person looked serene. "I thought she was lovely," Holt remembered.[1]

"She" would eventually become the correct pronoun for one of the key figures in the gender-identity education of Manhattan, even if at the time Alley Stoughton wasn't sure herself. A professor in Kansas State University's computing and information sciences department, Stoughton had come to Manhattan after a circuitous journey growing up as a child of the sixties in Los Angeles, knowing she was "differently gendered" since her early twenties, moving to Scotland for a PhD at the University of Edinburgh and then to England, where she spent seven years as a research fellow and lecturer at the University of Sussex. After Stoughton's then-wife had their daughter, the couple decided to move back to the States, and a colleague from Stoughton's doctoral-student days who was working at K-State told Stoughton about a job opening in Manhattan. Stoughton knew moving to a proudly agrarian city of fifty thousand people in Kansas would be a big change. "But it seemed like it was a good job.

Whatever gender or sexual orientation issues were going on with me I'd basically suppressed for years, so I wasn't thinking about whether it was a safe place to be LGBT or whatever."[2] Stoughton's family settled into a suburban neighborhood named Candlewood. "It seemed like it would be a good place for a child to grow up, and it was," she said. In one sense, Stoughton would grow up there too.

Over the next seventeen years, Stoughton earned tenure in the K-State computer science department; she also separated from her spouse and eventually filed for divorce. She began to think of herself as "in the middle" when it came to gender, still known professionally as Allen but dressing in a way that was clearly feminine. "I thought I'd carve out someplace where I wasn't a man but wasn't a woman," Stoughton said.

She was among those fighting the same-sex marriage amendment along with Christopher Renner and the Flint Hills Human Rights Project in the mid-2000s. "We did a tremendous amount of canvassing, talking to complete strangers, trying to educate them," Stoughton said, going so far as to call the marriage amendment "a kind of gift." Otherwise, "there's no way we could have gone around and talked to strangers about their attitudes toward gay or queer people. You don't just show up for no reason, but we had a reason." Stoughton remembers standing on a self-declared evangelical woman's doorstep a few days before the vote. She knows how odd she must have appeared: a willowy five-foot-eleven not-man-not-woman. Other people told her how gutsy she was going door to door. But Stoughton just had the nerve, perhaps subconsciously understanding the not-to-be-wasted opportunity to appear on a neighbor's doorstep as someone "who isn't managing to fit into the box that is assigned." The woman was respectful, Stoughton said, but told Stoughton that everyone she knew was planning to vote for the marriage amendment. A week after the vote, Stoughton ran into the woman at the Aggieville Chipotle. Based on their earlier conversation, the woman said, she had decided to abstain from voting. Stoughton knew that was a victory.

"We came damn close to beating it in the city," Stoughton said of the amendment. In the territory where the Flint Hills Human Rights Project had campaigned, the margin of loss was much closer than in the rest of the state; the amendment passed by just 53 percent in Riley County. "We influenced a lot of people," Stoughton said. Buoyed by those results, LGBTs and their allies turned their attention to city hall. They couldn't control the rest of the state, but maybe they could make Manhattan friendlier.

Over the next year, with Renner as chair, the Flint Hills Human Rights Project joined with the other organizations that merged to form Equality Kansas. That turned out to be a short romance. Equality Kansas kicked out the Manhattan chapter after disputes over strategy in the 2006 elections, and the Manhattanites regrouped as the Flint Hills Human Rights Project once again. Renner and Stoughton traded leadership for the next few years, sponsoring monthly educational programs and putting on LGBT film festivals. Renner's ally from the marriage amendment fight, Tammy Hawk, had started a Flint Hills PFLAG chapter, and together they hosted First Friday potlucks at the First Congregational United Church of Christ and staged plays by Kansas State graduate students at the Manhattan Arts Center.

Energized and organized, they wanted city commissioners to prohibit discrimination against LGBT people. Lawrence was the only city that had succeeded in such an effort, and its 1995 ordinance only covered sexual orientation, not gender identity. But other cities around the country (and some states) now had nondiscrimination ordinances protecting both categories, so the Flint Hills Human Rights Project took its proposal to the city's Human Rights and Services Board, which convened three public meetings.

"All the Bible thumpers were there," Holt remembered. She had gone to the last public meeting, intending to speak up about the need for protection from discrimination. Holt was an adjunct at Manhattan Christian College, teaching evening classes in economics and marketing. During the day Holt worked for the state, administering Medicaid for elderly and disabled Kansans; she was also finishing a PhD in adult education at Kansas State University. Holt said most of her students at the Christian College weren't especially religious; they were adults who had enrolled in the night school management program because it was convenient. "I had people who'd worked all day long, moms and dads who'd never finished school for whatever reason," Holt said. "They'd show up at six with their homework done. These people were on task."

As she walked into the Human Rights and Services Board hearing room, Holt saw several of her coworkers on one side. She imagines they thought she would sit with them, but she kept walking. "I could feel their eyes boring into my skin. I thought, 'Just ignore them, Cora, just ignore them.'" She listened as people who were sitting with the religious contingent testified that "those people" didn't need extra protection. Wanting to show that the argument was not hypothetical but human, Holt headed to the microphone. "I went up there and said, 'I work for Manhattan Christian College. I'm a lesbian. Tomorrow morning, they will fire me.'"

That was on March 9. The next day, Holt got a letter from the vice president for academic affairs at Manhattan Christian College informing her that she was now on paid administrative leave while the college investigated whether she had violated the faculty handbook. Six weeks later, Holt hired an attorney. It took until July for the college to decide she would not be allowed to teach classes due to "immoral behavior." The college settled her legal claim with a check for a few thousand dollars for classes she had been scheduled to teach in the fall.

Manhattan's Human Rights and Services Board, meanwhile, took no action on the nondiscrimination ordinance proposal. But at least one good thing came out of the whole exercise: after Holt started showing up at meetings of the Flint Hills Human Rights Project, she and Stoughton started dating. This complicated Holt's social life. Among her lesbian friends at K-State were some who, despite their academic work on gender roles, struggled with the idea of their friend dating a woman who hadn't been born a woman. She remembers a phone call from one who told her, essentially: "You're not really queer if you're hanging out with Alley, and we don't think we want to hang around with you anymore. If you stop seeing Alley we'll still be your friends." It reminded her of junior high school, and Holt ditched her friends. "I expected to get fired. I knew I would get fired. But I didn't expect the mean-girl thing at all."

Stoughton knew she was "probably the topic of a lot of conversations in Manhattan." A faculty member in the human ecology department invited her to visit a class and discuss the kind of clothing she had been wearing, which seemed to Stoughton like a positive opportunity to educate people. Stoughton later heard through mutual friends that the professor "said all sorts of nasty things about me, that I was really just a man." Even when people were nice to her in person and respectful to her professionally, Stoughton began to realize: "Not everyone is my friend."

But the two moved on with their activism. That fall, the Flint Hills Human Rights Project organized Manhattan's first Transgender Day of Remembrance, adding one more location to the hundreds of places around the world taking part in the annual ritual that had started with a candlelight vigil in San Francisco in 1999 (to honor Rita Hester, murdered near Boston). Now, fifty people showed up at Aggieville's Dusty Bookshelf to read or listen to stories of trans people killed in hate crimes around the world.

Activists in Kansas were making progress, and not just in college-town bookstores. The next year, Governor Kathleen Sebelius signed an executive order adding sexual orientation and gender identity to policies prohibiting discrimination against state employees. Holt was among those who attended the signing ceremony on August 31, 2007, and told reporters how she had been fired. Sebelius's order wouldn't have prevented that because it only covered the twenty-five thousand people working for state agencies, not private entities such as a religiously affiliated college. But, Holt told the Lawrence Journal-World, "the ripples from this are going to reach far and wide. So many people will have a safety net that they didn't have before." Sebelius said the order brought Kansas in line with thirty-one other states and most Fortune 500 companies. "We were out of date and out of step," she said.[3] Diane Silver, who was there and wrote up the day's events on her blog, noted a striking comment from the governor as she shook hands and handed out ceremonial pens: "Sorry it took us so long."[4]

It had been two years since the notable public distance Sebelius had kept from LGBT activists during the marriage amendment days. What had changed? For one thing, Sebelius had been comfortably reelected to a second term in 2006 and could not run for a third. For another, Cyd Slayton and a few others in Kansas City had stayed active in a local chapter of the national Human Rights Campaign, and the organization's new president, Joe Solmonese, had made several trips to Kansas City and Lawrence. One of those was an event with the governor at Slayton's house. Slayton stood at her patio door, thrilled to see her straight neighbors and a whole crowd of LGBTs enjoying appetizers as the governor talked about Kansas doing the right thing. That month, influential gays in Kansas City donated thousands of dollars to Sebelius's reelection campaign.

A few months after Sebelius's second term began, Slayton and Tom Witt were among those invited to meet with the governor about an executive order. Witt wanted to see the language before the meeting. The governor's chief of staff sent him the draft, which Witt remembers as thin, at best, with no mention of gender identity, no reference for training human resources departments in state agencies, no real mechanism for enforcement. He and others revised the draft and sent it back to Sebelius's office. Witt went to the meeting with the governor carrying a stack of exemplary statutes and executive orders from other states. A meeting originally scheduled for fifteen minutes had gone well beyond that when Witt pulled out the document he had been saving for last. It was from Ohio, Sebelius's home state, where her father, John "Jack" Gilligan, had been governor in the early 1970s, and where the current governor, Ted Strickland, had signed an executive order a few months earlier. "Look," Witt told her, "even Ohio has added gender identity to its nondiscrimination list." In Slayton's memory, Sebelius didn't need that much convincing. "The governor said firmly that she wanted the most progressive executive order for the LGBT community in Kansas," Slayton said. "She said she wanted it to be as progressive as Ohio. Given the firm conviction in her voice, I believed the governor had come to the meeting already prepared to do the right thing."

Whatever the LGBT team did, it worked. "I remember trying not to tear up when Sebelius told the group what she was going to do," Slayton said. "Maybe this was the first time ever that I felt welcome in my state." With Sebelius's signature, Kansas became the fourth state to prohibit discrimination against state employees based on gender identity as well as sexual orientation. These protections would later fall to a political pendulum that swung like a sledgehammer: eight years later, Governor Sam Brownback would make a dramatic statement by rescinding the Sebelius order. (In Ohio, Governor John Kasich would let Strickland's order expire in 2011 before reinstating protections based on sexual orientation only.) For the time being, though, Kansas had one of the most progressive policies in the country.

Three months later, Alley Stoughton decided it was time for her middle-gender phase to come to an end. She started taking female hormones. And already, the education of Kansas State University was underway. Stoughton had legally changed her first name to Alley in 2005, and she was already listed as "Alley" in course catalogs, thanks to university databases that allowed employees to select "Likes to be known as" rather than their legal names. But she needed the university's official records to match her gender, not just her name. She wrote to the university's affirmative action office to ask about the process. The director wrote back: "The decision to change one's gender is a personal one that does not initially require any action by an administrator."[5]

"So I just went about doing it," Stoughton said, "and various things went wrong." The chair of her department "was not totally actively hostile," she said, but most of her colleagues wouldn't use the correct pronoun. And inevitably, someone raised a bathroom objection. She had been using women's restrooms for about six months with no incident. Then, in the building where she worked, someone made a complaint. "Not that I'd done anything wrong, just that I was in the wrong place." Stoughton was summoned to a meeting with human resources. Rather than educating the person who had made the complaint (or the entire campus), administrators said that they planned to identify a small number of bathrooms where she could go. Anticipating a difficult discussion and knowing she might need a supporter, Stoughton had brought along a straight, cisgender female friend, a professor who also held an administrative position. "It took an hour and a half, but by the end we'd convinced them that going to the correct bathroom was a normal thing for a trans person," Stoughton said.

What "the correct bathroom" was for trans people would become a central—and politically manufactured—issue in the struggle for LGBT equality for years to come, as opponents cravenly conjured false images of men molesting girls in ladies' rooms. Stoughton is not sure what would have happened if administrators had insisted on a limited number of trans-allowed restrooms on a 556-acre campus. "I probably would have said, 'I'm not going to follow your rules.' I don't know if they would have fired me, but I felt like I had to keep pushing along and I did."

In February 2008, Stoughton wrote to the head of the university's human resources office, Gary Leitnaker, asking how to change her gender in all of the university's official systems. His reply suggested that it would be as easy as checking a different box in the human resources database. Later that same day, however, he had learned otherwise: "Alley, it has come to my attention that our legal office has already advised the university's administration that we should not list a preferred gender in our systems that is legally inaccurate. Therefore, I'll have to back off my previous comments to you and say that we can't change the gender (to a 'preferred' gender) in our systems until it's recognized by the state and/or federal governments."[6]

Stoughton knew what it would take for her gender to be recognized by state and federal governments: surgery, which she would have that summer. By August 2008 she was female on her driver's license, female on her Social Security card, and female on her passport. The university's lawyers, however, were advising Leitnaker that making the change at K-State would require a court order. Growing angry, and believing she was covered by Sebelius's LGBT protection order, Stoughton sought help from Topeka attorney Pedro Irigonegaray and the two began preparing legal arguments. Leitnaker, meanwhile, made an executive decision: the university's attorneys were wrong. He directed his department to change Stoughton's gender.

When she saw herself as female in the university's system, Stoughton cried. Her thank-you to Leitnaker, however, came with a plea that the university adopt "a simple, objective procedure for trans people who have satisfied the federal and state governments that they have changed sex/gender."[7] She noted, among other things, that the Social Security Administration "is unhappy" when an employer's federal tax reporting information for an employee does not match the SSA's information on record. And remaining "male" in the university's system could lead to serious errors when it came to Stoughton's university-funded health insurance ("Due to hormonal therapy and the loss of my testes, I will be at risk of breast cancer, just like other middle-aged women, and thus I'll be scheduled for regular mammograms. If someone like me is labeled as 'male,' my breasts will tend to be seen as pathological, not normal.") Leitnaker

Alley Stoughton, speaking at the first
Manhattan Pride Rally in April 2010.
Credit: Christopher Renner

understood. "It will be seamless for the next person in your situation," he replied, and acknowledged Stoughton's gratitude with his own: "Thank you again and it's a pleasure, Alley."[8]

The university's handling of her transition was "textbook how not to do it as an institution," Stoughton said. "I didn't know what to do. I really didn't," Leitnaker recalled, seven years later.[9] He had had a long career in the private and public sector by the time Stoughton's question came up, but had never been faced with that situation. By the time Stoughton's gender was correct with the other state and federal agencies, and knowing that the university's attorneys provide counsel but that final decisions rested with him, he said, "I thought holy cow, if she's able to do all of that, I'm no longer going to be a hindrance. Let's just get it done."

At the start of that academic year, Stoughton was pictured at the top of an article along with Joyce Woodford, a counselor who worked with transgender students, in Kansas State's faculty and staff newsletter. "It's hard for the individual to bear the weight of explanation," Stoughton said.[10] Her students had been wonderful, Stoughton continued, noting that after the semester she transitioned, her teacher evaluations "were at least as good as they had been." And she took the high road with regard to the faculty: "My colleagues have taken it in stride as well."

Woodford pointed out that Kansas State wasn't "the first or only university to move toward transgender accommodation," citing Newman University, a Catholic college in Wichita, which already provided gender-neutral, single-occupancy restrooms. "Nothing about being transgender is new," Woodford said. "The apparent current 'newness' stems from the availability of information, the willingness of people like Dr. Stoughton to become more public, and the rippling effect of normalizing what has seemed to be an exotic and rare gender status."[11]

Looking back, Stoughton said her public transition "somehow really wasn't as awful" as it could have been. She supposes her body type and body language must not have felt threatening. "People didn't yell things at me from cars or glare at me," she said, but she was always aware of possible dangers. One time in a grocery store parking lot as she was loading bags into her car, Stoughton noticed a man drive by in a pickup truck and look twice before driving on. Believing he was gone, Stoughton got into her car and was about to back out when he tapped on her window. For reasons she still doesn't understand, Stoughton rolled down the window even as she was thinking she shouldn't. "I know what you're doing and I think it's great," the man said. But he gave off a strange energy, and the incident frightened her. "It was like, if he didn't think it was great, he wouldn't have thought twice about beating me up." Eventually, Stoughton would have surgery that slightly altered the shape of her face to make it less obvious she is trans, which made her life easier.

What really made her life easier was moving to Boston in 2010. Stoughton and Holt had traveled to Massachusetts to get married in 2009. Soon, living in a place where their marriage wasn't valid became untenable. "Cora and I decided maybe we'd fought enough in Kansas," Stoughton said. She left the safety of tenured academia and now does computer science research and contract work for government agencies. In Massachusetts, she said, "being trans seems almost like a nonissue. I'm conscious of the fact that being white and middle class—professional class—makes a huge difference. I don't normally have experiences that are weird." The middle of the country was five or ten years behind the coasts when it came to understanding transgender, Stoughton said. Living in Kansas "feels like a weird snapshot of history." Still, trapped in that snapshot, somehow things were all right. "I would travel through Oklahoma and go to restrooms in truck stops, and I can't think of a time when anything strange happened. People didn't glare at me." But that was in truck stop women's rooms. Pretransition, men's rooms had been a different story. "There was one time at the public library in Manhattan. I was washing my hands and some man walks in, takes a look at me, theatrically steps back and looks at the sign like, 'what's going on here!'" Stoughton got out just in time, because theatrical bathroom reactions were only beginning in Manhattan.

Jonathan Mertz had returned to Manhattan in 2006, after seventeen years in Washington, DC. When family members asked him to come home and help care for his elderly parents, Mertz, the youngest of five, said one of the conditions was that he would not go back in the closet. "You guys need to be ready for that," he told them, "and they said okay."[12] He had grown up on a farm outside of nearby Wamego, a town of about four thousand people and one *Wizard of Oz* museum, and had gone to college and graduate school at K-State, staying closeted until his late twenties. "I wanted to try living somewhere other than Kansas," Mertz said.[13] DC's gay community was large, long-established, and energetic. Mertz considered himself a "midlevel activist"—not a leader, but deeply involved, going to rallies and volunteering at the Whitman-Walker Clinic, which was on the forefront of the national gay community's response to AIDS.

"I came back and was like, 'I want to meet people,'" Mertz said. Options existed, though they were limited. Twenty miles away at the Xcalibur Club in Junction City, an enthusiastic roster of drag performers regularly raised money for AIDS services. The annual Flint Hills Pride campout at Milford County Reservoir, which had started as a woodsy weekend getaway for the men in the Junction City Teddy Bears, had grown into a two-day minifestival of games, performances, and a barbecue, with as many as 150 people showing up during its peak years in the mid-2000s. And Mertz knew the Flint Hills Human Rights Project was a gay group, so he went to a meeting. Shortly afterward, one of the members asked him to lead the organization.

Since the previous effort to interest city commissioners in passing an antidiscrimination ordinance had stalled out at the Human Rights and Services Board four years earlier, the group had started screening candidates for city elections. Now, three out of five city commissioners were on record as supporting such an ordinance. The time was right to make another push. It was 2010, after all, and the world was clearly changing. As they geared up, Mertz asked group members how they felt about the tactic of incremental steps: getting the commission to add sexual orientation first, and then, when the heavens didn't tumble down onto the Flint Hills, pushing for gender identity protection later. "They said, obviously we're going to go for both. There was no discussion, no second thoughts. That's something I'm very proud of." At the time, Lawrence's ordinance only covered sexual orientation, and Mertz's group saw a chance for Manhattan to be more progressive than its college-town rival to the east.

They went to city hall with a genuine if not particularly heartwrenching example of basic discrimination: a graduate student whose landlord had denied his request to let his boyfriend move into his apartment. On the Kansas State campus, more students were coming out at the university. The gay-and-bisexual Lambda Delta Phi fraternity had been chartered in 2006, which is where a sociology major named Lukus Ebert found a home with ten brothers when he arrived in August 2008. After enduring years of bullying at Wamego High School, Ebert was a freshman ready to change the world. Besides the men at Lambda Delta Phi, he knew some of the women who had started the lesbian Gamma Rho Lambda (it would be chartered in December 2009), and Ebert was among the founders of a new student organization called LGBT and Allies. "There was just a lot of energy and need for LGBT support organizations," Ebert remembered.[14] "The people who started LGBT and Allies were all very type-A personality, go-get-'em, politically charged, and really caring about social issues and social justice."

Ebert's cohort included a political science major named Dusty Garner, who went to his generation's March on Washington in October 2009, where speakers included Matthew Shepard's mother Judy, openly lesbian New York City Councilwoman Christine Quinn, and Lady Gaga, who pressed the Obama administration to end "Don't Ask, Don't Tell" (the president would do so in 2011) and repeal the federal Defense of Marriage Act. After marching in Washington, Garner thought they should march in Manhattan. [15]

Ebert agreed, and was among three co-chairs who mapped a mile-long route from the Riley County Courthouse west along Poyntz Avenue, then north through Aggieville for a rally at the small Triangle Park across from campus. They guessed maybe fifty people would show up.

On the day of the parade, Mertz was driving his pickup at the end of the procession. "When I turned onto Poyntz to follow the walkers I had this view of a mass of people with signs and rainbow flags walking up the street and more people were running to join the crowd. It took my breath away," he told Christopher Renner, who wrote up the day's events for the *Kansas Free Press* website. The organizers counted two hundred people—a big number for the Little Apple. "This pride celebration will definitely be annual," said another one of the organizers, Samuel Brinton. [16] His promise would come true, but the high from that first parade was short-lived.

Mertz and the Flint Hills Human Rights Project anticipated opposition to their ordinance effort, but they were no match for more than two dozen ministers who soon organized against them. Mayor Bruce Snead, who supported the ordinance, wanted it to come directly to city commissioners for a vote. James Sherrow and Jayme Morris-Hardeman were also on board, so that vote would have been quick work. But after some debate about the process, commissioners once again sent the issue back to the city's Human Rights and Services Board for more study.

Manhattan's Code of Ordinances prohibited discrimination in employment, housing, and public accommodations based on the usual categories, such as race, sex, familial status, disability, religion, age, color, national origin, or ancestry, and in a nod to nearby Fort Riley, home to the army's vaunted First Infantry Division, whose twenty-five thousand military and civilian personnel lend this part of north-central Kansas a bunkered worldliness, the city had also added military status to the code. "Our thought was, they'd put a comma at the end of the list, then add sexual orientation, comma, and gender identity, and that would be it," Mertz said. "Instead, city staff came back with a major, major, major change to the city ordinance."

City hall staffers had identified a weakness in how such a law could be enforced. While Manhattan's human rights board had the power to hold hearings and levy fines if someone violated the ordinance, the guilty party could conceivably appeal to the state level. And with no statewide legal protections for employees of private companies, or laws securing equal access to housing and public accommodations, there would need to be a stronger enforcement process at the local level.

"Suddenly it was going around town that you were going to be fined $30,000 if you were found guilty of discrimination," Mertz said. "But, actually, that was the maximum amount, not the minimum, and even to get to that point would take several hoops of negotiations with city staff before you would ever get fined." Also, opponents griped that Manhattan shouldn't be adding categories the state didn't cover, even though the state didn't cover military status.

Commissioners scheduled a hearing for the end of August, setting up a contentious summer. On the side of equality, Mayor Pro-Tem Sherrow proclaimed June to be LGBT Pride Month. On the side of religion, a new organization called Awaken Manhattan emerged to combat the rising threat to morality—and bathrooms.

Awaken Manhattan was mostly ministers, along with the president of Manhattan Christian College and others who had been rounded up by the Kansas Family Policy Council, a Wichita-based operation manned by a political operative named Robert Noland and allied with national organizations such as Focus on the Family, the Family Research Council, and the Alliance Defense Fund (now called the Alliance Defending Freedom). Awaken Manhattan branded the ordinance a "bathroom bill" and got busy supplying opponents with talking points. "Aside from enacting protections for activity that is morally wrong," the Kansas Family Policy Council warned, "grave concerns have surfaced regarding religious liberties, rights of conscience and perhaps most troubling, questions regarding the gender-specificity of bathrooms and locker rooms in public facilities."[17]

Before anyone could get serious about bathroom questions, though, staffers in the city manager's office and legal department would have to define "gender identity," which was proving problematic. Manhattanites struggled with this and other aspects of the ordinance in public meetings that dragged on for hours on weeknights in August, September, and October. At October's meeting, city staffers finally had a definition of gender identity: "the gender-related identity, appearance, or mannerisms or other gender-related characteristics of an individual, with or without regard to the individual's designated sex at birth." When the meeting opened up for public comments, Daniel Blomberg, a Washington, DC–based attorney who flew around the country representing Alliance Defense Fund clients who said that their religious freedom was under threat from these types of ordinances, held the floor for half an hour warning about the dangers.

"If you go right outside the hall over here, just around the corner, you'll see there's a sign that says 'Men,' and right over there a sign that says 'Women,'" Blomberg helpfully noted.[18] "If you're going to use these definitions as they're written, eventually you'll have to get rid of men's and women's bathrooms." A court might eventually intervene to stop such an unthinkable future, he suggested, but only after Manhattan filled boxes and cabinets full of expensive litigation. His point was that sexual orientation and gender identity were ill-defined and malleable behaviors, which made them different from the other protected categories. "You wouldn't have out there a Baptist bathroom and an Episcopalian bathroom. This wouldn't make much sense. But there is a distinction, a very reasonable distinction, between men and women."

Blomberg had examples of trouble ahead. "In Maine, just last month, the human rights commission decided that a school had discriminated against a student because it wouldn't allow a sixth-grade boy to use the girl's restroom, and they punished the school for it. It was discrimination because it was a transgender child." He warned that owners of businesses who required employees to wear branded clothing could get sued over a "biological male, wearing your uniform, going into women's restrooms."

While Awaken Kansas brought in big guns from DC, supporters of the ordinance had reinforcements from Topeka: Stephanie Mott. Other transgender people lived in Manhattan, but since Stoughton's move to Massachusetts, Mott was the only openly trans person in Kansas who regularly testified in these sorts of situations (in addition to her appearances at pride parades and anywhere else where a publicly trans person might be helpful). Mott explained to commissioners over and over again that she wasn't pretending to be a woman—she was a woman; that only by living as a woman was she able to find health and happiness and to function in society. When city board members and commissioners asked her about bathrooms, Mott patiently told them that she used the women's facilities. The people of Manhattan didn't need to be afraid of transgender people in bathrooms, Mott told them—they just needed to be educated. Over the summer, Mott made three trips from Topeka to Manhattan to repeat these explanations.

By late October the human rights board had heard enough and forwarded a final version of the ordinance to commissioners. Meanwhile, Awaken Manhattan had been gathering strength. At a commission meeting in early November, Bob Flack of Grace Baptist Church read a letter signed by twenty-seven pastors, some of whom stood in solidarity as he spoke. The pastors rejected and opposed all forms of prejudice, they said. "But, advancing godly behavior does not constitute prejudice. God's design for human flourishing as revealed in the Bible includes the enjoyment of sexual intimacy only within the beauty and bounds of a marriage commitment between a man and a woman. All other sexual behavior is sin, subject to God's judgment."[19] They acknowledged that they, too, had sinned, and they were grateful that Jesus's death on the cross absorbed "the judgment due sinners," allowing them to "celebrate the forgiveness He offers to all who trust Him." The problem they had was that "creating protected classes in an antidiscrimination ordinance for self-selected behaviors and personally chosen identities would be bad law. We unite in concern that such an ordinance might silence individual Christians in response to the acceptance or practice of immorality when their silence would indicate consent."

The ministers, most from evangelical or Baptist churches, appeared to speak for all of Christianity while Manhattan's Methodists, Lutherans, and Presbyterians stayed quiet. "We heard the pastors of most of the

mainstream churches were in favor of the ordinance but wouldn't say anything out of fear of offending their congregants," Mertz said. "Even the
progressive religious groups in town were scared to say anything." The
parishioners at the liberal First Congregational United Church of Christ
and the Unitarian Universalists and the Quakers supported the ordinance,
but they weren't organized like Awaken Manhattan and they had little political weight to throw around.

It was standing-room only at city hall when the ordinance finally got
its official, mandatory first reading on December 7. It took hours for city
staffers to answer commissioners' questions about their months-long
process. At 10 p.m., Snead opened the floor for public comment. For two
hours, everyone listened to the same arguments they had been listening
to ad nauseam for months. Nearly forty people spoke.[20] One was a sixth-
grader at Lee Elementary (for). Another was an attorney representing the
Roman Catholic Diocese (against). Mertz and Brinton spoke (for). The
president of Manhattan Christian College spoke (against). A man named
Matthew Pennell (against) was afraid "a sexual predator could use the
ordinance to attack our children" and asked commissioners to consider
"children and adults sharing the same facilities." Stephanie Mott (for)
had once again driven over from Topeka, and Tom Witt (for) had driven
up from Wichita. Sue Gerth, president of Manhattan's PFLAG chapter and
mother of a transgender daughter, spoke (for); Mary and Bill Sier (for)
said they were blessed to be parents of an adult transgender child, but
their daughter didn't live in Manhattan because she didn't feel safe there.

The meeting lasted until 1:30 the next morning. When it was time
to vote, the same two commissioners who had always opposed the ordinance, Loren Pepperd and Bob Strawn, voted against it. The same
three who had always been in favor, Mayor Snead, Sherrow, and Morris-
Hardeman, voted for it.

Procedures dictated that there would be a second reading, but city
hall would get a breather from the subject until February 2, 2011, when
the ordinance was back on the agenda. After that commission meeting
was canceled because of a winter storm, the second and final reading, on
February 8, was a shorter (only two-hour) version of the same testimony,
from many of the same people. And the end result was the same: Pepperd

and Strawn voted no; Snead, Sherrow, and Morris-Hardeman voted yes. Manhattan would be the first city in Kansas to protect citizens from discrimination based on both sexual orientation and gender identity. The ordinance would go into effect six months later, in August 2011.

Except that it didn't.

City elections were in April. Supporter Sherrow would be the new mayor, but Snead had retired after sixteen years on the commission and Morris-Hardeman hadn't sought reelection. Pepperd remained on the commission. A new commissioner named Rich Jankovich had been lukewarm about the ordinance during his campaign, but two others, John Matta and Wynn Butler, were clearly against it. Opponents now held the majority. On the new commission's agenda for its first meeting in May: repealing the ordinance.

Everyone showed up to make their public comments all over again. Morris-Hardeman and Snead stepped up to the podium as private citizens, urging new commissioners not to negate everyone's hard work; others said the new commissioners had been elected in a referendum on this ordinance. Bob Reader of Awaken Manhattan warned that his group had collected 1,686 signatures on a petition, more than enough to put a repeal on a citywide ballot.[21] Commissioners and citizens endured another round of public testimony for the obligatory second reading a couple of weeks later, but the outcome was predetermined. The new majority voted for repeal. There would be no ordinance protecting LGBT people from discrimination in Manhattan after all.

Perhaps it was political naïveté that led the Flint Hills Human Rights Project to work so hard on passing an ordinance right before city elections. Perhaps it was lack of preparation for the inevitable backlash. Perhaps it was lack of campaigning to reelect allies. Maybe the original effort had exhausted the city's small group of LGBT activists and their allies—Mertz said he had trouble rounding up volunteers to campaign for city commission candidates. Maybe things might have been different if they had had some support from the national LGBT organizations. "Oh my God. I called and begged for help," Mertz said. He did speak with a representative from the National LGBTQ Task Force who came through town, but no one from the Human Rights Campaign ever returned his calls.

Still, the effort hadn't been a total loss. More people had joined the Flint Hills Human Rights Project and made donations and come out to testify. But now the organization lacked a clear direction. The Flint Hills Human Rights Project would put on events, but few people would show up.

While the organization retreated and city hall regressed, however, Kansas State University was continuing its profound transformation. Thanks to the efforts of Ebert and his fellow type-A personality activists, students who enrolled for the fall semester of 2010 arrived to find not only LGBT and Allies but also a brand-new LGBT Resource Center. Soon even more organizations would be up and running—a group for students in the high-profile veterinary medicine program, a group for alumni—and now there were events and awareness campaigns all over campus. "People don't call as many mean names, throw things, that just doesn't happen as much," Ebert told the K-State Collegian.[22]

Ebert and others attributed the friendlier environment to a new administration. In 2009, fusty Jon Wefald retired as the university's president after twenty-three years. His successor, Kirk Schulz, made a point of showing up to the LGBT and Allies' welcome-back barbecue, and forward-thinking leaders began taking over in key administrative roles (in April 2016, Schulz left Kansas to become president of Washington State University). The student newspaper was quoting Ebert and others for its July 2013 article because K-State had just earned an excellent ranking from Campus Pride, a national organization that assesses college atmospheres for LGBT students. When K-State first took part in the Campus Pride survey in 2009, it had earned an unhappy 1.5 out of a possible 5 stars. But now it was up to 4.5 stars—the same as traditionally liberal KU. And K-State was the only university in Kansas with a full-time LGBT Resource Center.

Running the center was Brandon Haddock, who had come to Kansas State in August 2007 after earning his bachelor's and master's degrees at Missouri State University. Though Missouri State was at the edge of the Ozark Mountains in Springfield—an Evangelical-Pentecostal-fundamentalist stronghold that is home to the national General Council of the Assemblies of God and the Baptist Bible Fellowship International—Haddock was used to more LGBT culture than he had found in Manhattan.

Despite its religious saturation, Springfield was a city of 164,000 people with five gay bars and an LGBT community center, and weekend getaways to Kansas City or Tulsa took less than three hours. Haddock had been active in the community, volunteering with PROMO—the Missouri gay rights organization—and the AIDS Project of the Ozarks, which served clients in twenty-nine counties.

"When I first moved here there was *no* LGBT community," Haddock said of Manhattan. "My friends were like, 'Why are you moving to the provinces?'"[23] Haddock had come to the Flint Hills to earn a doctorate at K-State. His undergraduate and master's work had been in geography and geospatial science, and Haddock was interested in why LGBT people stay in rural areas. He was already an authority on the subject, having grown up on a farm fifteen miles from the nearest gas station. "There were gay people all over," he said. "Everybody knows they're gay. They're just not waving a rainbow flag on their front porch." Haddock had graduated high school in a class of fifty-four people. "There were two lesbians who went to my senior prom together," he remembered. "No one said they couldn't attend prom." That was all the way back in 1993. Now, Haddock wanted to do quantifiable research that would help explain the obvious to all of those who might find it unfathomable.

Haddock had been recruited to Kansas State to study with a professor who ended up leaving shortly after his arrival, so he spent the next couple of years struggling to find other faculty members who believed his topic was worthy. After he had finally put together a dissertation committee and was settling into his research, the student government association was preparing to fund the LGBT Resource Center. Haddock's professors suggested that he apply for the job of running it, and a part-time graduate assistant job evolved into a full-time career in student services. Three years later, Haddock received a national leadership award from Campus Pride at the American College Personnel Association's annual convention in Las Vegas.[24]

Haddock finished his doctorate, but he doesn't see himself becoming a professor. He is finding more satisfaction in helping this new generation of LGBT students navigate their way through university life. "For a lot of these students," he said, "Manhattan, Kansas, is the biggest town they've ever been to." Each year, he said, the freshmen he's seeing are more secure in themselves. "They're more visible. So many high schools have gay-straight alliances. Parents got sick and tired of seeing their kids commit suicide—their neighbors, their nieces, their nephews. You have churches coming out as being open and affirming."

It's an odd moment for a place like K-State, which will always be a small-city ag school—that's the whole point of it. Even if gay and trans people ultimately achieve equal status, they'll be equals in a place best known for training future generations in the industries most associated with rural America and its mindsets. "The LGBT students who do well at K-State would not do well at KU," Haddock said. "There's still that social, political, religious conservatism they've grown up with and will carry the rest of their lives." He was talking about LGBT Republicans in Kansas, a phenomenon that has not changed much since the mid-eighties, when men like Bruce Ney studied agriculture law with future governor Sam Brownback. "It goes back to those family ties, what they've heard all of their life growing up: they're Republican first and foremost."

Thanks to his doctoral research and his conversations with students, Haddock has a deeper understanding of what he already knew about why LGBT people stay in Kansas despite its often unfriendly or outright hostile atmosphere. It's simple, universal, and not specific to LGBTs. "They stay because they love it. Just the landscape."

For now, Haddock is staying, too. He and his husband, Jacob Keehn, bought a house in Junction City, which is half the size of Manhattan. "I am not an urban person myself," Haddock said. "I'm the kind of person who likes to pee off my front porch"—though Haddock isn't making a habit of that, since their house is in town. It's unclear whether the ministers in Awaken Manhattan would have considered front-porch peeing to be a moral problem, but by then they were long gone, having turned their attention to bathrooms in Salina and Hutchinson.

7

Scott Graybeal headed to the Salina Community Theater in late February 2012. August Wilson's *Fences* had just ended a two-week run, and *Cabaret* wouldn't debut until April, so that night and for the next two Tuesdays, people in the auditorium's 330 tiered seats would see a different kind of drama: three public forums on whether LGBT residents of Salina should have protections under the city's nondiscrimination ordinance.

Just a few months after the newly elected city commission in Manhattan put a painful end to the year-long drama in that city an hour to the east, an Equality Kansas chapter in Salina had started a similar fight. Here, as in Manhattan, commissioners had scheduled public forums about the issue.

Graybeal was a single father, raising his daughter and working at Security Savings Bank. People close to him knew he was gay, and for everyone else, Graybeal figured there might be a giveaway in his sense of humor, the stylish way he had shaved his head, his designer glasses, and his fondness for 1970s white grommet belts and Chuck Taylors. But he hadn't been in a relationship for more than a decade, so there was rarely a need for his sexual orientation to be the subject of conversation. He had also kept a low profile while his daughter, Halie, was growing up, fearing that if he were too openly gay she might be a target for bullies. He certainly had been when he was her age.

It had been almost twenty-five years since Graybeal graduated from Salina Central High School, and from there he had followed the prescribed path for young Methodist men in small Kansas towns, getting married and having Halie, before his marriage imploded and Graybeal eventually stopped kidding himself about being gay. In recent years he had occasionally gone to an Equality Kansas meeting, though he had avoided joining the organization because it was too political for his comfort. But now Halie was a senior in high school and the generational shift in attitudes about LGBT people had reached even Salina: Halie had several gay friends, for example. Graybeal had begun to think about getting more involved.

Graybeal watched as the first few people made their way down to the floor and spoke in support of LGBT protections. Soon, however, speakers began introducing themselves as Christians and stating their opposition. Then the testimony went back and forth. After about an hour, a young man walked to the microphone. "I thought, 'Who's this cute guy?'" said Graybeal.[1] The speaker introduced himself as Sean Mune. He had lived in town for a little less than two years. "I don't believe that the information people have been getting about gays, lesbians, and transgenders is really informed. I am female-to-male transgender," Mune said.[2] "I've been this way my whole life. I'm not arguing about that. I don't oppose people who oppose me. I don't force them to participate, either."

Mune spoke about the possibility that he could lose his job by appearing in public, but said he wasn't afraid. "I'll find another job because I have to. But this is an issue that affects me every day. Our lives are on the line." Mune said he didn't make much money, that most trans people don't. He said he had lived all over the country and didn't know one transgender person who owned a home, so the issue of housing discrimination was real. "We have to fight for our jobs," he said. He cited a study that determined one out of every twenty-five transgender people would be murdered. "You don't have to face that," he told the audience. "I do." Mune said he welcomed the community dialogue. "I'm committed to bringing love to Salina, and that has to come through being allowed to live, and be normal. And right now I can't."

Mune's testimony was a surprise to the members of Equality Kansas, who didn't know who he was. Mune had made his way through childhood as a Mormon girl in Alabama, through Christian seminary school in New

York, through homelessness after being kicked out of a church in Colorado, through a gay-conversion program in California, through a gender transition that began in 2007 and took him back to New York, then to Chicago, then to tiny Lucas, Kansas, where he had gone to help out some "crazy trans women" who had bought some cheap property in the town of four hundred people that was, as Mune put it, "probably the only place nobody would know they were trans."[3] Now he was working in a Petro truck stop in Salina and had gone to the forum because he had been desperate to find anything resembling a queer community. When he heard about the forum, Mune thought, "I needed to be part of this conversation. One thing I've learned in my life is you can't argue with a witness. If somebody's witnessed a transgender, they can't say we don't exist, that we're not hurting, that we don't deserve these rights. A lot of violence happened to my partners. I've been homeless. You can't tell me I don't need these rights."

After Mune's testimony, the religious speakers began to pile on, and Graybeal's mood darkened. "I speak in the name of the Lord Jesus Christ," said a gravelly voiced eighty-five-year-old named Richard Main, who introduced himself as a born-again Christian. "I am definitely against a let-down in our morals any more than they've already been," Main said. "Personally I love all folks, the homosexual, the lesbian, because the word of God tells me to love them, and I do love them, I love them too much, and everyone else here, I love you, and I love you too much to not speak out against something that can cause ruination to our nation."[4]

Pastor Jonathan Presley also introduced himself as a born-again Christian. "I would challenge any of you who use the scriptures as a basis of saying the Bible does not say homosexuality's a sin should check again, but that's not what I want to talk about." His biggest concern was "issues with the bathroom," he said.

> I have a little niece, and the idea of her going into the bathroom and being followed by someone who is a man, it scares me. It really does. This is not to say that—I don't hate you. I want to apologize on behalf of every person who says they're a Christian or loves God and then says they hate somebody, or they're an abomination, they are absolutely just scum of the earth. They do not serve the same God that I serve.

Anyway, he said, the people should be allowed to vote.[5]

Ron Bowell, the ponytailed minister of CrossRoads Church, also stepped up. "I know a little bit about discrimination," he said.

> I've looked like this since 1960 and was run out of more than one town because I was a long-haired hippie. I hate discrimination. I have a degree in psychology so I know a little bit about how the human mind works. I also have a son who is gay, who I love very much, my wife and I do. I'm still in opposition to this ordinance because I don't think it's going to change the behaviors you really [want] to change. Laws don't change people, people change people.

Besides the potential for discrimination against people with "strong and deeply held religious beliefs," Bowell had another worry.

> We're on a slippery slope here. Fifteen years ago we talked about gay and lesbian people. Because my son is gay, I agree: I think we should not discriminate against them. But now we talk about the gay and the lesbian and the transsexual. So I would ask you what's next? Gay, lesbian, transsexual—pedophile? I mean, it's just children, they're just sexual objects, why not them? I mean, we don't have a good reason for that if we don't stand on some solid ground.[6]

Graybeal grew angrier each time some stranger made an absurd argument about his supposed lack of morality. Like many kids who struggled through junior high, Graybeal had found comfort and acceptance in his church youth group. Back then, he knew he should be liking girls, but he wasn't, so every time he went to communion at Grand Avenue United Methodist church, he would pray: "God, please don't let me be gay." He might have had better luck directing those prayers toward a girl in his seventh-grade gym class named Natalie, who turned Graybeal into Gay-beal. He couldn't walk down the halls without hearing, "Hey, Gaybeal!"

Despite the all-too-obvious nickname, Graybeal still didn't understand his own attractions. He had a crush on a girl who was his friend, and a crush on a boy on the swim team—there had been rumors about the swimmer and another boy in the shower together. "There was also this other guy who was just artistic and had a high-fashion haircut, so of course people thought he was gay." Nobody in his class of three hundred at Salina Central High School really knew what they were talking about. "I didn't know what those feelings were," Graybeal said. "I was just very withdrawn and alone."

After he got married and Halie was born, Graybeal tried to do the right thing, but the marriage deteriorated. He worked a second job while his wife, Graybeal said, preferred going out with friends to being part of the family. After seven years, they divorced. Graybeal lived in a house by himself, sharing custody of Halie with his ex-wife. Finally, when he was twenty-nine, he decided to make the hour-and-a-half drive to a gay bar in Wichita.

"It was a Tuesday night, of all nights." That was his only evening off, but it was successful: Graybeal met his first boyfriend. It lasted only a few weeks, but Graybeal had discovered J's Lounge. Soon he met the man who would be his first love. Graybeal stayed in Salina and the man he'll refer to only as "Junior" stayed in Wichita, but they saw each other on weekends when Halie was with her mother. After a few months, he introduced Junior to Halie. She didn't know he was her father's partner, only that he was a friend. "She was about seven, and he treated her like a little princess. They went to the mall, and he bought her an outfit, painted her nails, did her hair." Graybeal can still remember the outfit. When Halie's mother saw it, she threw a tantrum. She told Junior, "If you ever touch my daughter, I'm calling my attorney."

Graybeal ended the relationship, but a few months later he and Junior quietly got back together. Graybeal moved to Wichita but kept a weekend apartment in Salina. "I had the dual life. It was hard, and he was not openly gay." That went on for about two years while Graybeal struggled with being a part-time father; finally, with Halie headed into fourth grade, he moved back to Salina. Even though it meant he would be single, Graybeal said that was the best choice he ever made.

Graybeal landed a job as a teller at Security Savings. Headquartered in Kansas City with nine branches in the region, the bank would later be closed by federal regulators for engaging in unsafe business practices. The bank's founder, Don Bell, boasted that he had started the bank after receiving a message from God. According to Security Savings' genesis story, Bell's "revelation from God instructed him to forgo retirement plans and to take a leap of faith by purchasing a bank. This bank would have a mission to further the Kingdom of God."[7] Graybeal didn't have a strong opinion about his new bosses' orientation. "That's totally fine, whatever they choose to believe," he thought.

He had been working at the bank less than two weeks and had already been promoted to teller supervisor when an all-employee email came across his screen. "It was supporting traditional marriage, and had a link to the Alliance Defense Fund website," Graybeal said. Reading the intensely antigay email, Graybeal felt his adrenaline rise. He printed it out, scrawled his resignation across it, and headed for the human resources department. "I had no idea what I was going to do, but I thought, 'I can't work for this organization.'" The local branch president calmed him down. Rather than quit, Graybeal decided to write to the bank owner, his son, and the human resources department. The letter took a while to compose, but in the end, he said, "It wasn't one out of anger but one out of hurt, saying 'Let's not let this happen again.'" Graybeal didn't know it, but he was speaking for two other LGBT employees who had had similar reactions. Afterward, Graybeal said, "We did have some dialogue and I never had to see an email like that again."

Now, at the Salina Community Theater, he cycled back through all of those feelings. He hated being in front of crowds, but he couldn't sit still any longer. Graybeal walked down to the microphone. "I'm not a public speaker," he said—and began talking. His stream of consciousness wound around to "Yes, I am gay," and then Graybeal told the email story, and how he might have been fired if the conversation with human resources had gone in a different direction. "I had nothing to protect myself. I was dependent on the income, but I had something to stand up for and that is myself. I stand here today, but I am not protected."

It's one thing to figure everyone knows you're gay; it's another to have it confirmed on public-access television. At home that night, he had a talk with Halie. "I told her, 'We're just going to be careful for a few days. I don't think anything will happen.'" He was right. Sean Mune wasn't so lucky. At 4:30 a.m. the morning after the forum, Mune would be awakened by a phone call from a friend saying he was on the front page of the *Salina Journal*. Stacks of papers were delivered to the Petro truck stop, where Mune's boss was fine but none of his coworkers would talk to him. It got weird, so Mune quit and did temp work before leaving town.

For Graybeal, that speech was a first step toward activism. "It was so amazing to get up and take a stand," he said. Sure, his sister-in-law saw him on TV and told his parents, who told Graybeal they were worried about his influence on Halie. That made him angry, but, Graybeal said, "I realized my actions were having an impact. Even if the reaction was nega-tive, I was taking a stand for something that I firmly believe in. A couple of days into it, that fear became empowerment."

Graybeal's evolution was a success story for Equality Kansas's north-central chapter, which had been up and running since 2006. "We had a hard time getting the LGBT population to come forward," said Gary Mar-tens, the chair of the chapter.[8] "We have a ton of allies, and parents of LGBT kids who have moved away, but getting actual gays and lesbians and transgenders to do anything was a struggle."

The seventh-largest city in Kansas, with forty-eight thousand people, Salina is an oasis of culture in the center of the state. While it is possi-ble to see an old man in overalls driving a John Deere tractor down one of the older streets, the town also spreads southward with all the latest chains and big-box stores. Its agriculture-and-manufacturing economy gets diversification from a major regional hospital, a vocational-technical school, the Methodist-affiliated Kansas Wesleyan University, an outpost of Kansas State University, and a tiny branch of the University of Kansas medical school. Most of the storefronts along Santa Fe Avenue—down-town's classically wide, small-town main street—are filled with a healthy mix of businesses, along with the well-regarded Salina Art Center, and the city's annual Smoky Hill River Festival that draws thousands of peo-ple to Oakdale Park for three days of music, art, food, and kids' events every June. For years, Graybeal has chaired the festival's fine arts com-mittee, leading volunteers who organize performances across four stages and booths for nearly 150 artists and crafters. "It rivals anything a big city could have," he boasted.

Salina was not, however, an oasis of activism, as Martens and the other Equality Kansas members discovered. Martens might have agreed to chair the north-central chapter, but that didn't mean he was willing to take a

Larry Bunker (left) and Gary Martens in front of the Peaceful Body Wellness Retreat, a massage therapy business they started after Martens retired from his job as a federal bank examiner, on Santa Fe Avenue in downtown Salina. Credit: C. J. Janovy

public role in the effort to pass a nondiscrimination ordinance. A federal bank examiner, Martens feared he might lose his job if he told his coworkers he was gay.

Martens and his partner, Larry Bunker, who was also active in the chapter, had been together since the early 1990s. The two shared rural roots: Martens is from Jetmore, a town with about nine hundred people near Dodge City, and Bunker is from Wilson, population eight hundred, fifty miles west of Salina. They also shared winding paths to their relationship: Martens through Fort Hays State University, a marriage and children, and then a divorce; Bunker through Salina Area Technical College, a job in Kansas City, a move with a partner to Key West, and when that ended, a return to Wilson with plans to work in his parents' restaurant. On weekends he would go to the big city of Salina, which is how he met Martens.

When Kansas pushed to ban gay marriage in 2004, the couple had been together for a decade. Bunker thought, *Do I really want to be part of an institution that doesn't want me to be part of it?* He and Martens were already committed—they didn't need the state to make it real. As the anti-gay-marriage amendment campaigns intensified, Bunker thought, *Okay, those who want to get married, I hope they can. I didn't think I should be helping. We were just happy not to get beat up. Marriage? I just didn't want to get hurt, killed, harassed all the time.* His attitude had changed in the years since (before the two married legally in Iowa in 2013), but Bunker was shy and quiet, not the personality type to take the lead on introducing an ordinance at city hall.

So the job fell to Janice Norlin, a straight, sixty-year-old attorney with four kids and a dozen grandchildren. She was certain the majority of city commissioners would vote in favor, and that this would be the group's best chance, because there was no guarantee they would have any support on the commission after the next election. She had always worked for progressive causes—representing low-income clients at Douglas County Legal Aid while working on her law degree at KU, defending indigent clients for Salina's Municipal Court after joining a law firm in town, chairing the social justice committee for the local Unitarian church. The Unitarians had led Salina's fight against the anti-gay-marriage amendment, and 43 percent of Saline County voted no—the third-highest "no" vote in the state. Like activists in Manhattan, Norlin knew that losses by small(ish) margins were sometimes actual victories. "I figured I would be the least harmed, and I have a pretty thick skin," Norlin said.[9] "It looked like I was the safest one to do it."

When Norlin read the proposed ordinance in front of the Salina Human Relations Commission in February 2012, most of the forty people who showed up for the meeting were against the proposal, making arguments that would have been familiar to Manhattanites and would, in the months ahead, become well known to Salinans as well. Martens and Bunker were doubtful about the ordinance's prospects. "We all felt there's no way this was going to happen," Bunker said. "We figured, we'll make noise, get people talking, get things started."

Between the scheduled forums at the Salina Community Theater, Stephanie Mott of Topeka, who had made three trips to Manhattan the year before, booked a meeting room at the Salina Public Library, and about thirty people came to hear her talk about what it was like to be transgender. The *Salina Journal* covered the Q&A under the headline "Mott Tells of Being a Man, Then a Woman." When a woman named Cheryl Harp said that her boss was "too friendly" and discriminated against her because of her age, Mott pointed out that age and sex were legally protected categories.[10] "When asked by Harp whether she had a penis or had had surgery to become a woman, Mott said she is scheduled for surgery in May," the *Journal* reported. "When asked by Harp which bathroom she uses, Mott said the women's. 'I would be scared about going into the men's bathroom as a woman. I'd be afraid of being assaulted or laughed out.'" Another woman "said she wouldn't notice Mott was transgendered if she encountered her in the bathroom. Mott said she is always nervous when in a public bathroom, but feels she is in the right place as a woman."[11]

By May, the Salina Human Relations Department had finished with the public forums and compiled its report, and it was finally time for Salina's five city commissioners to vote on the ordinance. Martens was nervous about commissioner Kaye Crawford. "She's an older woman. She observed and listened very closely, kept it very professional and noncommittal in her comments and questions. We were a little worried." The night of the vote, Martens said, "She gave one of the most impassioned speeches in favor. It was very moving."

The ordinance passed 3–2. It went into effect on June 4. A week later, the newly formed Awaken Salina had packets ready for the forty or so people who would spend the summer collecting signatures on a petition to repeal it.

LGBTs and their supporters had to fight their battle all over again—and this time it wasn't just three out of five commissioners they had to convince. It was their whole town. And just like Awaken Manhattan had done, Awaken Salina embarked on a battle against the "bathroom bill."

With church members visiting city parks to collect signatures on a petition to repeal, the newly energized Graybeal made a decision. "I had to do something, so on the Fourth of July, I made a sign that said, 'With Liberty and Justice for All.' I went by myself with my sign and stood at a street corner opposite where they had been collecting signatures. That was a huge moment for me." Shortly after staking out his territory, Graybeal posted his whereabouts on Facebook and a friend arrived with a rainbow flag and an American flag. Over the next few weeks, Graybeal kept showing up, and sometimes a few other people would join him. Their signs urged drivers to honk if they supported equality. "It was so overwhelming to hear those honks as people drove by," Graybeal said. "Especially with the petition people right next to us."

Other members of Equality Kansas went door to door, canvassing neighborhoods with clipboards. "Our email list grew to two-hundred-plus, and we had several hundred on Facebook," said Norlin. Besides her fellow Unitarians, members of Trinity United Methodist were also trying to counteract the influence of other churches. Among the Trinity contingent was Beverly Cole, who had written two books: *Cleaning Closets: A Mother's Story* was in response to her son Eric's coming out and *Voices from the Kingdom: All God's Children Have Keys* consisted of interviews with gay and lesbian Christians, parents, and ministers. Cole joined Graybeal and others on the street corner. "Once in a while somebody'd stick their middle finger out, but for the most part we'd get quite a few honks, which was kind of fun," she said.[12] On the opposite corner, Cole remembered, "Those folks against it had such sour faces, when we were having the best time, laughing and joking. There was kind of this mood of negativity versus positivity in the issue. My husband, who's very ornery, stood right next to the opposing guy with his sign and got his picture in the paper." Other people weren't having such a great time. "There are really right-wing radio stations out here," said Norlin, who was the subject of discussion on some of them.

Awaken Salina needed 1,297 valid signatures within six months. Within eleven weeks they had twice that many. The repeal would be on the November ballot. In late October, Awaken Salina announced that its "Religious Liberty Rally," scheduled for Christ the King Lutheran Church, was moving to the city's 7,500-seat Bicentennial Center because of "overwhelming response."[13] The celebrity speaker was Congressman Tim Huelskamp, who represented the western two-thirds of Kansas and who, in his previous role as a state legislator, had proudly sponsored the marriage amendment in the Kansas Senate. His rally ended up in a second-floor meeting room, where only two hundred or so people showed up. Huelskamp was undaunted. "The threat to justice here is a threat to justice everywhere," he proclaimed. "Religious liberties are under assault. They're stopping at nothing. There is a reason the founding fathers protect religion. Without the acknowledgment of God, society can be crippled."[14]

Graybeal organized a counterdemonstration, and forty people rallied outside the Bicentennial Center. And as Election Day grew nearer, more gay people spoke out. "Whether they were mad, or ready to come out or whatever," Norlin said, "people finally outed themselves and were able to publicly tell their stories." By this point, Graybeal and Martens weren't afraid to be quoted in stories that ran on the front page of the Salina Journal.

From the beginning, Martens said, he and Bunker had braced for a backlash. "We were prepared for the real possibility of violence or more innocuous things like car scratchings, eggings, or obscene phone calls. I'm listed in the phone book, so people had plenty of opportunity." None of that happened. "Out and about, people were real civilized to our face and in letters to the editor. The opponents had a very negative campaign, but it wasn't shaking fingers and calling names to individuals—it wasn't, 'Gary, that faggot.'"

"That was uplifting," Bunker said. "You feared something that didn't pan out. As we talked to people it was amazing how many people understood and were what I would call living the Golden Rule—love everybody and do not judge. Gary and I were living out and we weren't getting harmed. But we met people who had been treated unfairly and really needed protection, so that kept me motivated."

Following advice from Tom Witt, they avoided getting dragged down into bathroom debates. "We got lots of compliments from both sides that our campaign was very positive," Martens said. Even though the chances of victory were slim, Martens and Bunker were optimistic. Heading into election night, Bunker thought there was no way Salinans would repeal the ordinance.

They did. It was 54 percent to 46 percent; 9,079 votes to 7,686. "It was devastating," Bunker said. "How could the majority of people think that I don't deserve to have rights?" Also defeated was Norlin, who over the summer had turned her energies to a race for the Kansas Senate. She was running against a conservative Republican named Tom Arpke, just so he would have a Democratic opponent. "I really did think I had a pretty good chance of winning," Norlin said. The moderate Republican who had failed to beat Arpke in the August primary had even endorsed her. "But even after all the work we did, I got the obligatory 35 percent," Norlin said of the vote percentage now common for Democrats in Kansas.

Martens took solace in the fact that at least Barack Obama had won reelection. Bunker reminded himself that, when the effort had started, they estimated they would lose with 30 percent. "To end up with 46 percent, it was a win. We accomplished a lot. We changed a lot of minds. It definitely boosted Salina's LGBT community because they finally realized that, even though it didn't pass, we have all these people behind us—you know you can find a friend." As the results settled in, it became clear that Bunker's happiness over losing by a less-than-anticipated margin wasn't just empty consolation. In the months that followed, even though LGBT Salinans had no official protections, they started hearing good news from city hall.

Salinans don't exactly elect mayors; each year, the five city commission members select one member to serve as mayor for a year. Starting in April 2013 the position went to Barb Shirley, who was one of the three city commissioners who had voted to pass the nondiscrimination ordinance. On her first day in office, Shirley signed the Mayors for the Freedom to Marry statement, joining 351 other mayors from around the country and putting Salina, Kansas, in the company of New York City (where Michael Bloomberg had signed on), Los Angeles (Antonio Villaraigosa), Boston (Thomas Menino), Newark (Cory Booker), and Chicago (Rahm Emanuel). Shirley made it clear that she was speaking only for herself, not the city.[15] "I have zero tolerance for any discrimination. As a mother, wife and community leader, I want people to know that no matter who you are, you are loved and deserving."[16]

In elections the following spring, commissioners Norm Jennings and Samantha Angell—who had voted against the LGBT protections—decided not to run again, so there was no way to gauge how voters felt about their time in office. But Kaye Crawford, who had voted in favor of LGBT protections, was up for reelection. "I was figuring, good Lord, there's going to be a huge backlash from the religious right to try to get in there and clean up that city commission," Martens said. But Crawford won easily, and the two new commissioners were also LGBT-friendly.

That summer, the north-central chapter of the Kansas Equality Coalition, flush with new members, began planning Salina's first gay pride celebration. Salina doesn't have any gay bars, but some talented young men had found other venues to put on drag shows and monthly socials, culminating in an annual December gala they called Glitter. Still, Martens was dubious about putting on a full-scale pride event. "I thought, 'Come on, it's Salina.'" But they booked a banquet hall at the Ramada Inn for June 29. Drawing on his logistics experience with the Smoky Hill River Festival, Graybeal organized it. They hoped for one or two hundred people. Five hundred showed up.

In the months that followed, Salina grew gayer and gayer. The city's first pride celebration was not a one-off consolation after a year of defeat. It would become an annual event. In June 2014 people packed the city commission chambers and cheered after Martens read a proclamation declaring all of June to be Lesbian, Gay, Bisexual, and Transgender Pride Month and Aaron Householter, that year's mayor, signed it.[17]

On downtown's main drag, decorating the industrial-metal arty overhang at one of the Santa Fe Avenue stoplights, was a banner with paintbrush-style swipes of rainbow colors in the shape of a heart, kissed by two strands of wheat, and the words "Gay Pride Salina: The Heart of Kansas." On the day of the city's second pride celebration, rainbow-colored streamers floated at the entrance to the Ramada Conference Center while the hotel's parking lot sign flashed "Welcome Pride."

Inside, organizers had rented a bigger space than the previous year and started an hour earlier, at 10 a.m. As they had done the year before, representatives from nonprofits and churches set up tables around the perimeter: the Saline County Democrats, the Salina Area Workers' Coalition, the Domestic Violence Association of Central Kansas, the local United Way, the city's human relations commission, the county health department, Stephanie Mott's Kansas Statewide Transgender Education Project, a Wichita-based internet portrait project called *The Face of Trans*, the local and statewide Equality Kansas reps, three churches, a home security company, a woman named Joan Jerkovich who hosted a show called *Empowering Talk Radio* on KSAL NewsRadio 1150, and a handful of badasses in the Cruisers Cult Bicycle Club, one of whom wore a T-shirt with huge letters saying, FUCK THE WESTBORO BAPTIST CHURCH. All day, people got their pictures taken with hats, costumes, and other props for a slideshow on Facebook; in the opposite corner was a play area for kids.

Graybeal and the ten other members of the pride committee worked the room in their rainbow-heart, blade-of-wheat-logo T-shirts while couples, families, loners, packs of teens dressed in goth-meets-*Glee* outfits, amateur drag queens, and khaki-and-polo-wearing average citizens wandered around or settled in for six hours of socializing and entertainment. Up front, a folk trio performed power-to-the-people standards like "This Land is Your Land" and "Get Together," then turned over the stage to lip-syncing drag queens and kings and a Katy Perry impersonator who at one point had been crowned Miss Gay LA. There was also a raucous live set by a drag queen named Honey Monet who collected a fistful of dollars. Then a woman from Wichita named Melissa Robinson, known for hosting that city's karaoke AIDS fundraisers, sang lesbian favorites by Melissa Etheridge, Bonnie Raitt, and Janis Joplin; she was followed by a singer-songwriter named Ashley Wheeler, a regular performer at Salina's coffeehouses who accompanied herself on guitar. Next, three poets delivered a set of spoken-word fireworks before the afternoon's finale, a set by the Heart of America Men's Chorus.

Witt spent the afternoon registering voters before commandeering the stage for a few minutes. "Things have changed a lot in the last decade," he boomed. Recounting his years of experience at the statehouse in Topeka, Witt cited a couple of notoriously antigay legislators whose behavior was growing more erratic. "We've gone from them looking for ways to attack us, to now looking for ways to run for the exits or run from their records."

Martens also jumped on stage for a short speech. In a voice less fiery than Witt's, he reminded the crowd how they had lost the nondiscrimination ordinance fight before noting that this year, the whole month was dedicated to LGBT pride in Salina. He thanked former mayor Shirley. "She's the only mayor in the state of Kansas to sign a letter for equality." The north-central chapter of Equality Kansas was now larger and more active than it had ever been. "Our opponents called themselves Awaken Kansas," he said. "The people they woke up were all of you."

Every once in a while, Scott Graybeal would take a seat and, for just a moment—before he had to get back up and take care of an entertainer or answer a reporter's questions or hug a supporter—he would catch a breath and enjoy the festivities. Now forty-four, Graybeal has never forgotten that when he came out at twenty-nine, he did not know a single other gay person in the town where he had grown up. There was no one to talk to about the feelings he was having. Awaken Salina's successful drive to repeal the short-lived nondiscrimination ordinance, Graybeal said, was the best thing that could have happened for gay people in Salina. "Had Awaken Salina not appeared, the [nondiscrimination] law would be on the books and it would be done," Graybeal said. "There would have been no coming together, no community, no Gay Pride Salina. Now I have all these new friends who are like-minded, and we are taking those acquaintances and making them into stronger allies and they are joining the quest. It's the best time to be gay in Salina."

An hour and a half to the south, the situation was more complex. In Hutchinson, Equality Kansas was fighting an additional foe: the woman who had spent her career trying to make sure there was never a good time to be gay in Kansas.

8

At forty-six, Jon Powell wasn't yet a candidate for residency at the Wesley Towers Retirement Community, a sprawling, United Methodist Church–affiliated campus where aging Kansans moved into ranch homes or patio apartments with bathing and medication management included in the rent and inevitably progressed to assisted living. Powell had not come to the chapel at Wesley Towers to pray, either. Instead, his business there was to document the offensive meanderings of one Jan Pauls, a Democratic member of the Kansas House of Representatives whose district included half of Hutchinson. His video camera was on.

With its hundreds of elderly residents, Wesley Towers was a reliable source of Republican votes and a popular site for legislative forums in Hutchinson. Pauls was the only Democrat among the five legislators seated on stage. It was February 2012, and the Kansas House was in the midst of a now-annual ritual: debating a "Religious Freedom" bill. Distilling several more-pointed questions that Powell had written on cards after a call for audience questions, the moderator asked, "Jan, what are your thoughts on House Bill 2260?"

Pauls, wearing a cobalt-blue suit, affected an air of powerlessness. She hadn't cosponsored the religious freedom bill, she said—it had come out of her committee, but the Republicans were in control. She wished the Democrats were in control, she joked thinly. Anyway, she explained, the Kansas Civil Rights Act protected people from discrimination based on their minority status—religion, gender, age, and so on—except for sexual orientation and gender identity.

"Say an employer didn't want to hire someone who was, for example, a cross-dresser," she began. "If someone had a religious belief, they had a business and felt that they did not want to have that person—or due to their sexual orientation—did not want to hire them based on their religious belief, that person could raise their religious belief on defense in litigation."[1] Squinting into the distance as if to underscore the effort it took to remember everyone lining up for special protection, she continued: "Sexual orientation, gay, lesbian, transgender—there's a whole list of—cross-dressing was covered in the Manhattan ordinance that was repealed." Her point was that the bill had received a lot of attention and she had heard a lot of testimony.

> The question is, the personal belief that you have as far as religion, should that be trumped by forcing people to then support a lifestyle that they don't support due to their religion as far as hiring? If you don't want to have someone in an apartment in your house—in Lawrence you would be compelled to rent to a group that shared an orientation that you didn't believe or want to have them employed by your business.

She said she supported the Kansas Civil Rights Act. "Kansas has not chosen to put sexual orientation, cross-dressing, transgender, etc., into our Civil Rights Act. I don't live in Lawrence anymore—I used to when I was in law school at KU"—her lips curled in the slightest of sneers, as if to remind her audience that she had escaped the gnarled clutches of gays, lesbians, transgenders, and cross-dressers in that Gomorra of a college town—"and I don't think an ordinance should trump other people's religious rights." Jon Powell posted this soliloquy to YouTube.

Pauls had held a seat in the Kansas House of Representatives for more than twenty years. She had first gone to Topeka in 1991, when her fellow Democrats appointed her to fill out the term of a state representative who had left office. It was apparently an odd moment in the annals of Reno County politics; a *Hutchinson News* editorial marking the occasion was headlined, simply, "Redemption." During her one acrimonious term as a county judge, local attorneys had complained to the Kansas Judicial Commission that Pauls took too long to handle cases, which led to a public censure and fine, and voters refused to reelect her. As the *Hutchinson News* put it, Pauls had "received the sustained negative attention usually accorded only to serial killers." But now, she had a new opportunity. "Having learned a hard lesson about the human condition, she should take that knowledge with her to Topeka, where interpersonal relationships, consensus building, and yes, politics are integral to success not only for elected or appointed officials but for the districts they represent. Mrs. Pauls does not go to Topeka alone. She takes her constituents with her," the article stated.[2] Serving with success, the paper editorialized, would silence her critics.

Given the ease with which she coasted to reelection through the end of one century and well into another, Pauls apparently redeemed herself. Her tenure was bureaucratic and generally unremarkable, except for one constituency. Pauls distinguished herself as the most antigay politician in Kansas.

For ten sweltering days every September, the forty-two thousand citizens of Hutch, as the city is nicknamed, welcome a full eighth of the Kansas population to wander and meet up amid the dusty, straw-covered grounds of the Kansas State Fair; to enter hogs, calves, quilts, crafts, and high school marching bands in competitions packed into historic prairie exhibition halls; to indulge the state's handshaking, butter-sculpture-admiring politicians; to seek thrills on the yellow-lit midway; and to hear headliners like Cheap Trick at the US Cellular Grandstand. A less-stereotypical Hutchinson attraction is the Kansas Cosmosphere and Space Center, a Smithsonian-affiliated museum boasting the largest collection of US spacecraft outside of the National Air and Space Museum in Washington, DC—including the battered Apollo 13 command module—and the largest collection of Soviet spacecraft and memorabilia outside of Russia. While this unlikely mid-Kansas cultural gem looks heavenward, Hutch's other distinctive destination lets visitors take a tram deep into the earth. The town's first industry was salt mining in the 1880s, and these days, Kansas rock salt helps de-ice highways all the way to the East Coast. And testifying to what some Kansans hope is their industrial future, next door to the salt museum is a Siemens plant where a few hundred workers assemble the engine-housing units for high-tech wind turbines. More visible evidence of Hutchinson's economy is the Archer Daniels Midland grain elevator, its concrete columns a white wall scraping the sky for half a mile along the city's eastern edge.

Growing up here, Jon Powell was oblivious to politics—except for his year as class president at Hutchinson High School. Charismatic and handsome, Powell enjoyed his status as a jock. But he carried a secret from the sixth grade, when he figured out he liked boys, through graduation in 1983. It ate at him as he went on to Hutchinson Community College, training to be a policeman and a paramedic. "Talk about two manly fields!" Powell said.[3] He loved being a paramedic, but police work was different. One night the cops planned a sting at the park: an officer would hang out in the bathroom and flirt with the men who came in. Everyone who touched the cop was arrested for sexual battery. Powell was not into casual sex and never cruised the park, but he felt for the men they caught that night. "One was a guy who owned a local floral shop but was married. He had kids. The next day at roll call, some fellow officers sent the cop who arrested him a dozen roses with a card that said, 'Thanks for the good time last night.'" Powell would never forget how the cops joked around after ruining a man's life.

He quit the force and headed out to Modesto, California, where he and a friend started a company that monitored prisoners on house arrest. On weekends, Powell made trips to San Francisco, where he went to his first gay bars. But California wasn't for him, and Powell came home after a couple of years. His father, a State Farm Insurance agent for nearly forty years, had died; his mother eventually understood the truth about her son and took to calling him a "confirmed bachelor." Everyone knew what that meant.

One night when Powell was in his mid-twenties, he heard a knock on his door at 2 a.m. It was Stephanie, his thirteen-year-old niece. A friend's mother had driven her up from Oklahoma, where, he learned, all three of his brother's daughters had been abused by their stepfather. "I hired an attorney and ended up raising my nieces," he said. Powell needed a new career fast. He landed at Conklin Cars, a long-established dealership. At first Powell thought, I'm not a car salesman. But it turned out he was. "In fact," he said, "I was very good at sales."

Within a couple of years, he was in management. At the company Christmas party, after several cocktails, Powell was having a heart-to-heart with one of the Conklin brothers and confessed that he was gay. "Well, tiger," the Conklin brother replied, patting him on the back, "I'm not but that's okay! It's okay!"

Powell helped open dealerships half an hour away in Newton and in Salina. But he was uncomfortable with the pressures of management and "demoted himself" back to sales—where he did well enough to keep his nieces in cars and clothes until they graduated. "I got them through school, walked two of them down the aisle," he said. "Now I'm a grandpa."

Despite Conklin's benign reaction to his Christmas party confession, Powell generally stayed in the closet. Hiding who he was helped him develop chameleonlike skills that served him well with his huge customer base. Lured by a recruiting call from an online vehicle auction company, Powell took a job that put him in charge of sales and marketing for the central United States and moved to the Kansas City suburb of Lenexa, which is where he was living when the gay marriage ban came up in 2004. One day after a week on the road, he came home to a sign in his neighbor's yard. "It had the outline of two men or two women with the circle-slash through it," Powell remembered. Besides being angry at his neighbor, he had a bigger problem. "I didn't even know what the hell was going on. I read the local fag rags. I would go with my friends to the bar on weekends and nobody—nobody—said a fucking thing to me about what was going on. Shame on me. Shame on my friends."

It would take a couple of years before Powell began making up for his obliviousness. Meanwhile, the former athlete's health was deteriorating. Powell was diagnosed with rheumatoid arthritis, lupus, and fibromyalgia, and at forty-five he took a medical retirement and returned to Hutch. Back home, Powell heard about some friends who had tried to rent an apartment and had been turned down because they were lesbians. He was incredulous. "I have never been discriminated against to my face. But after

I started asking around, the floodgates opened. I heard all sorts of stories. I thought, 'I can't let this go on.'"

Powell Googled "gay rights Kansas" and found Witt, who drove fifty miles from Wichita to meet with about eight people in the family room of Powell's comfortable home in one of Hutchinson's better neighborhoods. When Witt asked how many people they could round up, Powell knew he could put his sales skills to work. This was the beginning of Equality Kansas's Hutchinson chapter.

Having been gone for a few years, Powell had no idea how many gay people lived in Hutchinson. But after he started a Facebook page, they began to show up. His home, with its backyard swimming pool and its pine, oak, and maple trees providing shade and privacy, became a safe place for once-a-month gatherings. "We'd have barbecues in the fall. In the spring, we did a big Easter egg hunt—we grilled hot dogs and had Easter eggs for the kids. We had seventy-five or eighty people." While his guests were having fun, Powell would give his spiel. "We'd talk about how things needed to change, and they can't change until we speak up. Ninety percent of the people had no clue that they could be fired for being gay." They watched *The Times of Harvey Milk*. "We encouraged everybody to be out, be open, be who you are, it's okay." But they knew that without protection from discrimination, some people couldn't risk coming out.

So they decided to go for a nondiscrimination ordinance. As in Salina and Manhattan, city commissioners handed the question off to the local Human Relations Commission, which scheduled public forums where the "debates" were the same as the ones in the other two Kansas cities. Wichita-based Awaken Kansas cranked up a local chapter, Awaken Hutchinson, which started making noise about the "bathroom bill." Equality Kansas of Hutchinson countered. "We started getting members, meeting monthly, then twice a month," Powell said. "We went to town, let me tell you."

In June, city commissioners passed an ordinance protecting gay people only if they had been fired or evicted—no "public accommodations" protections to ensure gays were treated equally at any establishment that served the public. Also, the ordinance said nothing about gender identity—there were no protections for trans people.

Powell, having listened to all of the testimony and knowing commissioners were especially nervous about the transgender protections, thought he could come back later to work on adding gender identity. "I only knew one person who was trans," Powell said. "He said he understood. It's tough talking to someone and saying, 'We're not going to include you now.' But we needed to start somewhere."

Dueling petition drives ensued. Awaken Hutchinson, inflamed over the passage of any ordinance whatsoever, campaigned for repeal. Equality Kansas wanted sexual orientation protections across the board—not just in employment and in housing but also in public accommodations—but didn't press the issue of gender identity. Powell, Witt, and others would regret that for years. "I protested the decision," Witt said, but Equality Kansas's structure allowed local leaders to make those decisions. "I went ahead and wrote their petition for them," he said, "knowing I was doing the wrong thing."

The petitions put the question of LGB—but no T—protections to a citywide vote in November 2012. Powell and the city's newly rallied gay community and their friends took to the streets. Once a month, on third Thursdays, the businesses in downtown Hutch stayed open late and artists set up their easels along the strip of old-timey hardware stores, dime stores, insurance agencies, banks, and clothing stores that share Main Street's 1880s-vintage brick buildings with computer stores, coffee shops, galleries, and an organic market. The monthly street party drew thousands of people. This was where Equality's Hutchinson chapter would make a stand.

On the night of their first rally, Powell was hauling the group's signs in his pickup truck when he grew nervous on the way downtown. "Forty-some years old, and I'd never protested. I was scared to death to be on my hometown Main Street," he said. "I thought, 'I'll just drop off the signs and leave.'" But something kept him from being a no-show at his own rally. "I sucked it up. I gave out the signs, set up my folding chair, and held my sign proudly." And then, "I just bawled. I'd spent half my life peeking out of the closet. That night, I took the door off the hinges."

He went back month after month. "People would come from all over the state," Powell said. "To stand on our Main Street and hold signs—

we're here, we're queer—I'd never done that, and a lot of people from these rural communities had never done that. It was a huge step to say, 'We're not going to take it anymore.' One time we had 125 people there." No one from the nearby businesses complained, he said. "They supported us."

All summer, Powell had also been working on another campaign. As Hutchinson's gay citizens were growing more confident, they could no longer tolerate the fact that, in a statehouse filled with far-right Republicans, their Democratic representative was the most antigay of all. It had started in 1996, when Jan Pauls sponsored the state's first law banning same-sex marriage. Five years after the *Hutchinson News* editorialized that she had an opportunity to redeem herself after her stormy county judgeship, it published another editorial—one that now seems remarkable, given its time and place. "Why does Kansas, or any state for that matter, feel the obligation to prevent gay couples from showing their love and commitment to each other in the cherished tradition of marriage?" the paper asked. "Why such state-sanctioned fear?" Thanks to Pauls's efforts, Kansas had "officially declared that people who are different, people who don't think or act like the majority, are not to be allowed the same rights, freedoms and privileges as the rest of Kansas citizens. Gay couples got it first. Who will be next?"[4]

In the years following the constitutional marriage ban that bolstered her original law, Pauls's antigay efforts turned obsessive. During years when Witt was able to get legislative hearings on adding sexual orientation and gender identity to the state's Civil Rights Act, Pauls would show up to testify against it. "She's the only legislator to do so," Witt said. And that's not all. "She made sure that the same-sex sodomy law stays on the books here," he added of the legally unenforceable statute. He ticked off other mean-spirited efforts she supported: a bill that would ban domestic partnership registries; a bill that would have required fertility clinics to turn over the names of same-sex couples to the state health department; a moment in January 2014 when the Kansas Department of Health and Environment wanted some new rules for agencies that served as safe houses for victims of human trafficking. The proposal listed groups that would be protected from discrimination, including LGBT people. "Jan Pauls insisted that KDHE take that part out, because, she said, some people who are religious won't want to serve that kind of people."

Witt burned with a special anger over this one. "Human trafficking is really about prostitution—coercive prostitution—and the people who are coerced into prostitution are kids," he noted. "And half the kids who are on the streets are gay or lesbian kids who have been kicked out by their families." Pauls, he said, was "perfectly OK with gay and lesbian kids who have been forced into prostitution being thrown out on the street." The safe houses, he noted, "are supposed to be places of refuge, paid for by our tax dollars. She insisted that they take protections for LGBT kids out of the [state] rules and regs."

By the time Pauls was defending the Kansas Preservation of Religious Freedom Act at Wesley Towers, her fellow Democrats had officially grown exasperated. During the party's annual Washington Days meeting at the Ramada Convention Center in Topeka, Party Chair Joan Wagnon—who had been Topeka's first female mayor in the late 1990s—stood at the podium expressing her dismay about the bill. "It is targeted at members of the LGBT community," Wagnon told the assembled Democrats. "It just seems to me to be wrong. In fact, it's repugnant and it's hateful."[5]

Wagnon's voice grew shaky. "I get a little emotional about it because it's a very emotional issue for everybody. One of our legislators, and someone whom I've considered a friend, Jan Pauls, has been outspoken on this issue and she has supported it. Now, legislators who are elected officials, we don't all believe the same." Legislators were entitled to their opinions and to vote according to their own values and those of their constituents, Wagnon acknowledged. But the party's official platform statement supporting "equal rights for every Kansan" had added sexual orientation in 2006 and gender identity in 2010.[6] "I need to make it clear that what the KDP believes—the Kansas Democratic Party—we believe our platform statement, and we do not support House Bill 2260," Wagon said.

The bill died that year, but other "religious freedom" bills targeting LGBT people would rise like Jesus every year in the statehouse as legislators embraced the idea that equality for gays was an assault on Christianity. More troubling was that by the time Wagnon gave this speech in February 2012 the Kansas Democratic Party was basically irrelevant.

Wagnon's reprimand of the state's number-one gay basher—who was not Fred Phelps but a dowdy Democrat barely known outside of Hutchinson—was therefore mostly symbolic. But as a mile-marker for LGBT Kansans in the long fight for basic dignity, much less equality, it measured something significant if intangible.

It also fired up a twenty-eight-year-old gay man named Erich Bishop. Bishop was the son of a one-time (now repentant) Aryan Nations leader who had moved the family to Hutchinson from Idaho when Bishop was in sixth grade. After a chaotic childhood, Bishop had gone on to earn a philosophy degree, with high honors, from the University of Kansas. Uncertain what to do with that degree, he had come home to Hutchinson while he planned his next move. He worked as a home-health aide for a while, then got a maintenance job with the city. And he joined the Hutchinson Equality chapter. "I had political inclinations for quite a while," Bishop said.[7] "I'm sympathetic to working class and families and poverty, social justice issues. I grew up poor, and those are things that I hold very dear." Powell, putting his sales techniques to work, convinced Bishop to challenge Pauls, and a small army of volunteers went to work planting yard signs and papering the town with fliers.

Legally, Pauls shouldn't even have been running. Legislative districts had been redrawn earlier that year, and Pauls no longer lived in the district she represented. When she filed her election papers, Pauls had listed her residence as a three-story brick church fronted by a dramatic stained-glass window at 101 East 11th Avenue. The church was a few blocks south and west of where Pauls really lived, in a small, faded greenish ranch home at 1634 North Baker Street. Pauls and her husband, Ron, did own the church, and she said they were making plans to move in. Witt filed a complaint with a body called the State Objections Board, but that was an exercise in futility: the board consisted of the lieutenant governor, the secretary of state, and the state attorney general—three far-right Republicans. They ruled in Pauls's favor.

Pauls had promised she and Ron would be living in the church by election day, but years later the church would still be locked up, paint peeling on its wooden trim, a hole in one of the second-story stained-glass windows, while cars were parked in the driveway back at the faded greenish ranch home. Pauls had signed a voter registration card with the words, "I swear or affirm . . . that I have abandoned my former residence," the *Hutchinson News* reported.[8] She had lied, and everyone in town could see it. But the race went on.

"That July it was like a hundred degrees almost every day," Bishop remembered. All day, he worked outside at his city maintenance job. "Then I was going home, taking a shower, putting on heavier clothes, and going out and campaigning in the late afternoon, early evening heat." It was grueling, but Bishop felt genuine connections with people. Irked by arguments that he was a one-issue candidate, Bishop pounded economics. "People wrote letters to the editor—at least one was from someone I didn't know, who said they were going to back me because I talked to them." In the primary that August, Bishop came within eight votes of beating Pauls.

The philosophy major might not have been cut out for the rough-and-tumble of politics anyway. Late in December, after a night drinking alone at home, Bishop said he blacked out. He assaulted his father, which earned him a trip to jail, where, he said, rather than have someone bail him out, he chose to spend a month locked up, out of embarrassment. Eventually, Bishop moved out of state for graduate school. Pauls would cruise to reelection in November—the Republicans hadn't bothered to run a credible candidate.

Also on November's ballot was the nondiscrimination ordinance, which had caught the attention of editors at the *Kansas City Star*, who sent a reporter named Lee Hill Kavanaugh to write about how "culture wars" were raging in this small Kansas town. Kavanaugh met Jan and Ron Pauls at a coffee shop, where Pauls said she was the one being persecuted. "I have friends who have told me they worry that I'll be another Gabby Giffords, literally," Pauls said, adding that the fliers against her in the primary were "nasty."[9] "They're trying to intimidate and bully people who don't agree with them. Ironic, because, you know, they shouldn't be bullying at all."

Pauls told Kavanaugh a story now engrained in gay Kansas political lore. During Washington Days back in 2006, Pauls said, after she had written the same-sex marriage ban, Tom Witt came barreling out of the LGBT caucus room with fists in the air. "I backed up and yelled: 'Security!

Call security!' I think he was hoping he could throw me over the stairs,"
Pauls said. Friends of the irate man calmed him down. Witt told Kavanaugh it wasn't him (he said it was another man who has since moved out
of state). Besides, the closest stairs were through a door thirty feet from
the caucus room.

As Pauls was relating all of this, Ron kept interrupting—and Kavanaugh kept reporting. "Homosexuals don't love. Homosexuals are all about
the sex," he said. Pauls poked her husband in the ribs, Kavanaugh wrote,
describing Pauls as "giving her husband a look" and saying, "I would have
phrased that a little differently." Most Kansans' concerns, Pauls said, "are
not that the homosexuals want equal rights but superior rights. . . . Homophobia here in Hutchinson? I don't think so. We would have heard
about it by now if we were. Tom Witt would never let himself be a victim."

Ron Pauls couldn't contain himself. "How would you feel, he asks, if
your daughter's male gym teacher wanted to go into the locker room as
the girls were undressing? What about a female gym teacher? What if that
female gym teacher was a homosexual? She'd want those girls." Kavanaugh noted how Jan squeezed his hand in another unsuccessful effort to
quiet him, but he kept going: "People are afraid there won't be freedom of
speech anymore. Pretty soon you won't be able to quote Bible verses from
the pulpit if they're against homosexuality." With that, Kavanaugh wrote,
the interview was over: "The lawmaker stands up, pulling her husband with
her out of the shop. 'You've said enough, honey,' she says, still smiling."

Ron Pauls kept talking all over town. At a rally against the ordinance
later that month, he spoke on behalf of his wife, who was unable to attend, describing her as the "most prominent target of the militant homosexual community," reported the *Hutchinson News*.[10] "To much applause
and laughter after making a joke about belonging to the Democratic Party,
Ron Pauls read a letter written by his wife. 'Being a homosexual is not obvious to most people,' said the representative's husband. 'Laws should be
based on fact, not feeling.'" The irony of this respect for the law, from the
couple who had lied about their residency so that Pauls could keep running for office, was likely lost on this particular audience.

When the ballots were counted in early November, 58 percent of voters
agreed with Pauls. Gay people would not be protected from discrimination

in Hutchinson. "It was a big blow," said Powell. "Total defeat. So many people worked their tails off." He had grown up in Hutchinson. Everyone knew his parents. His father had served on the board of one of the city's largest Presbyterian churches. Powell thought that meant something. "Hell—I saved lives. It was okay when I was a paramedic and doing CPR and I was saving your kid's life in a wreck. But you don't think I should have rights just because of who I love? It was like we got kicked in the gut."

Witt took the defeat as a lesson about betraying his transgender brothers and sisters. He compares the Hutchinson ordinance to Salina's: "That was the full ordinance that included gender identity and public accommodations. And that was where we had the best performance. The city council didn't reverse itself, we didn't lose seats on the city council because of it. We lost at the ballot box in a fairly close election. I think that if we stay true to our values, that's where we have the best success. Trying to play little games with language or not being fully inclusive, that hurts us both with the general public and especially internally."

The internal distress was particularly acute because Equality Kansas had just revived a dormant chapter in Kansas City, thanks to the enthusiasm of a transgender woman named Sandra Meade. "Now she was ready to walk away from it altogether because of what happened in Hutch," Witt said. "I told her she was right. I was ashamed then and now." Meade demanded a bylaws change: No chapter could pursue a nondiscrimination policy without including gender identity unless the statewide organization agreed. She wasn't happy, but she stayed with the organization. "Let it serve as a warning to future activists who think dumping the trans community for expediency's sake is a good idea," Witt said.

Despite the painful lessons, Powell said they accomplished something important. "Even I didn't know how many LGBT people were in Hutchinson. Now we're out, we're proud." And although they wouldn't know it for a couple of years, Pauls's November 2012 election would be her last as a Democrat. Given her close call with Bishop, it was clear that Pauls would not survive another Democratic primary. She wouldn't admit that publicly, but in May 2014 Pauls announced she was switching parties. She won her next election, but at least she wasn't embarrassing Democrats anymore.

Powell, meanwhile, decided to concentrate on less-political efforts. Equality Kansas's Hutchinson chapter went dormant while he worked on starting a PFLAG group. "I've heard a lot of stories: 'What you guys did made my kid pay attention, he'd been asking a lot of questions, then he told us he was gay, now it all makes sense.' Those kinds of people are coming to PFLAG, which makes me feel good," he said. "I don't want kids to live double lives like I did." More and more, they don't have to.

On a hot, cloudy Tuesday in early September 2014, students spilled out of class early and into the grassy quad at Hutchinson High School for club signup day. The school had an array of organizations, some earnest (student council, the National Honor Society, the military club), some just fun (skateboard club, ultimate Frisbee club, video game club). At least one was new: the Hutchinson High School Gay Straight Alliance.

Working that table was Kara Vaughn, a petite junior with shoulder-length straight blonde hair, braces, and nerd-chic black glasses. Out in the crowd handing out fliers was her right-hand man, Eduardo "Eddie" Ibarra, also a junior. Ibarra said he could hear people saying, "Oh, faggots and queers and homos and fuck them, they don't belong here."[11] To his face, they told him, "Nobody wants to join your stupid fucking club, stop trying to act normal." But that was just ten or so kids, all of them jocks—Ibarra could tell by their jerseys and expensive shoes. He even saw some teachers roll their eyes at the GSA table and walk inside the cafeteria. But those people were in the minority. Mostly Ibarra felt an excited energy, along the lines of, "Hey, it's happening!" After all, he would say later, "Everyone knows someone who is LGBT or who has been affected by it." Two hundred kids signed up for the GSA that day.

The year before, Vaughn was president of the student council, but this year's project was closer to her heart. Originally from Utah, with some time spent in Indiana where her grandparents live, Vaughn and her mother and sister moved to Hutchinson when she was in seventh grade. By eighth grade she was starting to wonder whether she might be gay. Freshman year, she explored. Vaughn's mother and the new boyfriend who would soon become Vaughn's stepfather were supportive, but telling her religious grandparents was rough.

Vaughn raised the subject one day with them in Indiana. "I asked if being gay was against their religion and they said they hated homosexuals," Vaughn said.[12] "I waited a week or so, and when I was alone with my grandma I brought it up. I told her I liked girls. She didn't believe me. She was shaking her head, saying, 'No you don't.' I started to cry, like, a lot, and she realized I wasn't kidding." Vaughn was close with her grandparents—they were like her other parents—and the lack of acceptance was a struggle, but she said her grandmother was slowly coming around. Meanwhile, Vaughn kept moving forward with her feelings.

Sophomore year, Vaughn dated a girl for about a week. "She broke up with me because her parents don't like homosexuality," Vaughn said. "She was really scared about it." In high school, it's hard enough to approach someone you like if you're not sure whether they like you. Not knowing whether they're gay adds more uncertainty. "It's hard to know who is and who isn't," Vaughn said. "I don't want to embarrass myself, I guess."

Outside of school, Vaughn, Ibarra, and their friends had pieced together the basics of a social life in Hutchinson. They hunkered down at "the Metro" (Metropolitan Coffee), a spacious, homey hangout in a strip mall on the northwest side of town, with local art on the walls and shelves full of books and board games and poetry nights and live music on weekends (also the locale of Pauls's revealing interview with the *Star*'s Kavanaugh). Or they drove around, usually heading south through downtown, past the end of Main Street and on through the winding roads of Carey Park, with its baseball and soccer fields and skateboard ramps and shelters and ponds. Or they went to Walmart and looked around, or to Freddy's for frozen custard.

All of that was fine, but Vaughn knew there was a way to make school feel better. "I thought: 'I need a club so I don't feel awkward or shy about how I am. And there are other students experiencing that same thing.'" Besides the gay-straight alliance that Isaac Unruh had started at Garden City High School six years earlier, several other GSAs were now in place in high schools and colleges around the state. Vaughn heard about the clubs through her stepfather, who taught at Hutchinson Community College where there was a small GSA of perhaps a dozen students. The GSA's faculty sponsor invited Vaughn to one of Powell's PFLAG meetings, and one afternoon she found herself in a classroom at some church, surrounded by adults and feeling out of place, listening to a presentation she didn't really understand. Later, she looked at Powell's Facebook page and thought, *Wow, this guy knows what he's doing in the community.*

After some prep work with Powell, Vaughn went to the office at school and asked for information and forms to start a club. "I told them what it was, and the woman said, 'Oh I can't do that for you.' I think they felt it would offend people." She talked to Powell. Powell talked to the school superintendent. Soon Vaughn learned that the choir director would be the club's sponsor.

The GSA's first meeting was set for October 8 in the auditorium/drama room. In a twist of bureaucracy, Vaughn couldn't make it. (School administrators controlled the club schedules, staggering meetings so students could participate in as many organizations as they wanted, which meant clubs basically met for half an hour once a month.) She was booked for an honors biology field trip along the Arkansas River, and it was a substantial part of her grade, so she couldn't skip it. She was completely disappointed, but she drafted a to-do list: whoever comes to the meeting should write down what they want the club to accomplish and vote on club rules.

Eighty people came. When Vaughn checked in with people afterward, they told her the meeting was really fun. "I was so scared that people wouldn't like it," she said. Attendance stayed almost as high for the second meeting in November, when they worked on a T-shirt design contest with prizes bankrolled by PFLAG: the winner got $50 in cash; first- and second-runners-up $25 and $10.

Ibarra, also an honors student, and a member of the drama team, made time for the GSA in his already crammed schedule because, he said, a lot of students at school felt left out. "It sucks to not be a part of something you really want to be part of and you can't." He knows this from experience. His mother always warned him he was up against a stereotype: "Mexicans just come here to get papers, if you're Latino you're not going to get anywhere, this is white man's land, go back to where you're from." He understood what she meant one day in grade school when the teacher asked what everyone wanted to be when they grew up, and kids laughed when he said he wanted to be a surgeon. "These kids are like,

'Oh, Mexicans don't make it far so just shut up and sit down.' My teacher didn't defend me in that situation." Ibarra began to put his mom's advice to work. "Mother always taught me to be respectful and well-rounded and achieve things. What my mom says is, 'Hey, I'm getting better grades than you. I'm going to be something you wish you could be, but I have a better education.'"

His mother has always been his number-one supporter, Ibarra said, even after she noticed him flirting with another boy on Facebook. She asked if he wanted to talk. "Eddie? I see you think this guy's cute." Frightened, Ibarra broke down crying. But her questions were teasing, loving. "She said she went through a phase like that, where she wasn't sure. She says it's normal to question your sexuality and she said either way, it doesn't change who we are."

Ibarra had lived in Wichita until eighth grade, when his mother married a man who moved the family to Hutchinson. At first Ibarra missed his friends and the benefits of living in a bigger city, where there were "more different people who are able to express themselves" at school. But he found a way to make the best of his new situation. With smaller classes, he realized, he was getting more attention from his teachers and it would be easier to figure out his future. Now Ibarra was in the top 3 percent of his class. But he was worried about some of his schoolmates.

> I have a friend, his family's strictly Christian and their family is really wealthy. His parents are sending him to conversion therapy. He's a very quiet person and he's able to harm himself. He was putting some things on Snapchat that grabbed everyone's attention, like, "I am a male, I hurt myself. I'm going to therapy, my parents don't like me the way I am." So I'm just trying to slowly break the ice and see if I can become a friend, someone he can rely on, talk to, instead of bottling everything up.

Ibarra and Vaughn hoped the GSA could be a lifeline for kids who are struggling. But besides the jocks and teachers who sneered at them on club signup day, Vaughn found most of her schoolmates at Hutch High to be accepting. "People aren't really scared anymore. There's all this confidence that's been built up in people." Besides all the support for the GSA,

Kara Vaughn and Eddie Ibarra at the Hutchinson High School Gay Straight Alliance dance in April 2015. Credit: C. J. Janovy

she saw evidence on social media and in music. "There's 'Same Love' by Macklemore—that was a top song for a long time, and it talks about how, 'Hey I'm gay, I can't change, that's me, that's who I am.' So people are like, he's singing about it. Music is the way to explain it. People are standing up, now."

Vaughn had big ambitions for the GSA, but she was also learning about group dynamics. Over the winter, fewer people showed up for GSA meetings until only the most dedicated members remained. That was okay. It was enough to put on a dance.

On a Saturday night in April, the rented party room in Carey Park felt like a church basement except for the banks of windows overlooking the golf course. Jon Powell and others from the Hutchinson PFLAG chapter had strung Christmas lights around the windows and draped rainbow-colored plastic over folding tables. They had baked cookies and bought bags of M&Ms, gummy bears, Twizzlers, Doritos, Bugles, and donuts, piling them on plates in the small kitchen's serving window. In one corner of the room, wearing a ballcap and setting the mood from her laptop, was a DJ named Gina Johnson.

Vaughn ditched her glasses for the evening and was wearing tight jeans, a long-sleeved black T-shirt, and Vans with a bright flower pattern. Ibarra went hipster-chic, his black hair shaved tight on the sides and gelled up on top, a cross hanging from a long beaded string around his neck, his faded gray T-shirt screenprinted with a light blue swirling cloud pattern—a depiction, he said, of his soul. Lean and lithe, he buzzed with energy.

As sunlight through the windows faded, it was girls on one side of the room and boys on the other—three girls, to be specific, mostly in black, one in a vintage Misfits T-shirt, turned inward in conversation; three boys were spread around at an opposite table. As the room grew dimmer, a few other kids came in from outside, where they had been lounging around on the playground equipment waiting for something to happen. Somehow, now, everyone had glow sticks, which turned into fluorescent green radiating necklaces as they stood around, unsure of what to do with themselves as at the beginning of any high school dance. One extra-tall, burly boy in a gray T-shirt and faded baggy jeans, with the sun-hardened, short, choppy hair worn by farm kids all over the Midwest, finally broke the awkward stillness, floating to the center of the room and flailing freely, the neon ring around his neck bouncing rhythmically as his impressive moves and lack of social inhibition belied his tractor-driver facade. Perhaps inspired, a boy and a girl who had been hanging on each other in a conspicuously heterosexual display of affection joined him on the floor, finishing out the song in their own slow dance.

Surveying the scene, Ibarra decided that the long folding tables, set up in rows like diagonal parking spaces on either side of the hall, were too obtrusive. They must go, he told Powell, and the adults jumped into action, pulling off the colored plastic tablecloths, breaking down the tables, and stacking the chairs in the corner. Meanwhile, a delivery driver from Pizza Hut walked in with a stack of boxes, which put the early dance momentum on pause, and the newly rearranged tables became a buffet where kids loaded up on slices. By the time the pizza was gone it was finally dark outside and everyone headed out to the yard for the night's first game.

Off to the southwest, at the other end of the park, fireworks marked the end of a baseball game for the collegiate Hutchinson Monarchs. Here in the darkness, under a massive cottonwood, twenty or so teenagers gathered in a circle. This was as big as the crowd would get—all of them were from Hutchinson High School, but so far they had spent the evening in small separate clusters because few of them actually knew each other. This made Huggy Bear a good choice for the night's first game. Ibarra stood in the middle of the circle, his thespian projection skills on full display as he explained the rules: when he called out a number—two, three, four, whatever—everyone would grab enough partners to match the number. At the end of the scramble, anyone not locked in a right-sized group embrace would be out. A distant train whistle seemed to endorse the effort as Ibarra called the first number—five!—and the circle of high schoolers frantically rearranged itself into squirming, five-kid lumps. Three! Two! Four! Each time, someone was too late joining the nearest group hug; those already locked in the embrace hugged each other more tightly to keep the others from breaking in. After each round, more and more were out. The psychology of the game might have seemed dangerous for a group of kids who are outcasts in real life, but nobody seemed to mind because it was all just an excuse for desperate and intense physical contact. Ibarra went through this a few times, until only three kids were left, and then just two, each of whom got a ten-dollar bill from Powell.

As if to make up for expelling some of their own in Huggy Bear, the group spent the rest of the night as one organism. Back inside, they broke into loose rows as everyone did their best line-dance moves to V.I.C.'s "The Wobble," then dissolved into a mass of squiggles for the "baby let me love you down" lyrics of Usher's "OMG," then came back together for a bouncing "Blank Space," though this time Taylor Swift's ode to reckless youth was a Saturday night affirmation of each other's existence as everyone pointed heavenward and sang along to reinforce the chorus: "I'll write your name!" They reinforced each other's presence again and again, singing louder as DJ Gina's purposeful selections urged them to celebrate themselves—Katy Perry's "I am a champion! And you're gonna hear me roar!"—before crescendoing into the night's glow-stick-lit, Huggy

Bear–knotted, full-throated agreement with Pink's message: "If you ever feel like you're nothin', you're fucking perfect."

It was a triumphant feeling that Kansas LGBTs would, after years of hard work, share at least a few times in the tumultuous months ahead.

9

Christmas lights were still hanging in the window of The Roost, a trendy coffee shop and restaurant on Lawrence's Massachusetts Street, on a Saturday night in January 2014. Inside were a few punky undergraduate LGBTQIAs with shaved heads and face piercings, and a handful of graduate students wearing fashionable flannel amid a crowd of mostly middle-aged white liberals—University of Kansas professors and straight ACLU types—along with a strong contingent of gray-haired lesbians (one couple wore matching Carhartt hooded jackets). People surveyed the selection of cheese cubes on the bar, occasionally hugging folks they hadn't seen in a while.

At the back of the room, Kristie Stremel strapped on an acoustic guitar and stepped behind a microphone. It had been a long time since Stremel's days of outrage at the county attorney's sodomy presentation at Garden City Community College. Nestled into the long booth against one wall, Stremel's partner was busy keeping a bottle in the mouth of their four-month-old son as one "auntie" passed him around to the next. Stremel's apolitical love songs, delivered in a style more Paul Westerberg than Melissa Etheridge, weren't the type to get a crowd fired up, but the purpose of the evening was to raise money, which required people to turn out, and Stremel's strong lesbian following had obliged.

After her set, Stremel told the crowd she would split the proceeds of CD sales with the real stars of the show: Julie and Roberta Woodrick of Lawrence, and Michael Nelson and Charles Dedmon of Alma (population 800), tucked into the Flint Hills halfway between Topeka and Manhattan. "You just really have to have your shit together to sue the state of Kansas," Stremel said. "I'm so proud of 'em."

It was six months after the US Supreme Court's *Windsor* and *Perry* rulings, and gay couples in Kansas were now living in the bizarre marriage-isn't-legal-everywhere landscape. The Brownback administration's first post-*Windsor* insult had come in October 2013, when the Kansas Department of Revenue released an official notice ahead of tax season informing same-sex couples that even if they had been legally married in other states, they still had to file their Kansas returns "as they always have in the state, using the single filing status."[1] So the two couples now at the front of The Roost filed a lawsuit.

Plaintiff Michael Nelson took the microphone. A reluctant speaker, he reminisced about old times in the building that now housed The Roost. "We used to have LGBT history nights. People came to tell their stories—this was a safe place and it remains a safe place," he said. "Do all you can to make Kansas the progressive place we know it can be. Everything is connected to everything else."

Next up was someone much more at ease with a microphone: Diane Silver. Wearing a magenta long-sleeved shirt and a black vest, her hair now matching her last name, Silver joked that she would always make a speech if someone asked her to. "Thirty years ago, we wouldn't even think about marriage equality," she said. "Now 30 percent of people in this country live in a place where marriage equality exists!" A lot of people didn't know their Kansas history, Silver said, so she barreled through some examples of how "Kansas has been taking steps toward gay liberation since the sixties!" She recounted how gay students formed an organization at KU, how the Simply Equal campaign began at her kitchen table, how Equality Kansas had started. Now, she said, "I want to introduce these wonderful brave people: Michael, Charles, Jules, Roberta." The foursome stepped forward to raucous applause. "You could change the lives of thousands of people and make history," Silver told the audience while Nelson walked into the crowd with a donation bowl.

Next up was another one of the plaintiffs, Roberta Woodrick. "I don't know how to follow that," said the soft-spoken woman. She thanked The Roost, all the employees who had come in to work, and Stremel. "I think some of you came just to see Kristie, which is fine with me." She needn't have worried about following Silver.

> If any one of you, twenty-five years ago, would have come to me and my now-wife Julie and said, "Ladies, you're going to be married for twenty-one years, legally married for six, and the federal government will let you file your taxes together and you're going to sue the State of Kansas," we would have laughed and laughed and laughed for a very long time. We're not laughing now. The way you live your lives has a ripple effect on states, on the nation, on the world. We ride on your shoulders to Topeka and beyond if we have to.

Next the microphone went to David Brown, their attorney, a striking figure in black jeans, a black blazer, and black cowboy boots, his long gray hair woven in a thin braid like a rattlesnake slithering down his back. Brown explained that he had interviewed thirty potential plaintiffs before he found these two couples. "I said the Phelpses might show up and harass the shit out of them. People with kids said they couldn't put their family through that. Others said they weren't sure they wanted the state looking at their finances. Now we have four people." He asked the crowd to thank them for their courage.

Brown was convinced that a head-on challenge to the state's constitutional same-sex marriage ban wouldn't work, so he devised an indirect challenge. He planned to use Kansas's own laws, which said that the state had to follow federal definitions of marriage for state income tax purposes, to prove that the state was discriminating against its gay citizens. By creating a separate class of married taxpayers, Brown believed, Kansas was violating their rights to equal protection and due process. He predicted a long and expensive slog. It was inconceivable to everyone there that night, in the first weeks of 2014, how quickly and dramatically the legal landscape for LGBT people would change before the year was out.

A few days later, 165 Kansans—40 state senators and 125 state representatives—trudged back into their offices in Topeka, some traveling hundreds of miles from homes along the Colorado border out west, the Oklahoma border down south, the Nebraska line up north, and Missouri to the east. For his State of the State speech, Brownback earned howls in some quarters by equating the abolitionist movement to the 1991 Summer of Mercy protests (and, by implication, decades of violent antiabortion activity including the 2009 murder of George Tiller). "Kansas marked the bloody trail out of slavery," he said, continuing in overwrought prose, "The chains of bondage of our brothers rubbed our skin and our hearts raw until we could stand it no more and erupted into 'Bleeding Kansas.' The Summer of Mercy sprung [sic] forth in Kansas as we could no longer tolerate the death of innocent children."[2] That was because, he emphasized, Kansans depend not on big government "but on a Big God." Kansans, he warned, must listen carefully "to the voice of hope and not to the noise of decline. Which way to choose? We know the way. God wrote it in our hearts."

Days later, the Kansas House got down to business with the Kansas Religious Freedom Act, back for its annual resurrection. This time the stakes seemed higher than they did at the Hutchinson retirement home two years earlier, due to the supposed attack on Christianity posed by *Windsor* and *Perry*. This proposed law wasn't just about protecting bakers, florists, and ministers from forced gay-wedding cake decorating, bouquet arranging, and vow blessing. This proposed law said that no one could be punished in any way for refusing to "provide any services, accommodations, advantages, facilities, goods, or privileges"—including, but not limited to—"counseling, adoption, foster care and other social services," or "employment or employment benefits, related to, or related to the celebration of, any marriage, domestic partnership, civil union or similar arrangement" or "treat any marriage, domestic partnership, civil union or similar arrangement as valid."[3]

If it was sweeping, it was also barely coherent. "The people who push this stuff write it this way for one reason: to make it hard to talk about," said Tom Witt. That meant he needed time to make sure statehouse reporters understood—and could translate for newspaper readers—the bill's dangers. He heard that the Speaker of the House wanted the bill to move quickly. "The Speaker doesn't know how toxic a problem he's got on his hands," Witt remembered. "Of course, I know how toxic I'm going to make it."

Witt found people from all over the state to testify, which forced the committee chair to schedule more hearings out of respect for the citizens who had driven long distances to Topeka. He also got lucky when a blizzard shut down the capitol, pushing the extra hearings back a few days and giving Witt time to help reporters untangle the legislation's language. It was no surprise when the House passed the bill in mid-February, but by then news of its implications had been properly reported—and Kansas was once again the subject of national ridicule. "Denying services to same-sex couples may soon become legal in Kansas," CNN reported.[4] Critics called the Kansas legislation "a 'gay segregation' bill, allowing businesses, hotels and restaurants to deny services or accommodations to gays and lesbians based on an employee's religious convictions," wrote the *Washington Post*.[5]

What did come as a surprise was a statement from the president of the Kansas Senate, a rigorously conservative Republican from Wichita named Susan Wagle. "A strong majority of my members support laws that define traditional marriage, protect religious institutions and protect individuals from being forced to violate their personal moral values," Wagle said. "However, my members also don't condone discrimination."[6] The bill never made it out of the Senate's judiciary committee. Kansas turned out to be more progressive that year than Arizona, where Governor Jan Brewer was forced to veto similar legislation that made it to her desk in February.

What had inspired Wagle's remarkable "my members don't condone discrimination" statement? Witt had applied muscle from the ACLU, of course. But this time, even the conservative Kansas Chamber of Commerce had opposed the bill. The business community's opposition, Witt said, is what really got to Wagle. But what had inspired the business community's opposition? After all, it was essentially the same argument that had held little sway when Sandra Stenzel had made it in 2004, asking, "Would the highly valued employees of Fortune 500 companies want to move to Kansas?" Had the decade really made a difference? Yes, but there was also someone playing a crucial behind-the-scenes role, another veteran of the Kansas marriage amendment battles: Bruce Ney, the Republican attorney from Lawrence.

Though he had dropped out of politics after the painful experience of campaigning against the marriage amendment, Ney had continued to work for AT&T and was now the company's general attorney for Kansas, charged with keeping an eye on legislation that might affect the company. As a result, AT&T was one of the first big businesses to put out a statement against the bill. "As a major employer and retailer in Kansas, we strongly urge the Kansas Senate to reject HB 2453," said Steve Hahn, president of AT&T Kansas.[7] "This legislation is impossible to implement. The bill promotes discriminatory behavior by businesses against their customers; and, it interferes with AT&T's management of our employees. It eliminates the use of fair business practices with customers in Kansas." Soon, similar sentiments came from Sprint's world headquarters in Overland Park.[8] "It took a lot of people in the capital by surprise that a company like AT&T would step forward and take that public position to oppose what conservatives wanted to call just a 'social issue,'" Ney said. "I saw the bill as bad for the business, our employees, our customers, and terrible for Kansas."

If Governors Mike Pence in Indiana and Asa Hutchinson in Arkansas had been paying attention to Kansas they might have avoided the national ridicule and boycott threats that rained down on their states over similar legislation the following year. In North Carolina, Pat McCrory would make the same mistake in 2016. But the nation seemed never to learn its lessons from Kansas. The citizens of North Carolina would refuse to reelect McCrory after he became the public face of that state's cruel HB2. Pence's political fortunes rose, of course, but not without the drag of his anti-LGBT activities—and as LGBT activists knew, losses, in the long game, often built to victories.

A month after the disingenuously named Kansas Religious Freedom Act died, Fred Phelps took his last breath. Phelps's demise, on March 19, 2014, at Midland Hospice Care in Topeka, provoked an international shout of "good riddance." In a poetically perverse display of irony, the normally media-eager leaders of his church forwarded reporters' calls to voicemail, and the original funeral picketer would have no funeral.

Witt, who had been fielding a deluge of media requests and questions from LGBT Kansans after word spread that Phelps was in hospice, issued statements of extraordinary grace. "[Phelps] and his followers showed utter disregard for the privacy and grief of others for many years," Witt noted in an Equality Kansas news release a few days before Phelps's death. "This is our moment as a community to rise above the sorrow, anger, and strife he sowed, and to show the world we are caring and compassionate people who respect the privacy and dignity of all."[9] Equality Kansas asked that its members and supporters refrain from protests or demonstrations upon official word that Phelps was really gone.

When that moment came, Witt's second news release served two strategic purposes: it provided guidance for LGBT people wondering how to handle their emotions and perfectly eulogized their longtime antagonist. "Our position on whether or not to publicly protest, demonstrate, or celebrate his passing remains the same: Please don't," he wrote.

> Ultimately, the antics of Fred Phelps and his followers will be nothing more than an obscene footnote in the history of equal rights. In the end, Phelps and the Westboro Baptist Church protests will not have had any impact on LGBT equality. Our movement was making substantial progress before he began his protests in 1991, has continued to make progress over the past 23 years, and after his death we will continue to move forward. The best vengeance is knowing that we will prevail, his views will fail, and his life will be rendered meaningless.[10]

Witt included a web address where people could make donations to Equality Kansas. After all, Phelps's progeny were already planning their next protest.

On a cold Sunday as Phelps lay dying, ten Westboro members, several of them children, descended on a couple of churches in Roeland Park, a tiny, tree-shaded, inner-ring suburb of Kansas City, where the postwar ranch-style houses are generally home to placid retirees and young families in starter homes. It was St. Patrick's Day, so one Westboro girl held a yellow sign with a green shamrock and the slogan PAGAN IDOL as she stood next to other kids holding SAME-SEX MARRIAGE DOOMS NATIONS and GOD HATES THE U.S.A. signs.[11] The churchgoers of United Methodist and Saint Agnes Catholic Parish apparently warranted this visit because

Roeland Park city leaders were set to vote on an ordinance protecting LGBTs from discrimination.

Yes, Equality Kansas was trying to pass another city ordinance. Roeland Park seemed like an odd place for this effort. With only about seven thousand people, it wasn't the type of town that had weight to throw around the statehouse. In fact, it felt less like a town and more like a shady neighborhood in the northeast corner of Johnson County, whose twenty cities blend into one another as the older, inner-ring suburbs give way to strip malls and McMansions chewing ever farther into the prairie south and west of Kansas City. Roeland Park has no downtown, just a few blocks of Roe Avenue lined by a supersized convenience store, a few fast-food restaurants, a Walmart, a Lowe's, and a massive Price Chopper grocery store. Most LGBT people who lived in Roeland Park probably worked in one of the metro's other 118 cities, including those across the state line in Missouri. There had been no reports of gay or trans people getting fired from their jobs at the gas stations or the big-box stores, or having been refused service at the Taco Bell or the Burger King.

But Sandra Meade, the trans woman who had restarted the metropolitan Kansas City chapter a few years earlier and had become the statewide chair of Equality Kansas in January 2014, had a plan. The town's demographics looked good. Back in 2005 Roeland Park was the only city in Johnson County to vote against the marriage amendment. And despite all the work of activists and allies over the years, as of early 2014 Lawrence was still the only city in Kansas where it was illegal to discriminate against LGBT people. Equality Kansas wanted a win. "Loss after loss is a disincentive for other city councils to move forward," Meade explained.[12] "We wanted a confidence builder that another city council or county jurisdiction would look at as a positive." They had learned lessons about the opponents' methods in Manhattan, Salina, and Hutchinson. "We know the disinformation campaign," Meade said. If the Roeland Park City Council passed an ordinance and a religious contingent immediately organized to repeal it, Meade was certain the LGBT side could defeat it at the ballot box. "And we could win all the way."

Nobody on the council seemed against the idea when members Jennifer Gunby and Megan England introduced the ordinance, according to the *Prairie Village Post*, a news website that routinely beat the *Kansas City Star* on hyperlocal coverage. "People are born the way they are born, and we should respect that," said the mayor, Joel Marquardt. "I am completely all for this," said Councilwoman Mel Croston.[13]

Along with Meade in the audience was Michael Poppa, who had stepped up to chair the metro Kansas City chapter after Meade ascended to statewide chair. He had grown up in Johnson County, but gone to New York City to be an off-Broadway actor. He had also lived in Los Angeles for a year—the year of the devastating Proposition 8 vote, which politicized him. Now in his late thirties, living in Roeland Park with his partner of five years, and managing his father's doctor's office, Poppa was finally pursuing his political interests.

Poppa and Meade expected that they would just be on hand to answer questions, but Meade ended up speaking for about forty minutes. When Marquardt asked about shower facilities and changing rooms, Meade explained how other states, and even local high schools, had model policies for dealing with that—all Roeland Park needed to do was look across the state line at how the city of Kansas City, Missouri, handled the language in its city codes. Basically, she said, it just required education: transgender people use the facilities that match their gender.

Councilman Robert Meyers pressed the issue, looking Meade in the eyes and saying, "If you walked into a men's room, I would have a heart attack." (This ignored the fact that Meade, as a woman, would not be walking into a men's room.) Another council member, Sheri McNeil, agreed that "the restroom situation does unnerve me a little bit."[14] Meade remained patient. Some schools, she explained, created interim, separate single-stall bathrooms to allow students to adjust to having transgender kids at school. Across the state line in midtown Kansas City, she noted, some businesses already had unisex bathrooms.[15] After a few more questions, the council scheduled a vote for April 21—seven weeks. The debate would last five months.

In a repeat of the process that had played out in Manhattan, Salina, and Hutchinson, Roeland Park residents for and against the ordinance packed council meetings to speak during the time allotted for public comments. Opponents didn't bother starting up an Awaken Roeland Park, but

Kansas Family Policy Council Director Robert Noland came in for a town hall meeting on April 15. Meade had to sit next to him while speakers and questioners waited a dozen deep behind the microphone at an elementary school gym. The council put off the vote until May 6. That night, fifteen people stood up to comment, ten of them supporting the ordinance. Then the council heard from a special guest speaker, another attorney from Alliance Defending Freedom. Dale Schowengerdt had local connections, having grown up just west of Roeland Park in Mission (where his father, Steve Schowengerdt, had just been elected mayor). Citing a case in Canada in which a man went into a shelter and molested two women, Schowengerdt warned that the ordinance would allow biological men to use women's bathrooms.[16]

The council delayed action again until June. One Sunday morning, some Roeland Park residents woke up to find a missive on their doorsteps, signed "RP Residents for Non-Discrimination" with the Gmail address "rpequalrights." The flier urged citizens to show up at the June 16 council meeting "and speak out against discrimination." Despite its disingenuous signature and wording, the flier was not the work of Equality Kansas. Among its warnings about the ordinance: "This gives a biological male who identifies as a female access to women's bathrooms, showers and changing facilities. With this ordinance, an employee at a public pool could not question or stop a biological male from entering the women's shower. They would risk being sued."

That brought out Channel 41 Action News. At 10 p.m., reporter Jenna Hanchard stood live outside Roeland Park City Hall, where the council had been deliberating for three hours. That night, there was no public testimony, Hanchard said—instead, residents found "public comment" in their front yards. "The biggest concern with the ordinance starts here," she said, while the camera zoomed in on a white toilet, flushing for dramatic effect.[17] But a Roeland Park denizen named Kevin White told her bathrooms were a nonissue. "Even if there was a transgender male or female and they went into the restroom that they're comfortable with, most people are not going to know," he pointed out. Hanchard reported that she wrote to the email address on the flier and got an anonymous reply: "We are all Roeland Park residents that were given names at birth. As we said this group was formed for the sole purpose of notifying residents about the ordinance and encouraging them to attend the Council meeting next Monday. That goal was accomplished with the flyer. End of story."

In July, the council that had seemed so united when the ordinance was introduced back in March now rejected it on a 4–3 vote. In a dramatic twist, however, a car accident had kept Councilwoman Becky Fast from making it to city hall that night. Her hoped-for yes vote would have made it a tie, which Mayor Marquardt would have had to break, and he said he would have voted yes. Citizens demanded a revote when Fast could be there. Two weeks later, over gripes from council members who opposed the ordinance and complained that the issue had brought out the worst in people and divided their city, an exasperated council held another vote. Sufficiently recovered, Fast showed up to vote yes and Marquardt broke the tie. Roeland Park was now the second city in Kansas to protect all LGBT people from discrimination. There was talk of a petition to repeal, but nothing materialized.

Meade had endured months of insinuations that she was a bathroom predator. "As a transgender woman it's extremely offensive," she said, "but that's how they win. They don't win through giving truth. They win by giving misinformation and preying on the most base of instincts, which is fear. The only way to combat that is, number one, visibility of people like myself, but number two, we know the messages now and we've got better answers."

More than her own role in defeating the antitrans rhetoric, what struck Meade about Roeland Park was what she viewed as competing versions of Christianity. In meeting after meeting, she said, "you'd have the accepting and tolerant Christians and the intolerant opposition Christians. At some point, the truthfulness of what I had to say went by the wayside because people were locked into their ideology and they weren't going to budge. And in this case, the tolerant side of Christianity won." That was significant in a state where conservative-controlled rhetoric—that the LGBT movement is a threat to families and society—had prevailed, she said. "Once you see a corner of the state changing and bucking that rhetoric, that's going to be an incentive and enabler for people who haven't spoken up in other parts of the state to stand up and know they have a chance too."

After the Roeland Park victory, Meade said, politicians approached her about trying to pass similar ordinances in other Kansas City suburbs, though such campaigns did not surface any time soon. Meanwhile, Roeland Park had one more bit of business: city council elections in April 2015.

Michael Poppa, energized by the new friends and neighbors he met while mobilizing LGBT people and allies to show up at city hall to support the ordinance, resigned from his position as chair of the metro Kansas City chapter of Equality Kansas and ran for the council. In the primary, the incumbent city council president, Marek Gliniecki (who had voted against the ordinance) came in a distant third behind Poppa (44 percent of the votes) and a citizen named JoAnna Rush (41 percent) who had spoken against the ordinance at council meetings.

For the general election, Poppa campaigned mostly on economic development—though small and landlocked, Roeland Park had parcels of land just waiting for builders. He avoided bringing up the ordinance, but going door to door he heard about "the gay agenda," about how a vote for him would be "a vote for child rape," and about how Kansans for Life had been telling people, "Michael Poppa wants young women to have abortions."[18] He won by four votes. Understanding the implications in his margin of victory, Poppa's agenda, a few times a month, would involve stormwater management, street maintenance, redevelopment of an old swimming pool site, and hiring a new city administrator.

Two months after Roeland Park passed its ordinance, a year of intense but steady activism turned turbulent. On October 6, 2014, a year and three months after *Windsor* and *Perry*, the US Supreme Court refused to consider rulings by appeals courts that had allowed same-sex marriages in Indiana, Oklahoma, Utah, Virginia, and Wisconsin—states with constitutional amendments similar to the one in Kansas. The Supreme Court action—or more accurately, nonaction—immediately increased the number of states allowing marriage equality from nineteen to twenty-four, and the five new states were in federal judicial circuits that also covered other states, so legal experts were certain that the number would quickly grow to thirty states. Kansas was in the same federal judicial circuit as Utah (along with

New Mexico, Colorado, and Wyoming), meaning the Supreme Court's refusal to uphold Utah's same-sex marriage ban implied the Kansas ban was also unconstitutional.

In deeply religious Utah, the Republican governor said that he was disappointed but he accepted the decision, and the Utah attorney general, Sean Reyes, also a Republican, directed state and county officials to recognize same-sex marriages immediately. "It's time for people of goodwill on both sides of the issue to come together now and heal any rifts that occurred," Reyes said at a news conference. "We are all Utahns. I hope we will exercise a great deal of kindness, caring and understanding."[19] There would be no such compassion and humility from the deeply religious administration in Kansas.

Brownback's attorney general, Republican Derek Schmidt, appeared not to understand the Supreme Court's action, saying the court's "disappointing decision to avoid the issue" ensured that the "already uncertain legal situation for Kansas" would continue. "No Court has squarely decided whether the Kansas Constitution's prohibition on same-sex marriage—adopted by voters less than a decade ago—is invalid," he said, as if the Kansas ban were unique and special. He would deal with "pending or future litigation directly affecting the Kansas constitutional provision as it may come."[20] Future litigation came quickly, turning into a county-by-county battle as the state officially contested every inch in its death-throe opposition to gay marriage.

In Hutchinson, Julia and Gina Johnson (Gina was the DJ at the Hutchinson High School GSA dance) went to the Reno County Courthouse and applied for a license. They had already had one (nonlegal) wedding and renewed their vows in a second ceremony years earlier, and Julia had taken Gina's last name. They had both worked in various jobs that occasionally required trips to the courthouse, so they knew the women in the clerk's office. Grinning and congratulating them, the women handed the Johnsons their paperwork and told them to come back in three days, per the standard waiting period. "And then we get that devastating call that they're not going to give us a license," Julia remembered.[21] The clerk who called was so apologetic, Gina said, it was as if she was as disappointed as they were.

"It's been a busy 28 hours," Witt wrote later on the Equality Kansas Facebook page. All around the state, people had gone to their county courthouses to apply for marriage licenses. All had been denied. Clerks were sounding confused. "The 10th Circuit ruling applies to Kansas, but it's not self-executing," Witt explained. "It may take litigation. Or it may not. Kansas courts may decide that the US Constitution applies here as much as it does everywhere else, and start issuing marriage licenses."[22]

Everyone would have to wait and see what happened next, he wrote. "In the meantime, if you haven't married out of state, do this: Grab your partner. Go to your local county courthouse. Insist on being allowed to apply for a marriage license." If couples were turned down, he would put them in contact with an attorney. "If they say yes, tell everyone you know (and tell me, too, so I can keep track). The time to push this issue is right now. Don't wait. We've waited long enough."

From her computer at a clinical research lab, a woman named Angela read Witt's post and called her girlfriend Kelli. (Intensely private, the two women insisted on being identified by their first names only, and the media complied.) "Hey, honey," Angela said. "Want to go to the courthouse and see what happens?"[23] They had talked about the possibility. Kelli's antiestablishment streak made her skeptical about the whole institution, but she knew there were benefits. Besides, she wanted to be with Angela, and if Angela wanted to get married, that was all right with Kelli.

They had been together for a couple of years, blending complicated lives. Angela was deep in graduate school, without much time for dating, just looking for friends when she posted an ad on Craigslist. Kelli, raising two kids on her own, was cautious about involvements. But they emailed and realized how much they had in common. They liked being outside (on their first date, they went hiking in a city park). They wanted to live sustainably (later they would raise chickens and fill a backyard with rows of vegetables). And they loved Kansas. Angela was getting her master's in geology with a focus on hydrogeology: "Groundwater is the most important issue facing Kansas," she noted. Kelli had a black-and-white-spotted cow tattooed on her right arm: "They give so much," she said of cattle. "They're from the prairie."

If all that didn't qualify them as quintessentially Kansan, their first weekend together certainly did. They packed Kelli's kids in the car and headed out to the wide-open skies of rural Harper County to watch the solar eclipse of May 2012. On a road near the Oklahoma line, Kelli saw what looked like smoke up ahead. Then she realized what it really was: a line of tornadoes. Equipped with a hand-cranked radio, they learned that one had touched down a mile ahead of them. "I threw it in reverse and went as fast as I could on this gravel road," Angela remembered. Pretending to be calm, she heard Kelli's daughter saying she had to go to the bathroom. "Finally we got to this little town with a McDonald's. There were these old ladies in there eating fries. We said, 'There's a tornado.' They're like, 'Yeah.'" Some Kansans, she realized, were more used to this sort of thing than others. They paid $10 to camp at an RV park outside of Greensburg (a town still rebuilding after being erased by its own tornado in 2007). The clouds cleared out in time for them to watch the eclipse.

So now they were on another adventure, this one to the Johnson County Courthouse, which was about to close by the time they arrived to apply for a license from Chief Judge Kevin Moriarty. They expected the clerk to say no, but the woman told them to wait. Five o'clock came and the clerk's windows shut down. Finally, the woman came back with an application form. "The judge said he was going to think about whether to approve it," she said. "He'll give you a call tomorrow."

"I'm sitting here with your application, and I'm going to approve it," Moriarty said the next day, when Kelli answered the phone. He started asking: Did she understand what that meant? Did she want him to perform the ceremony? "I'm like, 'Oh my god, the judge is calling me,'" Kelli said. Moriarty told them to come back on Friday after the three-day waiting period, but first they had to go back to the courthouse to pick up their application.

Reporters were waiting. Kelli didn't want her children filmed, and neither woman felt qualified to speak, because they weren't among the activists who had worked on the issue for years. "We're not that brave," Kelli said. "There are people who sue the state—that's courage." But they felt trapped. "There are people who want to hear from you," a TV reporter yelled. "She was a woman of color, and when they speak I listen," Kelli said. She stumbled through some comments. Later, she would mostly re-member that she had called Brownback "senator" instead of "governor."

They braced for more reporters on Friday morning. They called Rev. Benjamin Maucere of the Shawnee Mission Unitarian Universalist Church, scrambled to find something to wear, and made sure the kids had clean shirts. Just before 9 a.m. on Friday, with Kelli's mom and kids and a few friends, they said their vows in front of the pay phones in the courthouse hallway.

One reporter from the *Kansas City Star* was there but few TV cameras were waiting in the drizzle outside. They walked around the corner to a café for coffee and hot chocolate, where the woman behind the counter gave them hugs when she heard the occasion. Then Kelli took Angela to work.

If their ceremony was perfunctory, that is not because they are not sen-timental. One of Kelli's wedding gifts was a necklace made of copper—but not just any copper. Over the last decade, a $330 million renovation had restored the Kansas State Capitol to an opulent turn-of-the-nineteenth-century grandeur. The restoration included a new copper roof. Seeking creative reuses for the old copper, the Kansas Historical Foundation had selected artists to make jewelry now sold in the statehouse gift store. One of the artists was Bailey Marable, who uses the metal to make tiny cutouts in the shape of the state. Now, a tiny piece of copper that endured more than a century under the Kansas elements and above its lawmakers was a wedding gift to the state's first married gay couple.

Kelli and Angela's wedding wasn't just about the two of them. "The instant we got married," Kelli said, "the court said no one else could." And so began six weeks of judicial bathos. Whining that Moriarty had overstepped his authority, Kansas Attorney General Schmidt begged the Kansas Supreme Court to make him stop; Chief Justice Lawton Nuss or-dered Moriarty not to issue licenses but said couples could still fill out ap-plications. Setting a hearing for November 6, Nuss warned Schmidt that he would need to explain why Kansas, in the federal 10th Circuit, wasn't bound by the ruling that overturned Utah's ban.

Inconveniently, or maybe conveniently, for Brownback, these gay mar-riage developments came in the final weeks of an unexpectedly close reelection race. In his first term as governor, Brownback had embarked on what he called a "real live experiment" with the state budget, hypothesizing that radically low taxes would lure businesses from all over the country.[24] The experiment had clearly failed, and now, with his state budget heading into an abyss, something politically unthinkable was happening: Brownback's challenger, Paul Davis, the squishy Democratic House minority leader from liberal Lawrence, was four points ahead of him in statewide polls. Brownback looked desperate when he responded to the US Supreme Court's nondecision decision with an October 18 rally at Wichita's Summit Church, where marriage-amendment crusaders Terry Fox and Joe Wright now ministered in diminished circumstances. (Just a year after the marriage amendment passed, Fox resigned suddenly from his six-thousand-member Immanuel Baptist, with congregational leaders complaining about Fox's misuse of church funds for his radio show, his "arrogant" attitude toward the congregation, and "the appearance of integrity failures," according to the *Wichita Eagle*.[25] Meanwhile, Wright had retired from the eight-thousand-member Central Christian.) "The people of Kansas have voted on this," the governor bleated to an unimpressive crowd of about 150, citing his favorite decade-old 70 percent statistic.[26] Congressman Tim Huelskamp joined him to deliver a familiar warning about activist judges.[27] Brownback might have broken a sweat in October, but come election day he racked up a four-point win, frustrating pollsters perhaps as much as Democrats.

But something else happened on election day: A federal judge stated the obvious, ruling the Kansas ban unconstitutional. But in a nod to protocol, 10th Circuit Judge Daniel Crabtree put his ruling on hold until Schmidt could argue his case against Moriarty to the Kansas Supreme Court two days later. That might have settled things mercifully, except the state Supreme Court, in circular logic, canceled the hearing because it needed time to decide whether it should defer to Crabtree's ruling. Desperate to keep Crabtree's order from going into effect, Schmidt filed an emergency motion with the 10th US Circuit Court of Appeals and the US Supreme Court. On November 12, the Supreme Court told Kansas it must abide by Crabtree's decision.

"GO GET MARRIED," Witt wrote to gay Kansans.[28]

The next morning, in Manhattan, on a sunny but cold and windblown sidewalk in front of the Riley County Courthouse, Darci Pottroff and Joleen Spain, who had been together for nineteen years, exchanged vows in front of a few dozen friends, family members, and reporters. First Congregational United Church of Christ pastor Caela Simmons Wood put her hand over theirs and blessed the rings they already wore.

Riley County chief judge Meryl Wilson had signed off on their marriage, but it might not have been technically valid, because in Schmidt's tortured attempt to interpret the instructions he had just received from the US Supreme Court, Crabtree's decision applied only in Douglas County and Sedgwick County, the home counties of two couples—Kail Marie and Michelle Brown of Lecompton, and Kerry Wilks and Donna DiTrani of Wichita—who, with the help of the ACLU, had challenged the marriage amendment in their counties and sued the state health department, which oversees vital records. (This case was separate from David Brown's suit against the Kansas Department of Revenue on behalf of Julie and Roberta Woodrick and Michael Nelson and Charles Dedmon.) Outside of Douglas and Sedgwick Counties, Schmidt contended, the ban still stood in the state's 103 other counties. A week later, the Kansas Supreme Court added another county to those where it was legal, ruling that marriages could proceed in Moriarty's Johnson County, but only there.

Schmidt expressed annoyance while declaring a sort of victory and telegraphing support to judges who didn't want to surrender: "Although we asked the Kansas Supreme Court to provide statewide uniformity, today's ruling leaves the decision whether to issue licenses in the hands of the federal judiciary and of district court judges throughout the state."[29] Meanwhile, he would keep fighting. On November 19, Brownback said that state offices wouldn't recognize same-sex marriages even if some county judges had.[30]

The state's behavior was as transparent as it was infuriating. "They don't get to make this stuff up as they go just because they don't like gay and lesbian people," Witt told reporters.[31] The ACLU now had a buffet of state entities to target. "We're trying to figure out who we sue, including possibly the governor," said Doug Bonney, the ACLU's legal director in Kansas.[32]

LGBT Kansans and their allies rallying at the Kansas State Capitol in Topeka on February 14, 2015. Credit: C. J. Janovy

Terry Fox of Summit Church wasn't happy. "I know that there's dancing in the streets from the homosexual community that this is over," he groused, "but until it gets settled I don't think government agencies should amend their policies."[33] He was wrong about one thing. Brownback's scattergun resistance had at least avoided the spectacle of mass nuptials on the steps of the state capitol.

Instead, news came in from quiet and unexpected places. By mid-December, Equality Kansas knew of forty-four counties where judges were issuing licenses, some for people Witt had never met. Out in the rural middle of the state, the *Marion County Record* reported that Kaci Miller and

Amanda Horacek had married on November 13; the story did not have comments from Miller or Horacek, but it did quote Chief Justice Mike Powers. Not all of the judges in his district "are of the same philosophical opinion with regard to same-sex marriage," Powers told the *Record*, "but all eight of them agree unanimously that that is what the law is at this point in time."[34]

In January, a year after the four plaintiffs in David Brown's lawsuit against the state's Department of Revenue gathered for a fundraiser at The Roost in Lawrence, the US Supreme Court announced that it would decide the issue once and for all. The holdout states would have their answer by June, and all the Kansas litigation hovered in suspension. The national gay rights organizations were counting Kansas among the thirty-six states where same-sex marriage was legal, though that wasn't entirely true.

On Friday, June 26, 2015, *Obergefell*'s timing seemed like poetic justice for Brownback, whose administration still seemed exhausted after the Kansas legislature had recently ended its longest session in recorded history, lawmakers finally putting themselves out of their misery after 114 days of trying to reconcile the irreconcilable state budget. Tea Partiers had been forced to raise taxes and the budget was still $50 million short. Making matters even harder for conservatives to swallow, *Obergefell* came a day after the US Supreme Court upheld the constitutionality of the Affordable Care Act's health insurance subsidies for those who qualified. Late in the afternoon that Friday, Schmidt released a two-sentence statement, remarkable in its suggestion of a state government bewildered by legal decisions it had had months to anticipate. "We are reviewing the past two days' opinions internally and with our various clients to assess next steps," Schmidt wrote. "Fortunately, tomorrow starts a weekend, and the courts should be done at least for this week with issuing decisions."[35]

Tom Witt went to work doing what the state would not do: ensuring that the law of the land applied in Kansas. On Monday morning Equality Kansas began, county by county, judge by judge, to obtain written confirmation that marriages would be allowed. Over two business days, Equality Kansas's Facebook page turned into an up-to-the-minute news source. "BREAKING," Witt posted at noon on Tuesday, "Minutes ago the chief administrative clerk of the 13th Judicial District, which includes Butler,

Greenwood, and Elk counties, called our office to let us know Chief Judge [David] Ricke has just now reversed his earlier ruling banning marriage licenses to same-sex couples." [36] At 2 p.m.: "BREAKING: We have confirmed the 24th Judicial District, including the counties of Edwards, Hodgeman, Lane, Ness, Pawnee and Rush, is now issuing marriage licenses to same sex couples. TWO MORE JUDICIAL DISTRICTS TO GO!"

By 3:30 p.m. Witt had confirmation from the 25th Judicial District (Finney, Greeley, Hamilton, Kearny, Scott, and Wichita Counties). "Our many thanks go to the judge who was kind enough to call our office with the news. This leaves just one judicial district where we have no confirmation: The 20th, which includes Barton, Ellsworth, Rice, Russell and Stafford counties." By 4 p.m. the 20th District had reported in. All counties were accounted for and on board.

Nearly a week later, however, Brownback's office was still "reviewing" its obligations. "You have to understand and get the mechanisms in place," Brownback told the press. "So that's what we've been studying in meetings with the attorney general and relevant Cabinet members. . . . We're just examining it carefully."[37] Witt instructed gay Kansans who were trying to "access any marriage benefit previously denied you by law" to get names and obtain written documents from government officials. "If possible, use your cell phone video to record any encounter that results in a denial of recognition of your marriage. Let us know if you are willing to talk to a newspaper or television reporter."[38]

By July 6 Witt had evidence that state employees were ignoring the governor. "We have statements from LGBT Kansans that they have either been able to get their license changed, or have been notified verbally or in writing that they may apply for their spousal benefits," he wrote on the Equality Kansas website. "Late yesterday, however, officials in Governor Brownback's office denied this was the case. This is no longer the State of Kansas. It's now the State of Confusion."[39]

The next morning, Brownback apparently surrendered. "In the past hour," Witt reported, "the State of Kansas has confirmed that same-sex couples may now update their driver's licenses, apply for health insurance on their spouse's state employee's health insurance, and adopt children as married couples."[40]

It was a week and a half after the Supreme Court's ruling. Later that day came Brownback's official response: an executive order prohibiting the state from taking action "against any individual clergy, religious leader, or religious organization" for acting on "a religious belief or moral conviction that marriage is or should be recognized as the union of one man and one woman."[41] This didn't just protect churches from being forced to provide "accommodations, facilities, goods, or privileges for a purpose related to the solemnization, formation, celebration or recognition of any marriage, based upon or consistent with a sincerely held religious belief or moral conviction." It also included organizations "providing social services or charitable services."

By executive order, Brownback codified essentially the same "religious freedom" laws that the legislature had defeated for years. And it wasn't just about churches, Micah Kubic, the executive director of the Kansas ACLU, explained to the *Wichita Eagle*: "A homeless shelter that received a state contract or grant could refuse family housing to a gay couple with a child, or a foster care agency could refuse to place a child in their custody with the child's family member just because the family member was in a same-sex relationship."[42]

Foreshadowing the backlash rhetoric that would whip around the country in subsequent years, Kansas's Catholic bishops weighed in:

> In America, religious freedom has not just meant the right to hold a religious ceremony in a private setting, confined to the four walls of a church. In this country, religious freedom has meant the right to live one's faith in one's daily life, at home and at work, in private and in public. . . . Kansans who believe that every child deserves a mother and a father should not be punished by the government for that belief.[43]

Brownback's order might have mollified his religious base and made headlines, but quieter reactions were winding their way through his administration. On July 9 the Kansas Department of Revenue filed a request asking a state judge to dismiss David Brown's lawsuit on behalf of the Woodricks and Nelson and Dedmon. The Department of Revenue had abandoned its 2013 instructions that same-sex couples legally married in other states must continue to file their federal and state taxes using the single filing status. "The state's filing puts an end to my clients' nearly two-year fight for marriage equality," Brown told the *Lawrence Journal-World*. He said he was happy that his clients now had the same rights as other married couples, although "it never should have taken this long for the state to act appropriately."[44]

Far away from Brownback's coldhearted office, the people of Kansas were starting to show that he didn't represent all of them. In Manhattan, something unusual began happening after Pottroff and Spain's ceremony on the sidewalk outside the Riley County Courthouse the previous November had put them at the center of a small-market media frenzy involving the *Manhattan Mercury*, the KSNT TV broadcast from Topeka, and some AM radio news stations. The two women hadn't been particularly aggressive activists. "We don't have rainbow flags hanging all over everything. I'm not out there going, 'Gay rights for everybody!'" Pottroff said. "The biggest thing we do, most importantly: We are at home. We do some really strange things like have picnics in the back yard. We mow our lawn. We keep a nice house, trim the shrubbery out front, maintain our vehicles, maintain our home. We have kids, and now five grandsons. We make a statement by being normal."[45] Getting married in front of the media was the most newsworthy thing either one of them had ever done (although Pottroff had managed to get appointed to a seat on the city council of Riley, population just under 1,000).

One day in the grocery store, a woman approached them. "I do not know this lady," Spain remembered. "She saw us, she looked, she went a little bit away, looked again, turned around, and came back. She put her hand on my arm and said, 'Are you the couple that got married?' I said, 'Yeah we are.' She said, 'Can I give you a hug?' She started bawling, just sobbing on Darci's shoulder. She was like, 'I'm so happy for you.'" Wedding cards and presents came pouring in, which wasn't surprising because the couple had a wide circle of friends. But then envelopes started arriving in their mailbox with no return address, wedding cards signed simply "Dave and Martha" or other names they didn't know. No last names. Quiet but solid, classically Kansan, gestures of support.

PART FOUR

THE TRANSFORMATION

AS GENDER IDENTITIES EVOLVE, SO DOES KANSAS

When Caitlyn Jenner introduced herself to a world that had formerly known her as Bruce, in April 2015, the reaction was, in some ways, as if that world had never heard about how transgender tennis player Renee Richards had been denied entry into the US Open forty years earlier, which had been big news at the time. Nearly a year before Jenner's big media rollout, *Time* magazine declared that the country had reached a "transgender tipping point" in "America's next civil rights frontier," with more trans people emerging into public life, fighting to equalize public policies, and facing predictable resistance. The magazine illustrated its May 2014 story with a gorgeous photograph of *Orange Is the New Black* star Laverne Cox on its cover.[1]

Two years after *Time*'s premature tipping-point prediction and a year after Jenner's debut, we were deep in the middle of what might ultimately be remembered as America's "Bathroom Spring," with the nation fixated on where transgender people could be allowed to perform one of life's basic necessities. In March 2016 the North Carolina legislature passed its notorious HB2, which, besides being another "bathroom bill" (removing protections that allowed trans people to use the facilities that matched their identities), also barred cities from adding gender identity and sexual orientation to their nondiscrimination ordinances, as more than a dozen North Carolina cities (including Charlotte, Raleigh, Chapel Hill, and Durham) had done.[2] The nation's obsession with the bathroom part of the conversation climaxed in May, when the Obama administration sent a letter to public school districts across the country, warning them to let students use the restrooms that matched their gender identity or risk losing federal education funds. More than twenty states (including Kansas) would sue the Obama administration in response, but not before the Republican governor of South Dakota vetoed a bill similar to the one passed in North Carolina, and celebrities, big businesses, and major sports enterprises punished North Carolina with boycotts.

Trying to explain how the issue of transgender people in bathrooms had made its way to the White House, the *New York Times* reported that "the current debate [had] its roots in Houston," where, the previous November, voters had repealed an antidiscrimination ordinance that included gender identity. "The law's opponents boiled their message down to a five-word slogan . . . 'No Men in Women's Bathrooms,'" the *Times* reported, helpfully adding that by the time of that vote, more than two hundred cities had antidiscrimination laws like the one Houstonians had repealed; Minneapolis, it noted, passed protections for transgender people in 1975. But the post-*Obergefell* backlash was in full fury. "The repeal of the Houston ordinance rattled national gay rights leaders," the *Times* noted, quoting Human Rights Campaign leader Chad Griffin as saying about organizations such as Alliance Defending Freedom, "I think they have now created a campaign in a box that we are going to see shipped from city to city and state to state."[3]

Griffin's assertion that Alliance Defending Freedom had "now" created that campaign in a box is the kind of comment that reinforces state-level activists' sense that the national LGBT organizations are insultingly out of touch with what is happening outside their blue-state big cities. It was a good thing activists in Kansas hadn't been waiting for help from Griffin's organization when they had fought those types of campaigns in Manhattan, Salina, and Hutchinson. And by the time of the Houston defeat, trans people had been *leading* the LGBT movement in Kansas for years. Stephanie Mott had her own (albeit Kansas-sized) media rollout four years before Jenner's, and Sandra Meade had defeated a Houston-style campaign in (admittedly tiny) Roeland Park. Though these contradictions to the Kansas stereotype played out well below the national radar, they are classic examples of American individualism—but directed, in this case, at great risk, toward a greater good.

10

Sandra Meade looks a lot taller than she is, especially wielding a microphone in front of a concrete wall etched with the Bill of Rights. A few hundred of us were once again at Ilus W. Davis Park, the stretch of lawn in front of the federal courthouse in Kansas City. A happy-hour breeze floated through the park. That morning, June 26, 2015, the US Supreme Court had legalized same-sex marriage nationally in *Obergefell v. Hodges*, and now everyone was hugging old friends and waving rainbow flags. Off to the side of the concrete Bill of Rights wall were musicians from the Mid-America Freedom Band—saxophonists, a French horn player, a flutist, a baritone player, a trumpeter, a double bass player, and a drum-kit drummer—whose refrain of "Here Comes the Bride" filled the space between speeches.

For Meade, the honor of emceeing this rally followed the obligation of organizing it. She is a short woman with perfectly straight long blonde hair and a warm voice. As if to compensate for her physical stature, her portable PA system, and her lack of an actual stage, Meade was wearing a brilliant orange sleeveless shirt and a light skirt with a zigzaggy pattern of red stripes that felt as electric as the day.

It had been less than a year since Meade's victory with the Roeland Park nondiscrimination ordinance. Meade was excited to read a statement from a political celebrity who regretted she couldn't be there in person: Kathleen Sebelius.

"I join you in celebrating today's wonderful victory for marriage equality nationwide," wrote the former governor. Sebelius was by this point a figurehead, having left public service bruised by the disastrous Obamacare rollout during her tenure as Secretary of Health and Human Services. But to this crowd, she was a star. "Throughout my career as a state legislator, insurance commissioner and governor and a member of President Obama's cabinet, I have been a proud LGBT ally working to eliminate discrimination and promote opportunity," Sebelius wrote. (Her revisionist statement assumed not many people in this audience would remember that a decade earlier, Sebelius was a lukewarm ally at best. But after all, she was not the only one who had evolved over the past ten years.)

Meade continued reading Sebelius's message, which reminded the crowd that LGBT Kansans who could now get married might still be fired for putting wedding photos on their desks. "It bewilders me why Sam Brownback cannot see this is bad for Kansas"—here Meade waved around the piece of paper and editorialized: "Mr. Brownback needs to pay attention!"—"but apparently he can't," Sebelius wrote. "We must acknowledge that the battle is not over. Our friends and family, our communities, and our country deserve our continuing dedication to equality under the law, to promoting lasting, loving relationships, and to valuing all families. So as we celebrate this amazing moment in history, please join me in rededicating yourself to the effort to ensure that these real family values prevail everywhere."

Not having been around for the Kansas same-sex marriage ban, Meade had no quarrel with Sebelius, whom she had met at a Planned Parenthood fundraiser a year before. Meade was just proud to be able to secure the statement (which Tom Witt read at a similar rally that morning at the statehouse).

Next up were the mayors of both Kansas Cities. Kansas City, Kansas, Mayor Mark Holland went first. A handsomely goateed man in his late forties, Holland had only been mayor for a couple of years—but he had a long career as a United Methodist minister, and is the son of a United Methodist minister and grandson of a United Methodist minister. "I'm honored to be here. It's an honor to be invited," Holland yelled. Referring to an earlier speaker who said it was a great day to be gay, Holland said,

"I would also say it's a great day to be straight in America." He introduced his wife and children. "I wanted our kids to be able to come today because I told them, 'This is a landmark decision in our nation and I want you to be able to tell your grandchildren that you were there the day the Supreme Court made marriage free for everybody.'" This earned enthusiastic whoops.

Holland wanted to make sure everyone knew that his church, Trinity United Methodist, welcomed everybody. He knew that wasn't true for all Methodists, but Holland brought good tidings from the denomination's annual Great Plains Conference a couple of weeks earlier. Holland was there, he reported, "with a thousand clergy and a thousand laypeople from around the states of Nebraska and Kansas, these two red states, and those two states passed legislation to send on to our international conference next year calling for the church to stop discrimination against ordination and marriage in the church. It passed in Kansas and Nebraska, among Christians by a 2–1 margin!" This got huge applause. Out here in the Bible Belt, even the unchurched and the atheists get excited any time religion doesn't get used as a weapon.

"We've come a long way but we have a long way yet to go," Holland said. As a Kansan, he continued, "I'm very discouraged that many people equate Christians with bigotry. We know that every bigotry in this country has been justified on religious grounds." He ran down the litany. Slavery: justified in the Bible. Segregation: justified in the Bible. Not allowing women to vote or be ordained: justified in the Bible. "The civil community has always been ahead of the church on social issues," Holland said. He knew he had brothers and sisters in Christ who struggled with the issue of homosexuality, but said that Jesus calls everyone to love and grace. Clearly looking ahead to the winter, when the Kansas legislature would reconvene, Holland proclaimed:

> Freedom to be Christian and to be free for religion is not freedom to be a bigot and to discriminate against gays and lesbian people at your barber shop, at your flower shop, at your bakery! Those of us who are people of faith need to continue to call people of faith, whether you agree or disagree, to a place of love and grace and welcome of all people because then, thy kingdom come. Thank you very much!

There was only one way Kansas City, Missouri, Mayor Sly James—an aggressive advocate for LGBT rights—could follow that. "I'm gonna kinda need your help. I'm gonna start off," James said when he grabbed the mic. He started singing: "All You Need Is Love." This went on for just one chorus, and then it was time for the rally's finale. The Heartland Men's Chorus took everyone out with "Somewhere over the Rainbow," and for once, in Kansas, dreams really did come true.

By this time, Sandra Meade had been statewide chair of Equality Kansas for two years and had led many rallies like this one. Meade's ability to summon big-city mayors and a former governor to stand with her is a testament to one remarkable journey in a decade of transformation not just for individuals but for the country.

Born a boy in the early 1960s to a carpenter and a homemaker and raised in small towns in Nevada and the mountains of New Mexico, Meade's childhood was defined by a moment around age six. Intractably drawn to his mother's and sister's clothes, the young Meade observed with fascination how his sister, who would later come out as a lesbian, hated everything feminine. "My mom would force her to wear a dress, and I would just be enamored with that dress," Meade remembered. "One day my mom put curlers in my sister's hair. Then my mom left and my sister was all pissed off and pitching a fit. I told my sister to put the curlers in my hair. So she did." Meade looked into the mirror and, for the first time, saw her true self. "It was just so validating—finally there I was, seeing the person I thought I should be." At that moment their mother, wondering why they were so quiet, came into the room. "Mom took one look at me and started laughing—it was funniest thing she had ever seen." Meade doesn't blame her mother for what happened next. Given the times, her mother wouldn't have known any better. She marched Meade into the living room, where her parents were entertaining friends, and everyone laughed at the little boy dressed as a girl.

"Within the course of two minutes I went from euphoria to utter humiliation," Meade said. And then she went into emotional hiding, seizing every secret opportunity to experiment with her mother's or sister's things while knowing something was terribly wrong. Meade remembered sitting on the edge of the bathtub when she was seven, rocking back and forth, praying to God: "Fix me, make it right, make my body match my mind." Her grandmother was religious and tried to ensure that her grandchildren were, too, but Meade concluded early on that nobody was up there listening, or else her prayers would have been answered.

Some relief came when Meade was a young teenager in the seventies and all the boys started growing out their hair. Meade talked her parents into letting her do the same. She was just being like everyone else, she argued, but the real reason was so that she could put her hair in curlers whenever she was home alone.

Meade was so deep in hiding that no one suspected any problems. That she grew to be only five feet, two inches tall was helpful after she transitioned, and in the intervening years served to explain why the young man appeared to be compensating for something. "Everything I did, I worked twice as hard. I raced motorcycles and was amateur state champion in 1976. I was the only kid on my baseball team who was selected for the Little League district competition. I was always trying to excel. I'm not sure if that was an effort to overcome the shame I had, but I was pretty ashamed."

When Meade was fifteen, her father's business failed. They moved to Houston and stayed with friends, but that didn't go well. Meade dropped out of high school, got into drugs and drinking, and went to jail more than once. For a while Meade and her father were homeless—they worked construction, and after hours they would meet at a work site where they could run an electrical cord to his van. "He'd sleep in his van and I'd sleep in my car. We'd eat sandwiches out of an ice chest. Before we'd meet for dinner, we'd go to a park and pay twenty-five cents each to use the shower." Meade knew it was time to get out of the situation. "I said goodbye to my dad and joined the navy." Meade was seventeen.

What followed was a redeeming and honorable six-year military career. Thanks to high scores on the entrance exams, Meade was in line for advanced electronics training. From Naval Air Station Whidbey Island in Washington State, Meade would be part of Carrier Air Wing 15, maintaining the electronics for A-6E jet bombers and deploying to the supercarriers USS *Kitty Hawk* and the brand-new USS *Carl Vinson* on its maiden voyage out of the Norfolk Naval Shipyard. "We took it around the world and then to its first home port at the Alameda Naval Air Station," Meade remembered, still sounding awestruck by the experience.

When Meade came home on leave, she would go to a storage locker and retrieve a small box of clothes. "In the privacy of my own home, I would have the freedom to dress as myself when I wasn't on base or at sea. I had manly hair because I was in the military, but I'd put on makeup and everything and just be myself—sometimes just for the evening, then I'd take it off and go back to work the next day." It was fleeting relief from an intensifying pressure. At the end of her six-year enlistment, Meade was twenty-three and starting to think seriously about "this thing"—her term for what would be an official diagnosis of gender dysphoria—and what might be ahead. "Whatever this thing was, I knew it wasn't compatible with this hypermasculine thing in the navy. I wanted to be able to experience myself before my fear got to me. I had to get out of the military and start exploring."

But Meade's civilian career turned in a direction only slightly less masculine. She went to work for a Lockheed Martin subcontractor at Vandenberg Air Force Base in southern California. It was the mid-1980s, and NASA was cranking up the space shuttle program, so Meade worked on the computer systems. Her team was six months from its launch at Vandenberg when the *Challenger* exploded after takeoff in Florida. A few months later, her plant was mothballed.

Meade, who had earned a secret security clearance in the navy, went to work on a top secret program at Edwards Air Force Base: the B-2 stealth bomber, Reagan's $2 billion trophy of Cold War weaponry. "It was a fascinating bird," Meade said. "To be working on this top secret plane that was going to change everything—it was one of the highlights of my career." But things were going well in the world, which meant things were going badly for the project. Mikhail Gorbachev came to power and dissolved the Soviet Union, the Berlin Wall fell, "and the B-2 went from a program where there were 170 planes to 130 planes to 70 planes to 21 planes," Meade said. Defense contractors in California were imploding, and Meade was on the most expensive program. She started putting out résumés.

But life had grown complicated. Working at Vandenberg, Meade had married a woman. "I'd told her early on in our relationship that I had this thing going on where I needed to dress as a girl sometimes, that it had always been with me and I thought it might eventually just go away, but I wasn't sure." The woman said she was okay with that, and they married and had a son. The family moved around for several years, with Meade's top secret clearance proving lucrative as they followed defense contracts around the country. Eventually Meade ended up at Whiteman Air Force Base near Warrensburg, Missouri, where the B-2 program was no longer top secret.

Meade was happy to be in a town with a college. Despite her technical education and success in the navy, it bothered her to be a high school dropout. She enrolled at Central Missouri State University, where, at the library, after finishing her assignments, Meade would look up books, scientific studies, "everything I could find about this condition I've got." All of it said the same thing: "Their distress is alleviated when they transition." In 1998, after working full-time during the day, going to school at night, and raising a son, Meade graduated summa cum laude with a degree in computer science and math. Meade's wife had also earned a degree, and both of them got jobs at Sprint headquarters in suburban Kansas City. For the first time in a twenty-year career, Meade had a job that wasn't associated with the Department of Defense.

After hours, Meade kept up her pattern of excelling at what were supposed to be manly endeavors, coaching her son's state championship baseball team. But she began to think more about transitioning. The man's-man father she had idolized had died in 2001. Her worries about disappointing him were replaced with a fear of disappointing her wife and son, but she was in her forties. Her father had died at sixty-five. "I started to realize that I might only have fifteen years left, that my time was almost up, that I was never actually going to live my life," she said. The ever-increasing pressure was agonizing.

Meade got a divorce in 2006. By then, all the information she had found at the Central Missouri State University library was easy to find online. "More people were starting to transition, and I fell into that category: I was exposed to more information, began to feel more comfortable and understand more about what I was doing." Still, she spent most nights crying herself to sleep. "I knew I had to transition or I couldn't continue living like I was," she said, but what if she transitioned only to lose her family, her home, her job? After seeing a therapist, in 2009 Meade had obtained the necessary doctor's clearance to start hormone therapy. She took her first dose in March 2010. The date, she said, was like a new birthday.

Meade remembered telling her therapist she was going to be an advocate. "Once I decided to transition, it's a really cathartic experience when you spend so much of your life in hiding and hate everything about who you are and the fact that you can't be honest." Now she wanted to be a voice for the community. "It sounds corny," she said, "but I honestly believe that all of my life brought me to that point."

A few months later, Meade saw a notice for an Equality Kansas meeting. "It was about learning your rights, getting involved, what you can do to help." She went. Not many people showed up, but Meade met Witt. Incredibly, Kansas City didn't have a chapter—there had been one, but it had gone dormant a couple of years earlier, after the death of its chair. Witt connected Meade with a few other people who were interested in starting it back up again, and in 2011 they all met on the patio at a brewpub to officially reinstate the metropolitan Kansas City chapter of Equality Kansas.

Meanwhile, Meade's determination to be a voice for the community became literal once she took over as host of "Trans Talk" on a community radio station. Once a month on KKFI 90.1 FM, Meade had the 1 p.m. Saturday afternoon slot. "Many of my guests were nationally known trans role models and experts," Meade said. She would get them on the phone to talk about topics in the news, or issues that were on her mind, seizing opportunities to help trans people reframe the negative messages they were constantly hearing about themselves. She is especially proud of a September 2013 episode about what happened to a popular New York disc jockey named Mister Cee, who ended his twenty-year radio career after a trans woman posted audio of him approaching her for sex. "After he was outed," Meade said, "he was crying and blubbering that he has issues. Wait a minute—going out with [a person like] me is 'an issue'? I'm a human being." She booked a show with the Los Angeles writer, producer, and activist Andrea James, an influential name in trans world, to talk about the "internalized transphobia" people might feel after the public shaming of a celebrity who wanted to spend time with trans people. She also booked

Sandra Meade, speaking at a rally at the Kansas State Capitol in February 2014. Credit: John Long, Camp Kansas City

a Kansas City author and psychologist to talk about overcoming guilt and shame. "It was important to have a venue where we were speaking in our own voice, about our own solutions, struggles, and successes," she said. "To have that program, with integrity, was extremely important."

It wasn't just important for however many trans people might have been out there listening. For Meade, it was just the latest experience that would steel her for what lay ahead. At Sprint, she had been a program manager at the same time that the global telecom company was spinning off a smaller, but still massive, local company called Embarq. This involved hundreds of projects that affected every department—HR, customer service, provisioning. Each week she got reports from a small army of project managers, and she would have to present status reports to directors, CIOs, vice presidents. "I had experience being clear, concise, and calm. I knew how to manage the message, manage the emotions in the room. In cases where the audience is going to be disagreeable, I was somebody who could keep my cool and stay on topic." This was necessary, because she was the one in front of reporters and cameras, representing the LGBT equality movement in Kansas during the climactic, news-heavy years of the same-sex marriage resolution and the intensifying "religious freedom" backlash.

Meade was the second transgender woman to chair the board of Equality Kansas; she ascended in the footsteps of Stephanie Mott. Witt had recruited them both. In finding trans people to be his bosses as board chairs, Witt wasn't just making amends for "throwing my trans friends under the bus" when he agreed to strike gender identity from the Hutchinson nondiscrimination ordinance in 2012. It's bigger than that. He recognized their journey. "I look at trans equality as being where the lesbian and gay population was thirty-five years ago," he said.

First, there was the violence. By the time the Supreme Court legalized gay marriage at the end of June 2015, national organizations had logged eleven murders of transgender women in the United States that year: Lamar "Papi" Edwards, 20, shot to death in Louisville, Kentucky; Lamia Beard, 30, shot in Norfolk, Virginia; Ty Underwood, 24, shot in Tyler, Texas; Yazmin Vash, 33, found dead of multiple stab wounds in Los Angeles; Taja Gabrielle DeJesus, 36, stabbed multiple times in San Francisco; Penny Proud, 21, shot multiple times in New Orleans; Bri Golec, 22, stabbed to death in Akron, Ohio; Kristina Gomez Reinwald, 46, killed in Miami; Keyshia Blige, 33, driving with a friend when shots were fired into her car in Aurora, Illinois; London Chanel, 21, found dead of two stab wounds in front of an abandoned house in north Philadelphia; Mercedes Williamson, 17, reportedly stabbed to death and buried in a field in Rocky Creek, Alabama. Most were women of color. Kansas City, Missouri, contributed to the awful litany with the murder of Tamara Dominguez, 36, run over multiple times in August.[1]

As 2015 went on, so did the killings, prompting a *Time* magazine article that tried to explain what was happening. "Transgender people are four times more likely than the general population to report living in extreme poverty, making less than $10,000 per year, a standing that sometimes pushes them to enter the dangerous trade of sex work," Katy Steinmetz wrote.[2] "Nearly 80% of transgender people report experiencing harassment at school when they were young. As adults, some report being physically assaulted [on] trains and buses, in retail stores and restaurants." Recent legal victories and a heightened media presence for LGBT people were positive developments, but the visibility increased the risk. Kris Hayashi, executive director of the Transgender Law Center, told Steinmetz that despite greater acceptance, "the majority of society does not understand who transgender people are in ways that lead to the violence and the murder and the harassment that we're seeing."

This might have been news to *Time* readers, but it was all too familiar for gay people at least old enough to remember the nineties. Aaron McKinney and Russell Henderson beat Matthew Shepard and tied him to a fence in Wyoming to die in 1998. That was only the most high-profile murder. "There was actual violence that people didn't care about because, 'Hey, it's the queers,'" Witt said. Back when he was living in Oregon, "two lesbian friends of mine were butchered in 1994 in Medford—some guy decided he didn't like lesbians, so he bound them, cut them up, and murdered them, and abandoned them in the back of a pickup truck." He was talking about Roxanne Ellis and Michelle Abdill, killed by Robert James Acremant. "Some bigots threw Molotov cocktails into a basement apartment and two people burned to death in an antigay attack in Salem." These were Hattie Mae Cohens and Brian H. Mock, who died in a September 26, 1992, firebombing. "That kind of stuff was happening around the country. It's the stuff that's happening to trans people right now."

The violence wasn't the only thing we'd seen before. "The other side is using the same scare tactics now against the trans community that they used against the gay and lesbian community thirty years ago," Witt points out. "The arguments are almost exactly the same: 'We can't let gay men into bathrooms because they'll rape your little boys.' Now we hear the argument against trans people: 'We can't let them into bathrooms because they'll rape your little girls.'" Given that rhetoric, Witt said he's amazed by the courage of people who transition. "Coming out and being themselves is an act of daily bravery. Just stepping foot out your door every day is an act of bravery."

It was standing-room only on January 14, 2016, in the chambers of the Kansas House Judiciary Committee, which was once again pretending to consider adding sexual orientation and gender identity to the state's antidiscrimination laws. Giving testimony first was the LGBT side—Witt, a couple of supportive ministers, former Salina mayor Barb Shirley, and Meade, who went first.

Meade started with a bit of her history. "I'm a navy veteran, having served six years. After that I served fourteen years working on Department of Defense programs for highly classified programs." She mentioned her time working on the space shuttle and the B-2 bomber. "That's how I ended up here in the Midwest. I'm a proud college graduate and a proud parent of a son who's also graduated college and also works in Kansas. I've been a resident of Johnson County for sixteen years," she said.

"The reason I bring this up is because I'm also transgender. And it seems like there's so much demagoguery about transgender people that I first wanted to humanize who I am." Meade noted the risks of publicly outing herself as trans, especially in a conservative state, and accurately predicted the tenor of what the committee would hear as soon as the opponents had a chance to testify. "Instead of being a veteran, instead of being a proud parent, instead of the contributions that I've given to my country," Meade said, "people try to replace all of those labels with the one that says 'predator.' I'm not a predator. I'm a proud American citizen. I'm a proud Kansan. I've given to my country. And I continue to work and pay taxes and I don't appreciate the demagoguery."

She refuted the argument that the bill in front of legislators would put young girls at risk by allowing men into their bathrooms. Federal and state laws are sufficient for dealing with predators in any setting, she noted. "What this bill does do is allow transgender men and women to use the bathroom that corresponds to their identity and access it safely. For somebody like me to be forced to use the men's restrooms because I was originally assigned male at birth puts me at risk." Meade said that Equality Kansas welcomed conversations with "reasonable people" who would work with the organization to strengthen religious protections while also strengthening LGBT protections. Mostly, though, "I ask this committee to reject the demagoguery on its face as unworthy of reasonable consideration."

Meade ended her testimony by saying that she was happy to answer questions. When no one had questions, the committee chair thanked her, just as he would everyone who testified that day, as the meeting slogged into overtime, hijacked by yet another attorney from Alliance Defending Freedom who came to Topeka from out of state to frighten the panel about threats to religious freedom and dangers to little girls.

For a while, it seemed as if Kansas legislators really might reject the demagoguery. Some would succumb to the bathroom panic, floating a "student physical privacy" bill that proposed allowing "aggrieved" students at public schools to sue their institutions for $2,500 each time they encountered someone of the opposite sex, as "determined by a person's chromosomes and . . . identified at birth by a person's anatomy," in a bathroom or locker room.[3] But Kansas students aren't dummies. "That's a $2,500 bounty, basically," a University of Kansas junior named Harrison Baker would tell the *Kansas City Star*.[4] The bounty bill wouldn't get out of committee, but on the last day of the session, with massive unfinished business (they would have to return for a special session to work out how to fund public schools), legislators would pass a resolution decrying Obama's public school bathroom stance, and Attorney General Schmidt would join the lawsuit challenging those rules.

But all of that was in the weeks ahead, after Meade spoke to the Kansas House Judiciary Committee in January. The committee chair that day was John Barker, a Republican from Abilene. And after her testimony, Barker said a few extra words to Meade that he hadn't said to anyone else who testified. To everyone, Barker said, "Thank you." To Meade, he added, "Thank you for your service." Saying those five words to veterans is reflexive to the point of cliché, but Barker sounded genuine. For a moment, a Republican in the Kansas legislature publicly recognized a transgender person for her contributions to society.

Only a couple of us in the audience noticed, but we recognized change occurring when we saw it, no matter how tiny and fleeting the evidence. I emailed Barker to ask him about that moment and never heard back. But Witt later wrote in the *Liberty Press* that Barker told an Equality Kansas representative that Meade's testimony had given him "a lot to think about."[5]

11

On a Wednesday morning in May 2015, Sam Brownback and a phalanx of Kansas politicians headed to Manhattan. Joined by Homeland Security Secretary Jeh Johnson and US Secretary of Agriculture Tom Vilsack, having accessorized their business suits with hard hats, they lined up in a field at the edge of Kansas State University and shoved ceremonial spades into a knee-high pile of fresh black dirt for the groundbreaking of the new National Bio and Agro-Defense Facility.

Celebratory dirt-tossing for the $1.25 billion science lab had been more than a decade coming. In 2004, George W. Bush declared the country's need "to defend the agriculture and food system against terrorist attacks, major disasters, and other emergencies."[1] (The country had been relying on the outdated Plum Island Animal Disease Center near Long Island, New York.) Kansas fought hard to win the contract for the state-of-the-art facilities—though that hadn't stopped all four members of the Kansas House delegation from voting against an appropriations bill containing the lab's final $300 million, citing their opposition to President Obama's immigration policy, just a few weeks before today's groundbreaking.[2] Now the politicians were eager to claim credit for helping to make the lab a reality. "This lab is the realization of all we hope for," said Republican Senator Pat Roberts, adding that it represented not just economic opportunity but "the preservation of our rural way of life."[3]

The politicians were long gone two weeks later, when evidence of another "rural way of life" pulled into the parking lot at the US Department of Agriculture's Center for Grain and Animal Health Research, a low-slung building on busy College Avenue: Stephanie Mott's maroon Hyundai, adorned with rainbow-colored stickers declaring that its driver is "Transgender and Christian."

Since she began to live as her true self in July 2006, Mott has gone to all corners of the state to try to educate Kansans about life for transgender people—driving from her home in Topeka to those Manhattan Human Rights and Services Board forums in 2010, to deliver the same testimony in Salina and Hutchinson in 2011, and giving speeches at pride parades like the one in Wichita, promising LGBT Kansans that things were changing for the better. Today, she was in a drab conference room where the only decorations besides the United States and Kansas flags up front were framed scientific posters explaining the missions of the scientists in these labs, such as, "To solve major endemic, emerging, and exotic arthropod-borne disease problems in U.S. livestock." One of those scientists, Kruger Bryant, had invited her to speak to his colleagues as part of the USDA's diversity efforts, in recognition of June as LGBT pride month.

Mott has perfected an endearing style for this sort of thing. Short and round through the middle, wearing black slacks and a sleeveless floral-print top modestly covered by a black short-sleeved button-down, her gritty voice soft and her eyes sparkling wryly, Mott comes across as a warm prairie grandmother. She thanked the dozen or so government workers who were quietly unwrapping their brown-bag lunches. "It's always an honor to have an opportunity to talk about what it's like to be transgender," she said. "You have permission to ask me anything." It might be rude to ask a transgender person some things, such as whether he or she has had surgery. "You can ask me that," Mott said. "You can ask me about relationships. If I'm not comfortable answering something I'll tell you, but so far that's never happened. There are no inappropriate questions in this space." With the noon hour to fill, Mott gave a more detailed version of the story she frequently reduces to a few minutes for hearings at city halls and rallies on the capitol steps.

Born in Lawrence in 1957 and growing up on an eighty-acre farm along the Wakarusa River, raised by a mother who embodied unconditional love and a stereotypically strict 1960s father, the child then known as Steven knew by the age of six that he was less like his brothers and more like his sisters—watching *The Brady Bunch*, for example, and identifying with Jan instead of Peter. "Not because I looked like Jan, but because she saw the world the same way I did. Any time I was around a group of people I would identify with the women." At first this wasn't troubling because life on the farm felt safe and secure. "I figured Mom and Dad had everything else in line, so everything was going to work out. I thought, 'I'll be able to be a girl sometime and everything's going to be all right.'"

Mott greeted each day with a mental adjustment she describes as "putting on my Steven suit"—going out into the world felt like walking onto a stage and pretending to be a boy. Mott was a teenager in 1976 when Renee Richards was denied entry into the US Open tennis tournament as a woman. "The news of this made it all the way out to the farm where I was growing up," said Mott, who at that point realized an authentic life might be possible—for some people, anyway. "I thought you had to have money, fame, and connections, and as a Kansas farm kid I didn't think it was possible for me."

Mott graduated from Eudora High School and headed to business school at the University of Kansas. College life gave her more freedom, but also made her more aware of how others would react if she revealed her true self. "People I knew, people who loved me and I loved, all thought someone like me was displeasing. So I was dealing with fear and shame."

Her life was traditional in at least one way, a fact she delivered with expert comedic timing: "I'm sure I'm the only nineteen-year-old student who discovered alcohol on a campus." This earned the laugh. Mott thought about suicide but instead, she said, "alcohol may have saved me—although it was killing me at the same time." For the next thirty years, drinking and drugs helped Mott hide from reality. And in an ongoing effort to learn how to be a man, Mott got married twice and had a son. Predictably, the marriages failed, and Mott figured she could never have a relationship because she would always hurt the person she loved.

By 2005 Mott was homeless in Pueblo, Colorado. As she had done before, she called her sisters in Lawrence and asked for money to come back to Kansas and get on her feet. "This time they said no. They knew I had something going on in the gender spectrum but didn't know what it was—they knew someone was stealing their clothes—and they were tired of watching me kill myself with alcohol and didn't want me around their teenage kids."

She ended up at the Topeka Rescue Mission. It sounds sad, Mott said, but this was the best thing to happen to her. "For the first time in my life, I didn't have anything left to lose." If she knew anything at that point, it was that pretending to be a man wasn't working. "I realized that 'if I'm going to be okay, I'm going to have to figure this out, how to live authentically as the woman I've always been.'" Mott uses the phrase "if I'm going to be okay" frequently in her talk, and it is an effective way to connect with her audiences: people might not be able to understand being transgender, but an effort to simply be okay? That quest is universal.

"The rescue mission was probably not the place to start that little journey, but it was a great place for me to be," Mott continued. The facility felt almost like a jail, and Mott was surrounded by potentially dangerous men. So she escaped to the chapel every day. On the third day, someone asked if anyone wanted to accept Jesus as their savior. "I thought, sure, I'll do that. I wanted to do something different because what I'd been doing wasn't working." Mott started going to a tiny Southern Baptist outreach church near the mission where the pastor seemed respectful of everyone. The congregation was only a handful of people, and when they found out she could play the piano, she became the pianist. By then she had gone several months without a drink. Mott moved into a residential drug and alcohol treatment program at Valeo Behavioral Health Care, a nonprofit mental health agency, where she met a counselor with "long braided hair, a careworn face, tired eyes, and a heart [like] gold." The scientists were rapt, as Mott's voice dropped almost to a whisper. "I sat down at the table across from him and he created a space where I could talk about what I needed to talk about without feeling judged. And I'd never had that."

Next came Mott's salvation. She met a woman who invited her to Topeka's Metropolitan Community Church—the gay church. "She said there were transgender people at this church. I said, 'No there's not!'" Mott's repeated internet searches for support groups had come up empty. "I didn't understand why, but now I do. In 2006, all the transgender support groups were clandestine. If people knew where the support group would meet, no transgender person would go because of fear of violence." She took this opportunity to provide some data: "In the United States today, one transgender person is murdered once a month. In 2006, those statistics were even more frightening."

The woman who had invited her to the Metropolitan Community Church took her to a thrift store. "She bought me a dress, and some shoes, and a purse, and just the right pair of earrings. I stuck them behind the seat of my pickup truck because I was living in a men's halfway house—it did not seem like a good idea to get dressed at the halfway house," she said, earning more laughter. On Sunday she drove to the church and spent fifteen minutes arguing with herself: she knew this was right for her; she worried about hurting others; this felt like her only chance. "I went in and got dressed in the basement of the church. Another transgender woman guarded the door because we didn't want a cisgender woman"—Mott had already explained that *cisgender* means having a gender identity that matches one's biological sex, or, not transgender—"walking in and seeing a man in the bathroom. Turns out it wouldn't have mattered because in that church the cisgender women and the trans women mix in the bathroom. Everybody goes in there for the same reason"—Mott waited another comedic beat—"to fix our hair."

Newly dressed, Mott went upstairs where the pastor hugged her and people shook her hand. "I sat in a pew and looked up at the cross and I felt truly myself in the eyes of the Lord for the very first time." When the attendance book came around, Mott signed her name as Stephanie.

I can't tell you what the pastor said because I was being Stephanie in front of God and everybody, and it was so amazing and so beautiful that I don't even know if there was a sermon that day but there was communion. The pastor who served my communion put her hand on my shoulder and said, "God, bless your daughter for the faith she has shown in you." And Stephanie was born. I was forty-seven years old.

It was like walking through a door and "the nightmare was not allowed to follow." The next week, Mott went back to the church. "The pastor did a sermon on Second Corinthians 5:17, which says, 'Therefore if anyone is in Christ, old things are passed away, behold all things are become new.' I thought he was talking about me."

Mott was a little nervous about telling her religious story to a room full of scientists. "My story is a Christian story," she acknowledged.

It's a faith story. I needed a place and it didn't need to be a church—it could have been a school classroom, could have been a conference room in the Agricultural Resource Services section at the USDA. I just needed someplace to be me and not feel judged. I'm not one of those people who believes it matters what you believe. I think it's cool to have conversations with people who don't believe and people who believe differently from me because I learn, I get to be a bigger person.

The point is, Mott said, "when I took off all the facade, pretense, got down to the core of who I am and exposed her to the sunlight, I started growing and being alive and being happy. Amazing things have happened since then."

Not too long after that first day at the church, Mott said she was invited to tell her story at a gay-straight alliance meeting at a high school in Topeka.

There was a seventeen-year-old transgender girl there that day. My presentation was horrible, but she came up to me afterward and said I changed her life. I'm like, okay. I didn't realize at the same time she changed my life. She taught me that everything that I had gone through had prepared me to do something different, which is to come to places like this and share my story. That I'd been empowered to make a difference for people who need somebody to make a difference for them.

Mott ticked off the tangible signs of a successful life: gainful employment as an office assistant, a return to school to earn a bachelor's in social work, a master's degree now nearly complete. Later that summer, she told the group, she would go back to Valeo Behavioral Health Care—where she first talked with that long-haired counselor with the careworn face who didn't judge her—to do her master's in social work internship. The scientists broke into applause. "I've been sober for nine and a half years, done hundreds of presentations like this, started a couple nonprofit organizations," she continued. "I'm part of the world today, which is something I wasn't before."

The discussion that followed was friendly. Mott answered questions about what percentage of the population is transgender: the statistics vary, she said, but it's somewhere between two or three people per thousand. "So in Manhattan, with a population of fifty thousand, you've got between 100 and 150 people in the city." There was a question about the suicide rate. Mott said 41 percent of transgender people will attempt suicide at least once. Someone asked whether she ever sought psychiatric help, and Mott talked about how the American Psychological Association, the American Psychiatric Association, and the American Medical Association agree that being transgender is not a mental disorder. When the hour was over and the workers needed to get back to their labs, a few of them came up to Mott and thanked her.

Lingering at the edges of the group, waiting until everyone said their goodbyes, was a man who looked to be in his mid-forties, muscular, with a military crew cut and an aggressive stance. He had been sitting in the back of the room and walked out before the end of Mott's talk. Having returned, he looked as if he might be hostile—but it turned out he was just eager. The man told Mott that he had a gay son and that he and his wife were being supportive. He, too, thanked her for coming.

Mott had not looked afraid of this man, even before she heard his story. Maybe it was because she knows she walks with God. Maybe it was because she knows her Buddha-like, grandmotherly presence defuses hostilities. Most likely it was because of her experience on what she now refers to as the Transgender Tour of Kansas.

When the long Fourth of July weekend arrived in 2011, Mott had been living authentically—and publicly—with the zeal of the born again. In 2008, she had started writing a column for the Liberty Press called "Trans-Formative." Every couple of weeks, Mott would get a phone call or an email from someone who was trans and looking for information or support—folks who had never spoken to another trans person. Her rising public profile made her think she could do more. The next year, Mott read a newspaper article about Tom Witt testifying in a state senate committee. During the hearing, Dennis Pyle, a Republican state senator from Hiawatha, a town of three thousand people near the Nebraska line, asked whether the statewide nondiscrimination ordinance would "protect bestiality."[4] Disgusted, Mott decided she wanted to be able to testify at the legislature. Later that year she got her first taste of public speaking when the Lawrence Human Relations Commission held hearings about adding gender identity to the city's nondiscrimination ordinance. Mott testified, but commissioners told her they couldn't give much weight to her comments because she didn't live in Lawrence.

"I thought, 'that's horrible,'" Mott said.[5] She liked public speaking. She knew her story was compelling, and if she wanted to keep telling it for all different audiences and occasions, she would need credentials. So she started a nonprofit called the Kansas Statewide Transgender Education Project. As president and executive director of KSTEP, Mott reasoned, she would have standing to testify anywhere gender identity was the subject. Now, every time she accepted an invitation to talk to a college class or visit a church group or sit on a panel at a conference or attend an organizing meeting, she was officially representing KSTEP. Mott would rack up hundreds of these talks, while going back to school to earn her advanced degrees in social work.

Witt, meanwhile, had been reading Mott's columns in the Liberty Press and invited her to a statewide Equality Kansas meeting. Watching him in action, she could see that Witt could help her understand politics and strategy. "He's perfectly constructed for what he does. You have to be able to be very willful, you have to be very sure of yourself, have that ability to speak powerfully," she said. "You've also got to be brilliant, and Tom is brilliant. You have to be smart enough to understand when to fling bags of poop—that's Tom's term—and when not to. And understand how one thing affects another, and how everything is interconnected. I was in awe."

The next time Equality Kansas held elections for statewide officers, Mott put in for vice chair. Not that it required much campaigning. "There wasn't really anybody standing for it. I said, 'Well, I'll do that.'" That was commitment enough, so Mott still can't entirely explain why she did what she did next. But when that Fourth of July weekend rolled around in 2011, what seemed like a good idea was driving 1,600 miles to thirty cities and stopping to talk to random people about being transgender.

In retrospect, she said, "I wanted a better understanding of how the average person in Kansas might feel as opposed to what I was hearing from conservative pastors and government officials." She also needed to draw attention to the fledgling KSTEP and figured she could generate media coverage. "Part of this was about me making a name for myself," she admitted. If headlines along the way educated the public or conveyed a bit of comfort to some isolated trans person, even better. Mott started sending out press releases, and it worked. The *Topeka Capital-Journal* reported on the tour,[6] and Mott was hearing from trans people and their families before she even left town.

On Friday morning, July 1, with a longtime male friend named Chris riding shotgun, Mott drove an hour west to Manhattan. It had been just two months since the newly elected city commission repealed the nondiscrimination ordinance before it could go into effect. Given all the trips she had made there over the previous year, Manhattan felt like a second home to Mott—the perfect place to kick off her tour. A dozen of her supporters, still stinging from the defeat, held a sendoff breakfast at the Bluestem Bistro in Aggieville, and the *Manhattan Mercury* and the local ABC affiliate both did stories. Mott delivered her TV sound bite with that grandmotherly smile: "There's nothing about who I am that has anything to do with whether or not I can do a good job, or whether I'll be a good tenant, or whether I'll come into a place and be an appropriate customer."[7]

Mott had mapped out the route with stops in towns where she had heard from somebody who was transgender and felt alone. Rather than setting up meetings with those people, though, her plan was to pull into a gas station or a Walmart or some other easily accessible public place and approach strangers in parking lots. While Chris stayed unobtrusively vigilant in the car or hung around nearby as a silent, almost ghostly presence, Mott would identify herself as a writer traveling across Kansas and ask her interviewees whether they knew the word *transgender* and what it meant, and what they thought about people who are transgender. Depending on how that icebreaker went, she would ask if they knew anyone who was transgender. If they said they didn't, she would tell them that actually, they did: they had just met her. Her goal was simply to let average Kansans see someone who was transgender, and let transgender people read something about her in the newspaper.

From the breakfast rally in Manhattan, Mott and Chris headed twenty miles west on I-70 to Junction City, the military town of twenty-three thousand people near Fort Riley. Just off the interstate, they pulled into the parking lot at Stacy's Restaurant, a classic diner that boasts of its clientele: "From military personnel, farmers, construction workers, and business men; you'll see them all at Stacy's."[8] Mott approached a man who said he didn't know anyone who was transgender. But after she told him she was, he changed his story and started telling her about a trans friend he had who was having a hard time. She gave him information about KSTEP and got back on the road.

By midmorning they were in Salina, where Mott had booked a room at the public library. Four people showed up, along with a reporter from the Salina Journal, whose coverage of Mott's presentation included a quote from eighty-seven-year-old Marge Streckfus: "We need conversations—it's good she's willing to do this." Streckfus added, "There's nothing like meeting someone face to face. I wanted to learn, pure and simple."[9]

After leaving Salina, Mott turned onto Route 81 and drove an hour north to Concordia (population 5,200), arriving just in time for lunch at Kristy's Family Restaurant, a storefront in a cowboy-era building downtown. Then they continued twenty miles farther north to the Casey's General Store in Belleville (population 2,000), then thirty miles west, skimming the Kansas-Nebraska line on two-lane Highway 36 to the Buffalo Roam Steakhouse in Mankato (population 900) and another thirty miles to Duffy's Steakhouse in Smith Center (population 1,600). Late in the afternoon they turned south on 281 toward Russell—home of Bob Dole and Bruce Ney—and Meridy's Restaurant & Lounge, another highway shack, extra-noticeable thanks to its name carved into a van-sized slab of Flint Hills limestone in the parking lot. Soon they were back on I-70, driving half an hour to Mr. Goodcents in Hays.

Throughout the day, some people had given her polite enough brush-offs, saying they didn't have time to talk; one woman said the question was "too personal" and one man told her, "You don't want to know what I think about that." But most of the conversations went better than anyone might have predicted—at least anyone not buoyed by Mott's faith in God and God's creation. Maybe the question was such a surprise that it proved disarming. "People in places like Coffeyville, Kansas, don't expect you to walk up to them and start talking about transgender," she would write later. "Almost every time, you could see them mentally processing the question, accessing a place that perhaps had never been touched. Speaking feelings, rather than thoughts."[10]

People generally had one of two responses when she asked what they knew about transgender. One was to say something like: "That's like gay, right?" This reaffirmed the need for education. The other response was some variation of, "To each their own." Mott started to believe that the politicians of Kansas weren't really representing the more open-minded people of their state.

The next morning, Mott and Chris headed thirty miles west on I-70 to WaKeeney, where it had been six years since Sandra Stenzel lost her job. (Oblivious during the marriage-amendment days of 2004–2005, Mott had never heard of Stenzel.) They stopped at the WaKeeney IGA, then drove fifty miles farther west on I-70. Mott had intended to stop at another Casey's in Oakley (population 2,000), but instead drove on twenty minutes to Colby (population 5,400), where she had booked another library event and the Colby Free Press had run a story. Dominating the front page that day was a black-and-white photo of a combine, its front blades churning up field dust under the headline "Wheat Harvest Underway." Just below the fold was a story about Mott, headlined "Awareness Tour Comes to Colby." It quoted Mott's estimate of as many as five thousand trans people living in Kansas. She said she hoped people in Colby would come out to meet her. "There is so much misinformation about transgenderism. We are pretty much like everybody else," Mott said.[11] Four women took her up on the invitation, going to the library at ten in the morning.

After that it was a long hundred-mile stretch through Anne Mitchell's old territory. They drove south on Highway 83 to Garden City, then fifty miles along Highway 50 to Dodge City, fifty miles to Greensburg, and then seventy miles east to Pratt, stopping at more kitschy-postcard-worthy restaurants before the day's eighty-mile final stretch to Wichita.

"Today's journey was mostly positive," she wrote on Facebook. "The negatives have not been rude or threatening. I did choose to skip the Oakley stop because I was not comfortable with what I perceived as a potentially unsafe situation. I have to respect my instincts."[12] At the Casey's in Oakley, they'd come upon six hypermasculine guys and Mott decided not to stick around. But she kept thinking about the nonencounter. "I couldn't help remembering my visit to a church a few years back," she would write in a later newspaper column.

> I had been living as Stephanie for over a year. I was so moved by the music that I sang out loud, in my slightly-lower-than-tenor singing voice. The moms in nearby pews pulled their children in tight to them, and slid just a little bit further away from me. There is a part of me that will forever wonder if one of those big, burly guys might have known someone who was transgender. There is a part of me that understands the necessity of taking precautions, as a transgender person in Kansas. And there is a part of me that knows that one day, moms won't be afraid of me, and I won't be afraid of letting a group of big, burly men know who I am. That day is not yet come.[13]

Mott greeted the next morning excited about the itinerary: "First stop—Daylight Donuts in Yates Center. Yummy!"[14] The day was good before they even set out: "The nice woman at the Econolodge in Wichita this morning read one of my articles from *Liberty Press*. She said, 'I never met a transvestite before.' ☺ Then she said, 'People should be happy.'"[15]

Yates Center (population 1,300) was ninety miles east—and disappointing, but only at first: "Daylight Donuts was closed in Yates Center, but Casey's saved the day. Met a lady there from Missouri who has a transgender friend who is having kind of a hard time. Gave her my card. God is AWESOME!!!!"[16] Out of Yates Center they drove fifty miles south on Highway 75 to Independence (population 9,200), near the childhood home of Laura Ingalls Wilder. Twenty miles farther south, at the Oklahoma line, they stopped in Coffeyville (population 10,000), where Mott posted

Stephanie Mott, at Tropical Sno in Coffeyville, Kansas, in a photo posted to her Facebook page during her Transgender Tour of Kansas over the weekend of July 4, 2011. Credit: Photo courtesy of Stephanie Mott

a picture of herself at an ice cream stand, its bricks painted in rainbow-colored stripes advertising hundreds of flavors of Hawaiian shaved ice. Since hitting Colby in northwest Kansas the day before, they had essentially made a diagonal line back across the state, and now they began moving north along its eastern edge, making a forty-mile zigzag up and east to Parsons (population 10,000), with Mott's Facebook travelogue beginning to sound more like a Yelp guide to Kansas mom-and-pops. Her status update: "[Stephanie Mott] is at Pizzo's Corner Restaurant in Parsons. Meatball sandwich coming up!"[17]

Fortified, they drove thirty-five miles nearly due east to Pittsburg (population 20,000), where a woman named Kim in the Walmart parking lot told her, "People need to be who they are." [18] After another thirty miles straight north to Fort Scott (population 8,000), notable in American history as the hometown of Gordon Parks, Mott proclaimed it an "awesome day." Three times, she wrote, "the journey has crossed the path of the friend of a transgender person. Three times, I have given out my card and asked the friend to share with their friend. OMG. Literally."[19]

Mott began the Fourth of July with strong feelings. "Today is Independence Day," she posted, "but my people are not free. We are not free to marry. We are not free to love who we love. We are not free to serve our country. I love my country. I support our freedom fighters." But Mott was also thinking about Africa, where anti-LGBT rhetoric exported by evangelical ministers from the US appeared to be fueling government-condoned violence. "If we are going to fight for freedom," she wrote, "then let's go put an end to the genocide in Uganda."[20]

Before Uganda, though, there was Emporia, the college town of twenty-five thousand people at the eastern edge of the Flint Hills and home of the original "What's the Matter with Kansas?" writer William Allen White. Mott stopped at a fireworks stand, where the woman didn't know what transgender was. "After I explained it she said, 'I've never been in a situation where I would have a feeling about this, but, I wouldn't have anything against them.'"[21] Fair enough. Mott and Chris headed fifty miles northeast, to the Old 56 Family Restaurant in Ottawa (population 12,000), then another thirty miles to the sprawling Kansas City suburbs of Olathe (131,000) and Overland Park (181,000). "Man and wife in Olathe: Woman: You mean like Chaz Bono? Me: Yes. Woman: I think he's awesome. Man: You mean she."[22]

They turned westerly and drove twenty miles up the freeway, past strip malls and beige subdivisions to Bonner Springs (population 7,400), where, once again, the quest for food led to a profound moment. "The woman in Bonner Springs who took my ticket at the Waffle House, is the ex-wife of, and co-parent with, a transwoman. I am in tears at the power of God."[23] They went on twenty miles to Lawrence, then an hour north to Valley Falls (population 1,100) before one last restaurant check-in: "1608.3 miles later, I am sitting at Denny's on Wanamaker in Topeka."[24] After a night's sleep, Mott wrote to her followers: "It will be months before I can truly begin to understand the happenings of the last four days. I can say that there will be a Trans-Tour Two."[25] Mott had made it home not just physically unharmed but spiritually nourished, as if she had walked across the state on water.

Given her estimate of a possible five thousand trans people in Kansas, it wasn't surprising that on her tour, Mott met people who knew, or were related to, trans people. In any case, there were enough for Mott to convene a TransKansas Conference in Lawrence in fall 2013. Over two days at Bert Nash Community Health Center, trans people, allies, healthcare professionals (who got continuing education credit), and students heard presentations from other trans people, parents of trans people, pastors, counselors, and the owner of an electrolysis clinic. Sandra Meade spoke, as did Tom Witt, the attorney David Brown, and Brandon Haddock from the Kansas State University LGBT Resource Center. At lunch, they socialized and checked out tables stacked with information about supportive organizations around the state. Keynoting the event was Fred Phelps's son Nate, who had left the Westboro compound at midnight on his eighteenth birthday and had been an advocate for LGBT equality ever since. Mott counted a hundred people throughout the weekend, which was so successful that the TransKansas Conference would become an annual event, each year in a different city so more Kansans could attend: 2014 would be in Wichita, 2015 in Manhattan, 2016 in Topeka. These meetings were strictly educational and not especially political (apart from Witt's legislative updates), but would have ripple effects throughout the state.

Among the attendees was a trans woman from Wichita named Elle Boatman, whose entry into activism had been her website *The Face of Trans*, where she posted a series of high-quality portraits of trans people with a few words about themselves. Hers was the first: "I love supporting our local shops, taking walks through College Hill, and cheering on my Wichita State Shockers," it read. "I am a transgender woman. I am Wichita."[26] Eventually there would be twenty-nine of these images, with trans men and women and their allies from all of the state's major cities.

Boatman, along with her future partner Brenda Way, would go on to organize the Wichita Transgender Community Network, or WitCon, which they envisioned as a place where trans people in the state's biggest city could find friends and support. Boatman and Way had a lot in common: difficult childhoods; attempts to man up via military service (Boatman in the air force, Way in the army); unhappy marriages; repeated suicide attempts. They wanted to make the journey less difficult for other trans people.

Starting WitCon earned them a story in the *Wichita Eagle* on July 4, 2015. Under the headline "Wichita's Transgender Community Strives to

Become More Visible" was a color photo of Boatman, in a short black-and-white-flower-printed spaghetti-strap summer dress, and Way, wearing a psychedelic-colored tank top, both women's tattoos complementing the patterns of their outfits, and both smiling.[27] Reporter Denise Neil began by revisiting Caitlyn Jenner's April interview with Diane Sawyer and subsequent *Vanity Fair* cover. "I think trans celebrities definitely have their place in the moment and in society," Boatman told Neil. "But I'm not a trans celebrity, and so my place is to raise the awareness and visibility of more everyday, typical trans people who don't have the resources and the support that often comes with high-profile transitions. Because that's where things need to change."

Neil contrasted Jenner's professionally styled and art-directed media rollout with an anecdote about Way's recent experience at a Wichita grocery store, where she had needed to use the ladies' room. Way was less than a year into her transition and had been thrown out of her house by her then-wife and fired from her job as a dishwasher. In the grocery store bathroom, a woman told her she was in the wrong one and ordered her to get out. Way had taken care of business and was leaving anyway; a few minutes later in the coffee aisle, though, was the woman with a security guard, saying, "That's him! That's him! That's the man who was in the women's restroom!"

Neil's article was long and deep, introducing several trans people to tens of thousands of Wichitans who would never have known there were any outside of Hollywood. Describing a WitCon meeting, Neil wrote: "Katie said she had recently transitioned and didn't know any other trans people in town. Karen had been going to support groups for years and had high hopes for this one. Thomas was one week on hormone replacement therapy. Finn said he'd heard about the group and wanted to see what it was all about."

"The fact that the article made the front page was crazy," Boatman told me.[28] Two years after the story ran, WitCon's support group attendance had settled in at about fifteen to twenty people, down from a high of as many as forty when the organization started. "We have our regulars, and some people who come a few times and you never see them again," Boatman said. She reported no negative consequences as a result of the article;

instead, the visibility boost helped WitCon make connections with other activist groups. "It's been really cool to see where we have gotten our support," she said. "It's not all been within the LGBT community. The intention from the beginning was to make the trans community in Wichita more visible and make the trans community really part of the greater Wichita community, and I think we're starting to kind of see that."

Another of Neil's interviewees, Grayson Barnes, was a humanities and art appreciation teacher who reported having no major problems when he transitioned at Butler Community College in El Dorado, an oil refinery town of thirteen thousand people thirty miles northeast of Wichita. Barnes announced his transition at a college all-staff meeting where everyone had nametags. He picked up the one for "Helen" Barnes, crossed out the name, and wrote Grayson—taking Gray, the middle name of his father, and adding "son" (Barnes had cleared the idea with his father, who said it was an honor). "I marched up to the vice president of academics before that meeting ended," Barnes told me, "and said, 'I'm trans, I want to be Grayson, I want a new sign [for my office door] and new business cards.' She said, 'Okay.'"[29]

Three years into his transition, Barnes didn't think he looked masculine enough for his students to immediately know how to address him, so he started classes with a preamble: "'When you signed up, you signed up with Helen Barnes. I want to let you know that I'm not an extremely masculine woman, I'm a trans man, so I would prefer you use masculine pronouns. If you have any problems with that, there's always "professor."' I haven't had a lot of them challenge me." Some students have asked him questions—not in class, but in private. Barnes said there are six or seven trans students on a campus of nine thousand.

On another campus halfway across the state, another trans man had also made an impression—on a billboard, in Manhattan, a full year before Jenner spent a month on the cover of Vanity Fair. "I am an art student at Kansas State University and an avid tattoo designer. I am an older brother, a best friend, and a full-on nerd. I am a transgender man. I am Manhattan," said the text accompanying a photo of Adam O'Brien, an adorably handsome young guy with messy dark hair, sky-blue eyes, and deep dimples framing a smile that does his dentist proud. O'Brien had posed for

Adam O'Brien, on a billboard above Manhattan in April 2014. Credit: Photo courtesy of the Flint Hills Human Rights Project

a picture in Boatman's *The Face of Trans* photo booth at Mott's first Trans-Kansas conference in Lawrence. A few months later, Boatman called. She had been talking with the Flint Hills Human Rights Project, now chaired by a Kansas State University biology professor named Michael Herman, and the group had the resources to put one of the images on a billboard for a month. Would O'Brien be willing? "I was like, 'Um, well, that would be good,'" remembered O'Brien, who was finishing his senior year as a fine arts major at the time. "I'm always happy to educate people."[30]

The Flint Hills Human Rights Project unveiled the image during a small gala at an Aggieville art gallery. That was when reality set in, O'Brien said. "My face is going to be on a billboard forty feet long, right by the highway. I'll be outing myself to my entire city." That night, people kept telling him how brave he was. Nerve-racked, O'Brien shook off the feeling and focused on school—it was the last few weeks of his final semester, and he had "projects out the wazoo." But he couldn't avoid the inevitable for long. He was sitting in class when a friend texted: *I just saw your billboard.* It was on Highway 177, just across the Kansas River east of downtown.

O'Brien had been in Manhattan for four years. He had grown up in Lawrence with parents who understood and supported him, so the University of Kansas might have seemed a natural choice for college. But like many others, O'Brien wanted to go to college somewhere other than his hometown. K-State was in-state and affordable, and it had resources for LGBT people, which was important because he knew he would begin his transition at college.

O'Brien lived in a women's scholarship house for freshman year and joined the queer student organizations. It was about five years after Alley Stoughton had pioneered trans faculty life at K-State; now O'Brien was doing the same for students. "I think I was one of the first, certainly one of the few, trans people who participated heavily within the LGBT and Allies student organization," he said. That involved educating the Ls, Gs and Bs. "In a way I almost became the token trans member, and a lot of the people within that circle couldn't see the me beyond that. I encountered some unfortunate transphobia from within—that's a common problem, transphobia within queer circles—but I'm pretty sure that was nipped in the bud by everybody else."

For his sophomore year, he moved to the women's floor of a dorm. "I let my RA know that I did not identify as female," O'Brien said, explaining that while he had started to transition socially, he had not legally changed his sex, so it would have been difficult to live on the men's floor. The RA was unfazed by the information, and O'Brien soon began his medical transition. He didn't really know most of the women on the floor, he said, so, "I don't think many noticed that one of them was slowly turning into a dude." There, in real life, contrary to the Alliance Defending Freedom rhetoric, was the not-shocking truth: no problems in the bathrooms. O'Brien moved into an apartment for his junior and senior years. When the billboard went up, he expected the worst. Bracing for whatever might happen, he went to his shift in the kitchen at Applebee's, where he wasn't out to his coworkers. Nobody said anything. Nothing bad happened.

"We understand many of you may have questions," wrote Herman, the Flint Hills Human Rights Project chair, in a *Manhattan Mercury* op-ed on April 1, 2014.[31] Herman introduced Manhattanites to O'Brien, explained the point of the billboard, and invited the public to upcoming events. O'Brien and Boatman, along with the director of K-State's counseling services office and a local physician who worked with trans people, spoke on a panel later that month. "It was really interesting," said O'Brien, who, in retrospect, guessed that the billboard was "one of those things that brought awareness about something people don't typically think about and made them go 'Huh, interesting,' and keep on driving, but they weren't so offended by its presence that they would lash out."

O'Brien had done something profound in Kansas, but after graduation he was ready to get out of Manhattan. He moved to Minneapolis, where he had friends, and went to work as a baker for a small organic restaurant chain. In his early twenties, his existential questions would be post-transition, such as whether to tell people he was trans or whether to live in stealth. "That's a big question for trans men in particular," he noted, "since it's easier for us to appear to be cisgender. 'Passing' has negative connotations, but it's a good describer for what it feels like to have society see you, yourself, like how you're supposed to be." He will never forget that he is trans, but it's just one piece of his identity, another part of which is Kansan. "Minnesota really isn't that different, but it's different enough," he said. What he misses most, O'Brien said, is the landscape.

That's a feeling Stephanie Mott understands. In the summer of 2015, Mott set out on her promised second transgender tour. While Jenner was securing the surreal world of television, Mott was plowing much more difficult terrain: churches in the Bible Belt. She called this expedition the Transgender Faith Tour. It might have been stopping at friendly, liberal, mostly Unitarian Universalist churches, but they were in places like Tulsa; Little Rock; Columbus, Ohio; and Springfield, Missouri.

And her home state. On July 12, Mott visited the adult Sunday school class at Peace United Church of Christ in the tiny Flint Hills town of Alma, about thirty miles south of Manhattan. She had been there before, she wrote on Facebook. "Must have been in the early 1980s, when my brother Dan was the pastor there. Dan and I both struggled with alcohol and demons unknown to ourselves and each other. He lost his battle, indirectly related to alcohol in 2000, and never got to meet his sister Stephanie."[32] Twenty years earlier, Mott wrote, Dan had some work to do at the church and she had tagged along and played the piano while she waited for him. Now she anticipated an emotional return. "I believe that Dan will be in attendance that day, in whatever way that might be possible. I believe that he will be very proud of his sister Stephanie."

Mott said the response from the fifteen or sixteen people who showed up for Sunday school that day was entirely positive, and some of them remembered Dan. "One talked with me about how he had been there for her and her family at a time when they were losing a family member, how much that meant to her," Mott said. "I walked out of that place knowing his love for me was enhanced by my authenticity."

If Mott is effortlessly certain about the feelings of those now living in the great beyond, there are things about this world she still can't get her head around. "When I first started doing this, I would speak to a college class and nobody in the class would know anyone who was transgender," she said. "Today, a third or a half of the class knows somebody. It's amazing to me that it's changed that much in that amount of time." It's not that there are more transgender people in the world now. It's that they are more free. After all, as Mott points out, given the vast diversity of Creation, with so many beautiful variations in all living organisms, it makes no logical sense that humans would have only two narrowly defined genders.

Another thing always amazes Mott, something she feels after her travels around the state. She might have grown up on a farm outside Lawrence, but it was Topeka where she found salvation. She lives in a small house across the street from the old Monroe Elementary School, where she used to vote. In 2008, it was where she first voted as Stephanie. "I hadn't legally changed my name yet, but I was presenting as Stephanie. The lady handing out ballots was like, 'How can you be Steven?' I explained that I was transgender. She got a confused look on her face, but this other lady where you pick up your ballot was just smiling. I had to publicly explain what transgender was." Then, in the home of *Brown v. Board of Education*, she voted for the man who would become the first black president. These days, the rest of the world might know the capital city of Kansas as the home of the Westboro Baptist Church and a scary legislature, but that's not all it is. Heading back into Topeka on evenings after trips west, as her Hyundai tops the hill just outside of town on Interstate 70, Mott always catches her breath at the sight of the city's lights. "Wow," she thinks. "This is my home."

Kevin Stilley pointed his 1973 Buick Century north out of Manhattan. A hot breeze blew through the open windows of the car-club-contending, caramel-colored beauty he calls Butterscotch as its eight powerful cylinders hauled us past the chain motels and their nearby chain restaurants, past the 1960s-era Vista Drive-In burger joint, past the new churches and the housing developments and the self-storage units and the bait-and-tackle shops, out into the emerald pastures and farm fields lining Highway 24.

Stilley is one of the many people I came to know over three years of research for this book. I met him at the Flint Hills Pride campout in June 2015 at Milford County Reservoir, outside Junction City. Its Facebook flier had promised a "laid-back" event with a potluck, a biscuits-and-gravy breakfast, games, karaoke, and a drag show, but the weekend was a lot more laid-back than perhaps Stilley had planned, because not many people showed up. Besides Stilley, there were Darci Pottroff and Joleen Spain, the couple who had gotten married outside the Riley County Courthouse the previous November. They had parked their enormous travel trailer in the clearing and barbecued an industrial barrel of brisket for a small handful of folks. But there was no karaoke, no drag show.

So I sat in a lawn chair and listened to their stories. Stilley was a gracious campout host. I could tell he was one of those guys who had spent decades working to make things happen but letting others enjoy the attention. Not that he hadn't had his time in the spotlight. Tall and lean, his gray hair cut tight with a stylish tuft up front, he had a pocketful of one-liners and he punctuated each one with laughter as sturdy as winter wheat. He had been a stripper in his twenties and, after having his mustache shaved for an AIDS fundraiser years ago, he had allowed himself to be dressed in drag, which had given rise to the character Allie Monet (a play on *alimony*), who, through no particular character development effort on Stilley's part, reminded audiences of Carol Burnett.

The Flint Hills Pride campout had been going on for a decade, but after that weekend organizers voted to disband the event. It was bittersweet, Stilley said.[1] He was proud of what they had accomplished, but he knew the run was over. I had seen Stilley a couple of times on visits back to Manhattan, and I knew there was one more reporting trip I wanted to make, which was why I was now riding shotgun in Butterscotch.

It was Memorial Day weekend 2016, and Stilley was reminiscing at my request. On the way to our destination, he slowed down and pulled over on the shoulder to point out an old white frame house at the end of what used to be a lane, now overgrown with tangles of locust, elm, mulberry, hackberry, walnut, and Osage orange trees. It's where he lived until he started school. "There was no indoor plumbing," he said. "We had a path instead of a bath." There was also no furnace, so they heated it with wood. The rent was $20 a month for his twenty-one-year-old father, whom Stilley described as "a bit of a goof-off" with young twins to raise. Despite the lack of amenities, Stilley said, "we were very, very happy."

Stilley's happy childhood continued even after his father drowned at Geary County State Lake some years later. His mother was strong and independent, and all four of his grandparents were nearby. Stilley and his maternal grandfather grew especially close the summer he was thirteen, when he moved out to their farm to help with the chores. His grandfather was the father Stilley didn't have, and Stilley, whose mother was an only child, was the son his grandfather never had.

Stilley knew that he liked boys by the time he was in junior high, though he "didn't know what the hell that was." Others appeared to know sooner: Stilley's third-grade teacher had told his mother she thought Kevin was gay because he didn't like to play sports. His mother didn't tell him about that little parent-teacher conference until years later, but Stilley always knew his mom would be cool. He had seen her watching Anita Bryant on the TV news, and still remembered her response: "I don't know why that bitch can't just leave people alone."

Stilley fell in love for the first time when he was twenty-two, in 1980, with a man he had met through the personals in a gay magazine he bought every month at a chain bookstore in the mall. When it was time to tell his mother he planned to move to Kansas City to live with this man, he spent a weekend trying to get up the nerve. On Sunday night she put an end to his stalling. "She says, 'Kevin, there's something bothering you. I wish you'd tell me what it is.' I said, 'Well, I really need to come clean about something and I haven't quite figured out how to bring it up.' She says, 'What, that you have a boyfriend?'"

The man broke his heart badly. Over the next year, construction jobs sent Stilley all over the Midwest, then he went to work for a friend who was opening a mobile home dealership. Stilley saved his money and made plans to move. His options were Dallas and Denver—he had friends in both cities—and he decided on Colorado. The day after Christmas in 1982, he headed west on Interstate 70. It was snowing, with a wind chill below zero. "I got to Salina and thought, 'Denver will be there in the spring.' I hung a left."

He arrived in Dallas in the early days of AIDS. "We all assumed we had it," Stilley said. "Let's face it: we weren't monks." He started helping out with fundraisers and volunteering at a hospice house. "This is how ignorant society was: they wouldn't deliver mail," he said. "I could see them not picking up mail because, my god, it could be tainted—but they wouldn't even deliver mail. We had to have a post office box."

Every week he went to a funeral. "A lot of them were for people I didn't even know. So many of these boys, their families and their friends had abandoned them. I just got to a point where if it was an AIDS death and I knew it, I went. It was one tiny little thing I could do. I went to a few funerals where there were maybe six people."

Stilley got sick in the summer of 1985. "I went to the ER with horrible cramps, which they diagnosed as a kidney infection. And informed me I had pneumonia." He had been having trouble breathing, he said, "but I smoked like a chimney, I worked long hours, I partied long hours. The fact that I was run-down came as no surprise." Though he hadn't been tested, the hospital workers immediately treated him as an AIDS patient.

"I laid in a hall on a gurney for twenty-two hours while they supposedly were trying to find a room. I told myself, 'My god, they've decided I have AIDS and they're just going to let me lie here and die.'" Someone finally started wheeling him somewhere. "They were concerned about TB because my lungs were in such horrible shape, so they put me in isolation. Everybody had to be gloved and gowned and masked to come see me. After I finally got in the room and got in bed and everybody got gone, I rolled over and bawled for about thirty minutes. And then I kind of shook myself out, said, 'You're bigger than this, get over it.' I've never looked back."

He had had good Kansas role models for that sort of attitude. His dad's father had survived a horrific accident while working for the USDA in the 1950s, when his crew was filling a grain bin and the auger was caught in overhead electric wires. "I don't know how many thousands of volts were shot through him," Stilley said. "The only thing that saved his life was, he fell off the bin and when he hit the ground his heart started again." He spent eighteen months in the hospital enduring countless skin grafts; his left ear was burned off so he had no sense of balance; and one leg, pinned from hip to ankle, never bent. "Eight years after that his only son, my father, drowned. Three years after that his only daughter, my aunt Carol, was killed in a car accident," Stilley said. "But you never saw Grandpa unhappy. He accepted the hand that life had dealt him and he played it out as best he could." Having done the same, Stilley had been living with HIV for more than thirty years. "I figure I was put on Earth to accomplish a certain number of things," he said, "and I'm so far behind I'll never die."

He came back to Manhattan in the late eighties. Hs grandfather was ill and he knew his mother and grandmother would need help. Stilley kept quiet about his HIV status for a decade, but eventually he joined the board of the regional AIDS project. When the Ecumenical Campus Ministry at Kansas State University hung a dozen panels of the AIDS quilt in 2001, Stilley gave a speech and the *Mercury* interviewed him. Then his case manager at the Riley County Health Department asked him to go with her to speak at a high school. Then Allie Monet arrived on the scene for those drag fundraisers, and the Flint Hills Pride campouts needed organizing. In 2006, when the Flint Hills Human Rights Project made its first push for a nondiscrimination ordinance, Stilley was in the audience at the meeting when Cora Holt, whom he had known his whole life, made the speech that got her fired from Manhattan Christian College. "I totally admire Cora's courage," he said. "I mean, I always knew she was a gutsy broad, but for her to do that at that time in that climate, it was absolutely huge."

Stilley had a similar moment when, several years later, the Flint Hills Human Rights Project convinced the city to declare an AIDS awareness week. "They asked me to speak at the proclamation. I announced to the city commission, the local TV channel, and the whole wide world that I was HIV-positive." Stilley had been telling his story for years, but only on invited occasions. "I would never deny it, but I didn't always throw it out in your face. I did that night." By then, the city's mayor was John Matta, one of the commissioners who had been elected in the spring of 2011 to repeal the nondiscrimination ordinance before it had a chance to take effect. "I gotta give it to Mayor Matta. He shook my hand afterwards and didn't immediately look for the hand sanitizer." Other people thanked him for speaking. "One had worked with my dad's mother—she was a nurse at Saint Mary's Hospital. She asked, 'Do you happen to be Agnes's grandson?' I said yes, and she said, 'I was pretty sure you had to be, the way you care about public health.'"

Stilley made plenty of trips back to city hall in 2015 and 2016. That was because the LGBT citizens of Manhattan and their allies did something beautifully masochistic: they went back to the commission to fight for another nondiscrimination ordinance. Once again, new commissioners had been elected, and this time the members of the Flint Hills Human Rights Project knew that at least three out of the five commissioners would vote in their favor.

"We immediately began to push for it," said the organization's current chair, Katie Jordan, a graduate student working on wheat genetics in the plant pathology department at Kansas State University.[2] Besides having allies on the commission again, they had built a stronger foundation several years earlier, quietly and without controversy convincing the Manhattan-Ogden School District, which was working on its antibullying rules, to add sexual orientation and gender identity to its nondiscrimination protections. "That was huge, because we were able to keep referring to that," Jordan said. "Now all the major employers here have those protections—K-State, the school district, Fort Riley."

Also not lost on anyone was the fact that Roeland Park had passed its ordinance. If tiny Roeland Park, about an eighth the size of Manhattan, with no Big 12 university, could pass such an ordinance, why couldn't Manhattan? (In other words, Sandra Meade's strategy of getting a victory in Roeland Park so it might inspire other cities appeared to have worked.) Then came *Obergefell*, and after another long meeting, commissioners made it illegal to discriminate based on sexual orientation in the city's hiring policy—which only made sense, if some gay city employees were now legally married. But that wasn't the same as a citywide ordinance.

LGBT Manhattanites started showing up for every commission meeting. Even when there was nothing LGBT-related on the agenda, they stood up and spoke during the time allotted for public comments. And in December, nine pastors sent a letter supporting the cause. It wasn't nearly as many as the twenty-seven pastors who sent a letter opposing the "bathroom bill" five years earlier, and three of the pastors were from First United Methodist Church and two were from the Manhattan Mennonite Church, so they were only really representing six congregations. But still, they were clergy.

Meanwhile, the ministers from last time were conspicuously absent. "We had no opposition from them," Stilley said of Awaken Manhattan. "At one commission meeting when the ordinance was on the agenda a lot of them were there and they did speak out against it, but they weren't organized. And for every one of them, there were six on our side."

In July, the ordinance passed. Unanimously. Even Wynn Butler, one of the commissioners elected to repeal the 2011 ordinance, voted for it this time. (Butler said he approved of this version because it had a different enforcement process and significantly lower penalties for offenders.[3]) As of November 2016, Manhattan would join Roeland Park and Lawrence in protecting lesbian, gay, bisexual, and trans people from discrimination.

Stilley said Manhattan—and Kansas—is more progressive and accepting than people give it credit for. But he had also been around long enough to see how much the world has changed. "It's just a totally different environment than it was ten years ago," he said. "Young people are so much more open about it, so it's getting harder and harder and harder for hatemongers to say they don't know anyone who's LGBT—and it may well be someone they love."

Stilley didn't say this, but it is people like him, and all the people I met while reporting in Kansas, who created that safer world for young LGBT people. The task of securing that safer world, let alone expanding it, will remain daunting after the November 2016 elections called many of their gains into question. Interestingly, though, while the federal government took a hard right turn, Kansans spent that high-drama political season quietly moving back toward the center: fourteen moderate Republicans knocked off conservatives in the Kansas House and senate primaries that August, and in November, Democrats gained a dozen seats in the House. Moderates and Democrats were still in the minority, but they were stronger. Among those who would not return to the Kansas legislature in 2017: Jan Pauls of Hutchinson, who lost her seat to a Democrat named Patsy Terrell (in a bizarre turn of events, Terrell died of natural causes at age 55 on June 7, 2017, near the end of her first session in office; Pauls, 64, died a month later).

It will be a long time before we really know what the end of the Pauls era meant, if anything, for LGBT Kansans. Equality Kansas chapters scattered around the state still struggle to find people willing to get involved, and Tom Witt will not lead the organization forever. "My time is growing shorter," he told a strikingly young crowd at an Equality Day rally on the statehouse steps in March 2017. "My husband is retired and my daughter got married. One day I'll want to spend time with my grandkids, and it's going to be one of you up here. Good luck! It will be easier!" he promised.

Other activists simply deserve a rest from politics. By the time she read Kathleen Sebelius's post-*Obergefell* congratulatory statement for hundreds of people at Ilus W. Davis Park in June 2015, Sandra Meade had begun seriously dating for the first time since her divorce. Her boyfriend lived in another city a few hours east of Kansas City, so they logged a lot of phone time in between weekends together. The relationship gave her new hope that there was someone out there for her. "There just aren't that many people in my age bracket who are going to be accepting or tolerant of someone like me," she said. After her transition, Meade's activism had fulfilled her need for human connection—meanwhile, she met too many straight men who were in the closet about their attractions to trans women (as was the case with the New York hip-hop DJ Mister Cee, whom Meade discussed on her radio program in 2013). Finally, Meade met this man online. "He's a scientist, so he's not afraid of difficult concepts like the fact that somebody's brain might have organized differently in utero than their genitals already had." She began to consider a new idea: "I don't have to die alone." Two years later, the couple moved to California after he was recruited to a job there. Meade had served Kansas with distinction, and now she would enjoy a well-earned personal life.

It's easy to imagine that someone who spent half her life waiting to live as her true self might feel resentment about so much lost time, but for Meade, it's not that way. "I feel lucky," she said. "I've lived such an interesting life." When she first began transitioning, Meade had some hard feelings, but she doesn't call them regrets. For one thing, she has a son of whom she's proud, and they're on good terms. She would wonder, though, about what could have been. "What if I had transitioned already? What if, when I got out of the navy, I'd made the decision right there, before it went any further? What would my life have been like if I'd had the body that I should have? I spent a lot of time thinking about all of that, which wasn't really helpful." Now she sees how her life fits in a much bigger story. "This is who I am. This is the era I grew up in. I'm one of those people in history who was in the middle. Going forward, I'm hoping people won't have the kind of shame and discomfort that I grew up with. I can look back and know that, under the circumstances, I did the best I could. I lived a great life and feel like I contributed to my country. I love my country."

And her country was more inclined to acknowledge contributions such as the one Meade had made. In June 2016 Defense Secretary Ash Carter announced that trans people were welcome to serve openly in the US armed forces. "We're talking about talented Americans who are serving with distinction or who want the opportunity to serve," Carter said in his statement. "We can't allow barriers unrelated to a person's qualifications prevent us from recruiting and retaining those who can best accomplish the mission."[4]

That equal-rights victory was endangered at the dawn of the post-Obama world, but by then, generals as well as the general public were perfectly fine with transgender people serving.[5] Still, many of our gains felt threatened. None of us in Kansas were surprised when one of the people who had a role in what felt like a backlash administration was the Kansas Secretary of State, Kris Kobach, whose many insults to his state's non-straight-white citizens had included that line, "If a person wants to live in a San Francisco lifestyle, they can go there. If they want to live a Kansas lifestyle, they can come here."

I knew Kevin Stilley's story told another truth about us and about Kansas, which is what inspired me to ask if I could tag along on his Memorial Day weekend drive.

Now we are at our destination: the Grandview–Mill Creek–Stockdale Cemetery, a sun-soaked, grassy rise alongside a two-lane highway, final resting place of (so far) 923 souls, mostly guarded by a chain-link fence.

There is no fence at the east end, so Stilley steers off the highway, Butterscotch bouncing gently over the thick green lawn and coming to a stop in the middle of the cemetery's unoccupied ground. Half a mile to the west is a caretaker's farmhouse and shady yard; in the treeless stretch between here and there are dotted lines of white stones and waist-high monuments, their edges rounded by 150 years of prairie weather. "We'll start up here with my family," says Stilley.

His first relatives arrived before statehood, in 1858. "Most came right at the end of the Civil War, because Civil War veterans could get the quarter section of land that anyone could get, plus another quarter section as veterans. So they could get a half section of land free." His great-great-great-grandfather, Timothy Lewis, came from southern Indiana and staked a small claim on the Blue River.

Over the past few years, Stilley has been staking his own type of claim. "When my dad died—he's the furthest one up the hill—Mom bought a block of lots," he explains. "When Aunt Carol was killed, my grandparents

Kevin Stilley, near the Rainbow Plot at Grandview–Mill Creek–Stockdale Cemetery in Riley County, on Memorial Day weekend, 2016. Credit: C. J. Janovy

bought the next block." Stilley figured each block had eight graves. "So I'm thinking, two parents, four grandparents, three kids, spouses—sixteen may not be enough." He called the cemetery manager and asked if he could buy the third block in their row. "He said, 'Okay, but you're gonna have to pay more than your mom and your grandma did. They each paid $15.' He says, 'I'm gonna have to charge you $30.' I said, 'I think I can handle it.' It's the only real estate I've ever owned."

Stilley and his mother were out here yesterday—by the end of the Memorial Day weekend they'll have decorated two hundred graves in Riley County—so the markers for his father, his Aunt Carol, and their parents, and his mother's folks already have flowers. "That's my great-great-grandfather's sister, her son, her grandson, and then a sister of my great-grandfather. This is my great-grandparents, Tim and May." As we walk back closer to the highway, he pulls a handful of something bright and yellow out of Butterscotch's back seat. "My great-grandmother absolutely hated artificial flowers. This year there was nothing blooming, so I stopped off the highway and pulled weeds," he says, tucking the arrangement beside her marker.

Stilley points west, to a little pink flower at a stone by itself: Rev. Timothy Lewis, the first arrival. He was a Baptist preacher, born in New York State; his family moved to southern Indiana where he grew up, married, and had the first of several children before coming to Kansas. From reading Baptist histories, Stilley learned that Lewis was nicknamed "the marrying preacher" because younger couples would ask him to perform their services. "So he must have been a cool dude, not a fire-and-brimstone type."

That theory is a comfort, anyway, to a man who has spent decades hearing Baptist preachers say unkind things about the other branch of his family. Not the blood relatives, but his gay brothers and sisters. Some of them are buried here too. Stilley knew Dan Bodenhamer through the Junction City Teddy Bears, a men's group. "He lived a couple miles north of here in a trailer house. And he had cancer. The fall before he died, he called me one day. He said, 'Who do I call about buying into that cemetery there where your folks are?'" Stilley, who had ended up with more plots than he needed, told Bodenhamer not to buy. "Just use one of mine," he told Bodenhamer, who said he would pay for it. "I said, well, okay, Dan, but I gotta tell you, I paid thirty dollars for my block. That's three dollars a grave!" Stilley's laughter rises to the bright blue sky, an answer to the meadowlark that has been chiming in from a fence post opposite the highway. "Of course I didn't let him pay me for it. He died much sooner than he thought, and Mike, his partner, came up and picked out the space."

A few plots down the gentle slope are Grace and Maxine, who rented a mobile home from Stilley and his mother. They had been together for forty-three years when Grace died in 1990. "Everybody in Manhattan knew 'em. They were old-school lesbians—blue jeans, flannel shirts, short hair—and they were just completely accepted, nobody thought anything about it. They never had any trouble," he says. "When Maxine got Grace's ashes from the funeral home, she didn't want them in the house. I said, 'Well, Maxine, I think there's still one space left on my great-grandparents' block up at the cemetery where we are. We could bury her up there and there'd still be plenty of room for you, too.' So we drove up here and she looked around and said, 'Yep, this is actually the direction we used to go when we thought the car needed exercisin'.'" Maxine lived another sixteen years; she died in 2006.

Stilley has reserved the next space for Bodenhamer's partner, Mike. "And then Darci and Joleen'll use that third one," he says of Pottroff and Spain. "They're gonna be cremated so they'll share one." That leaves five spaces still available. "Daddy Ron, he has nowhere to go," Stilley says of the man who's currently president of the Junction City Teddy Bears, "so he thinks he'd like to come up here with us."

Stilley, a sixth-generation Kansan, has nicknamed his land the Rainbow Plot. He's thinking of getting a corner stone, and he wonders if it can be made in color. If so, he says, "I want to do rainbows. My mom says, just think of some future genealogist, wondering, what're all these people doing here?"

They're belonging to Kansas. Just like they did when they were alive.

ACKNOWLEDGMENTS

First, I'm profoundly grateful to everyone who shared their experiences with me. And there are many others whose names do not appear in these pages but by all rights should: people who considered speaking to me and then changed their minds for whatever reasons; people I spoke with whose stories I did not include; people I was never able to reach; people who made specific contributions to this narrative but are no longer alive. Deep gratitude goes out to all of these people for working toward justice and equality.

Thank you to Kim Hogeland, Kelly Chrisman Jacques, Colin Tripp, Karl Janssen, Mike Kehoe, and Derek Helms at the University Press of Kansas for giving this book a home, and to copyeditor Amy Sherman, proofreader Caitlin Armbrister, and indexer Doug Easton. Thanks also to Lynn Johnston, whose time and consult made it a better book before it found a home, and to Joanie Shoemaker and Jo-Lynn Worley for midproject advice. Thanks to early readers Justin Kendall, Karl Hamann, Diana Hamann, and Patty Spiglanin.

Much respect to the statehouse reporters of Kansas, without whom this book could not have been written. Thanks to Deb Nuss, for helping me understand Manhattan. And thank you to my supportive colleagues at KCUR, particularly Donna Vestal, Sam Zeff, Laura Spencer, and Peggy Lowe.

This project reaffirmed my immense appreciation for librarians everywhere, and especially Tami Albin of the University of Kansas's *Under the Rainbow: Oral Histories of Gay, Lesbian, Transgender, Intersex and Queer People in Kansas*, and Stuart Hinds of the Gay and Lesbian Archives of Mid-America at the University of Missouri–Kansas City.

Terri Heibert and Rhonda Reist, thanks for putting up with all of this during vacations. Danny Alexander, John Boyd, David Cantwell, Amy Elliott, Nicole Esquibel, and Doris Saltkill: thanks for so many helpful conversations on the phone and at meals, holidays, and baseball games. Jena Janovy, Karen Janovy, and John Janovy Jr., thank you for always being there. Thanks as well to my compatriots in the Stratlist brain trust. Special thanks to Daniel Wolff for constant mentorship and encouragement, and to Emily Levine for friendship above and beyond.

To Lori Bednar, thanks for making me an honest woman before and after it was legal.

NOTES

INTRODUCTION. A STRANGE FEELING IN MIDDLE AMERICA

1. Thomas Frank, *What's the Matter with Kansas?: How Conservatives Won the Heart of America* (New York: Metropolitan Books, 2004), 31.

2. Obituary, "Alf Landon, G.O.P. Stand[ard]-Bearer, Dies at 100," *New York Times*, October 13, 1987, http://www.nytimes.com/learning/general/onthisday /bday/0909.html.

3. Craig Miner, *Kansas: The History of the Sunflower State, 1854–2000* (Lawrence: University Press of Kansas, 2002), 291.

4. Ben Brantley, "Critic's Notebook; Why Oz Is a State of Mind in Gay Life and Drag Shows," *New York Times*, June 28, 1994, http://www.nytimes.com/1994/06 /28/movies/critic-s-notebook-why-oz-is-a-state-of-mind-in-gay-life-and-drag -shows.html.

5. Sandra Stenzel, email to the author, May 11, 2014.

6. Ian Crouch, "Viagra Returns to the Bob Dole Approach," *New Yorker*, October 7, 2014, http://www.newyorker.com/business/currency/viagra-returns-bob -dole-approach.

7. Beccy Tanner, "Coming Home: Nancy Kassebaum Reflects on Her Political Legacy, Life (+video)," *Wichita Eagle*, November 11, 2015, http://www.kansas.com /news/state/article44227929.html.

8. Chris Wallace, "Sens. Graham, Durbin Talk DOJ, IRS Scandals; Rare Interview with 'America's Veteran,' Former Sen. Bob Dole," *Fox News Sunday*, May 26, 2013, http://www.foxnews.com/on-air/fox-news-sunday-chris-wallace/2013/05 /26/sens-graham-durbin-talk-doj-irs-scandals-rare-interview-americas-veteran -former-sen-bob#p//v/2411280923001.

9. Jane Mayer, *Dark Money: The Hidden History of the Billionaires behind the Rise of the Radical Right* (New York: Doubleday, 2016), 332.

10. Frank, *What's the Matter with Kansas*, 91–92.

11. Ibid., 102.

12. Dave Helling and Steve Kraske, "Kansas, Missouri Remain Solid Red States," *McClatchy DC Bureau*, November 12, 2012, http://www.mcclatchydc.com /news/politics-government/article24740083.html.

13. Gary J. Gates and Frank Newport, "LGBT Percentage Highest in D.C., Lowest in North Dakota," *Gallup*, February 15, 2013, http://www.gallup.com/poll /160517/lgbt-percentage-highest-lowest-north-dakota.aspx.

14. Scott Herring, *Another Country: Queer Anti-Urbanism* (New York: New York University Press, 2010), 4, 43.

15. Ibid., 183.

16. Carol Mason, *Oklahomo: Lessons in Unqueering America* (Albany: State University of New York Press, 2015), 157.

17. Rebecca Barrett-Fox, *God Hates: Westboro Baptist Church, American Nationalism, and the Religious Right* (Lawrence: University Press of Kansas, 2016), 115.

18. Lucas Crawford, "Snorting the Powder of Life: Transgender Migration in the Land of Oz," in *Queering the Countryside: New Frontiers in Rural Queer Studies,* ed. Mary L. Gray, Colin R. Johnson, and Brian J. Gilley (New York: New York University Press, 2016), 126.

19. Larry Bunker, interview with the author, January 27, 2014. Recollections and quotations by Bunker here and in chapter 7 are from this interview.

20. Debbie Cenziper and James Obergefell, *Love Wins: The Lovers and Lawyers Who Fought the Landmark Case for Marriage Equality* (New York: William Morrow, 2016), 249.

21. Linda Hirshman, *Victory: The Triumphant Gay Revolution* (New York: Harper Perennial, 2013), 341.

22. Dana Milbank, "Supreme Court Gay Marriage Rulings Lead to Celebrations," *Washington Post,* June 26, 2013, http://articles.washingtonpost.com/2013 -06-26/opinions/40199446_1_california-s-proposition-marriage-laws-california -ban.

23. Elizabeth Weise, "San Francisco Celebrates Gay Marriage Rulings," *USA Today,* June 26, 2013, updated July 5, 2013, http://www.usatoday.com/story/news /nation/2013/06/26/san-francisco-celebrates-gay-marriage-ruling/2461259/.

24. Gilbert Baker, interviewed by Tami Albin, June 19, 2008, "Gilbert Baker Oral History," *Under the Rainbow: Oral Histories of Gay, Lesbian, Transgender, Intersex and Queer People in Kansas,* University of Kansas ScholarWorks, https://kuscholar works.ku.edu/handle/1808/6895.

25. Tom Witt, interviews with the author, October 27, 2013, May 13, 2014, October 1, 2014, and July 22, 2015. Recollections and quotations by Witt in this and subsequent chapters are from these interviews unless otherwise noted.

PART ONE. THE DEFEAT

1. C. J. Janovy, "Behind the Veil," *Pitch,* November 18, 2004, http://www.pitch .com/news/article/20608232/behind-the-veil.

2. "Bush Calls for Ban on Same-Sex Marriages," *CNN,* February 25, 2004, http://edition.cnn.com/2004/ALLPOLITICS/02/24/elec04.prez.bush.marriage/.

3. Tim Hoover, "State Argues Gay Marriage Vote Timing—Nixon Sues Blunt over Amendment Ballot Date," *Kansas City Star*, May 21, 2004.

4. Alan Cooperman, "Gay Marriage Ban in Mo. May Resonate Nationwide," *Washington Post*, August 5, 2004, http://www.washingtonpost.com/wp-dyn /articles/A38861-2004Aug4.html.

5. Monica Davey, "Sharp Reactions to Missouri's Decisive Vote against Gay Marriage," *New York Times*, August 5, 2004, http://www.nytimes.com/2004/08/05 /us/sharp-reactions-to-missouri-s-decisive-vote-against-gay-marriage.html.

CHAPTER 1. TROUBLE IN TOPEKA

1. Chuck Kennedy, "First Lady Michelle Obama Tours the Brown v. Board of Education National Historic Site in Topeka, Kan., May 16, 2014. Stephanie Kyriazis, Chief of Interpretation and Education, leads the tour," Official White House Photo, Flickr.com, May 16, 2014, https://www.flickr.com/photos /whitehouse/14358465770/in/photostream/.

2. Michelle Obama, "Remarks by the First Lady at Topeka School District Senior Recognition Day," *The White House: President Barack Obama*, May 17, 2014, https://obamawhitehouse.archives.gov/the-press-office/2014/05/17/remarks -first-lady-topeka-school-district-senior-recognition-day.

3. "Legally Recognize Westboro Baptist Church as a Hate Group," *We the People*, December 14, 2012, last accessed December 30, 2016, https://petitions.whitehouse .gov/petition/legally-recognize-westboro-baptist-church-hate-group-0. Since the change in presidential administrations, the content is no longer posted on *We the People*, but a previous version is available via the Internet Archive *Wayback Machine*, last captured January 28, 2017, https://web.archive.org/web/20170118092233/https:// petitions.whitehouse.gov/petition/legally-recognize-westboro-baptist-church -hate-group-0. For more on the petition, see "White House Responds to Westboro Baptist Church Petitions," *Huffington Post*, July 3, 2013, http://www.huffingtonpost .com/2013/07/03/white-house-westboro-baptist-church_n_3540814.html.

4. Michael Paulson, "Fred Phelps, Anti-Gay Preacher Who Targeted Military Funerals, Dies at 84," *New York Times*, March 20, 2014, http://www.nytimes.com /2014/03/21/us/fred-phelps-founder-of-westboro-baptist-church-dies-at-84 .html?emc=edit_th_20140321&nl=todaysheadlines&nlid=63647470&_r=0.

5. Pedro Irigonegaray, interview with the author, August 11, 2014. Recollections and quotations by Irigonegaray in this and subsequent chapters are from this interview.

6. Harry W. Craig, "To Whom It May Concern," letter regarding an amendment to the City of Topeka's municipal code, July 12, 2002.

7. John Fish, "To Mayor Butch Felker and the Topeka City Council," letter regarding an amendment to the City of Topeka's municipal code, July 13, 2002; John McKelvey, "To Whom It May Concern," letter regarding an amendment to the City of Topeka's municipal code, July 15, 2002.

8. Tiffany Muller, interviews with the author, July 2, 2014, and July 16, 2014. Recollections and quotations by Muller in this and subsequent chapters are from these interviews unless otherwise noted.

9. Norris did not respond to my requests for an interview.

10. Rick Ellis, interview with the author, August 27, 2014. All recollections and quotations by Ellis in this chapter are from this interview.

11. SharpConnections, "GOP Sen. David Adkins on Marriage, March 2004," Soundcloud, last accessed September 9, 2016, https://soundcloud.com/sharp connections/adkinsonmarriage.

12. Scott Rothschild, "Senate Advances Amendment against Gay Marriage," Lawrence Journal-World, March 25, 2004, http://www2.ljworld.com/news/2004/mar /25/senate_advances_amendment/.

13. Ibid.

14. John Ballou, interview with the author, April 12, 2017.

15. John Hanna, "Research, Discomfort Caused House Switches on Marriage Amendment," Lawrence Journal-World, May 9, 2004, http://www2.ljworld.com/news /2004/may/09/research_discomfort_caused/.

16. Ibid.

17. Kendrick Blackwood, "Ministers Hate Fags Too," Pitch, July 22, 2004, http://www.pitch.com/news/article/20609077/ministers-hate-fags-too.

18. Ibid.

19. Ibid.

20. Ibid.

21. Editorial board, "Tiffany Muller—Yes, but Wait: Tiffany Muller Is More than Just Topeka's First Gay Council Member," Topeka Capital-Journal, September 19, 2004, http://cjonline.com/stories/091904/opi_muller.shtml.

22. Tim Hrenchir, "Narrowed Plan Passes: Discrimination Ban Limited to City Hiring Practices," Topeka Capital-Journal, November 17, 2004.

23. Ibid.

24. Jodi Wilgoren, "Vote in Topeka Today Hangs on Gay Rights and a Vitriolic Local Pastor," New York Times, March 1, 2005, http://www.nytimes.com/2005/03/01 /us/vote-in-topeka-today-hangs-on-gay-rights-and-a-vitriolic-local-protester .html.

25. Sandra Stenzel, interviews with the author, March 2, 2014; March 14, 2014; March 15, 2014; April 8, 2014; and February 3, 2015. Recollections and quotations

by Stenzel in this and subsequent chapters are from these interviews unless otherwise noted.

CHAPTER 2. HEARTBREAK IN TREGO COUNTY

1. Supreme Court of the State of Kansas, Original proceeding in discipline, no. 103,195, In the Matter of David J. Harding, January 22, 2010, http://www.kscourts .org/cases-and-opinions/opinions/SupCt/2010/20100122/103195.pdf.

2. Associated Press, "Ex-Trego County Sheriff Convicted," Lawrence Journal-World, May 20, 2004, http://www2.ljworld.com/news/2004/may/20/extrego _county_sheriff/.

3. Associated Press, "Ex-Sheriff Guilty of Molesting Adopted Girl," Topeka Capital-Journal, October 19, 2006, http://cjonline.com/stories/101906/bre_molest .shtml.

4. Kari Blurton, "Former Trego School Board President Accepts Plea Agreement on Drug Charges," Hays Post, February 26, 2014, http://www.hayspost.com /2014/02/26/former-trego-school-board-president-accepts-plea-agreement-on -drug-charges/.

5. Supreme Court of the State of Kansas, In the Matter of David J. Harding.

6. Jon Schmitt, interview with the author, March 14, 2014. Recollections and quotations by Schmitt are from this interview.

7. Dave Schneider, interview with the author, March 15, 2014. Recollections and quotations by Schneider are from this interview.

8. John Hanna, "Kansas Ponders Saying 'I Don't' to Gay Marriage," Lawrence Journal-World, February 8, 2004, http://www2.ljworld.com/news/2004/feb/08 /kansas_ponders_saying/.

9. Associated Press, "Gay Marriage Ban Could Hurt Business Growth, Say Critics," Lawrence Journal-World, March 17, 2004, http://www2.ljworld.com/news /2004/mar/17/gay_marriage_ban/.

10. Joy Leiker, "People Show Up in Droves for WaKeeney Meeting," Hays Daily News, August 18, 2004.

11. Ibid.

12. Gwen Schmitt, interview with the author, March 14, 2014. Recollections and quotations by Schmitt are from this interview.

13. Joy Leiker, "Trego County Residents Not Happy with Budget," Hays Daily News, September 1, 2004.

14. Mike Corn, "Meeting Draws Big Crowd," Hays Daily News, March 1, 2005.

15. Mike Corn, "Sexual Politics? Ex-Economic Development Director Claims Dismissal Not Job-Related," Hays Daily News, March 16, 2005.

16. David J. Harding, interview with the author, April 26, 2017.

17. Sandy Schneider, interview with the author, March 15, 2014. Recollections and quotations by Schneider are from this interview.

CHAPTER 3. COLLEGE TOWNS AND RIVALRIES

1. Diane Silver, interviews with the author, June 23, 2014, and April 18, 2015. Recollections and quotations by Silver in this and subsequent chapters are from these interviews unless otherwise noted.

2. Nancy Smith, "GAY: Homosexuals Say Lawrence isn't San Francisco, but It's a Place They Can Call Home," *Lawrence Journal-World*, June 19, 1988.

3. "Doria Services," *Lawrence Journal-World*, February 7, 1993, http://www2.lj world.com/news/1993/feb/07/doria_services/.

4. Bruce Ney, interviews with the author, October 26, 2014, and June 28, 2015. Recollections and quotations by Ney in this and subsequent chapters are from these interviews unless otherwise noted.

5. Joel Mathis, "A Place for Us?," *Lawrence.com*, January 23, 2005, http://www .lawrence.com/news/2005/jan/23/onlylawrence/.

6. Cyd Slayton, interviews with the author, May 27, 2015, and October 12, 2015. Recollections and quotations by Slayton in this and subsequent chapters are from these interviews.

7. Associated Press, "Amendment Supporters Outspent Opponents More than 2–1," *Pittsburg Morning Sun*, April 26, 2005.

8. Christopher Renner, interview with the author, November 2, 2014.

9. Christopher Renner, unpublished interview with Tami Albin, January 2008, for *Under the Rainbow: Oral Histories of Gay, Lesbian, Transgender, Intersex and Queer People in Kansas*. Quoted with Renner's permission.

10. Lena Williams, "200,000 March in Capital to Seek Gay Rights and Money for AIDS," *New York Times*, October 12, 1987, http://www.nytimes.com/1987/10/12 /us/200000-march-in-capital-to-seek-gay-rights-and-money-for-aids.html.

11. Renner, interview with the author.

12. Hawk died of pancreatic cancer in 2010.

13. Renner, unpublished interview with Albin.

14. Ibid.

15. Ibid.

PART TWO. THE DUSTOFF

1. Tom Witosky and Marc Hansen, *Equal before the Law: How Iowa Led Americans to Marriage Equality* (Iowa City: University of Iowa Press, 2015), 4.

2. Linda Casey, "Independent Expenditure Campaigns in Iowa Topple Three

High Court Justices," Followthemoney.org, January 10, 2011, accessed December 18, 2016, http://www.followthemoney.org/research/institute-reports/indepen dent-expenditure-campaigns-in-iowa-topple-three-high-court-justices/.

3. Alexis Levinson, "Huckabee Makes Himself Heard in Iowa," *Daily Caller*, October 29, 2010, accessed December 18, 2016, http://dailycaller.com/2010/10/29 /huckabee-makes-himself-heard-in-iowa/.

4. Sheryl Gay Stolberg, "Obama Signs Away 'Don't Ask, Don't Tell,'" *New York Times*, December 22, 2010, http://www.nytimes.com/2010/12/23/us/politics /23military.html?_r=0.

5. Barack Obama, "Remarks by the President and Vice President at Sign-ing of the Don't Ask, Don't Tell Repeal Act of 2010," White House Office of the Press Secretary, December 22, 2012, accessed December 18, 2016, https:// www.whitehouse.gov/the-press-office/2010/12/22/remarks-president-and -vice-president-signing-dont-ask-dont-tell-repeal-a.

6. "The First It Gets Better Video: Dan & Terry," *It Gets Better Project*, October 13, 2010, accessed December 18, 2016, http://www.itgetsbetter.org/blog/entry/the -first-it-gets-better-video-dan-terry/.

7. "What Is the It Gets Better Project?" *It Gets Better Project*, accessed December 18, 2016, http://www.itgetsbetter.org/pages/about-it-gets-better-project/.

CHAPTER 4. AN AWAKENING IN WICHITA

1. Abe Levy, "Christian Leaders Chastise Senate on Gay Marriage," *Wichita Eagle*, March 31, 2004.

2. Opinion, Memo: Student Views, "Should Gays Be Able to Marry?" *Wichita Eagle*, March 10, 2004.

3. Bruce McKinney, interview with the author, November 18, 2014. Recollec-tions and quotations by McKinney in this chapter are from this interview.

4. Jeffrey Stinson, "City Commission Sets Hearing on Gay Rights," *Wichita Eagle*, August 17, 1977.

5. Gordon Atcheson, "Bryant Says Gays Ordinance Affords 'Special Privilege,'" *Wichita Eagle*, December 6, 1977.

6. Emily Behlmann, "Health Care Heroes—Dr. Donna Sweet," *Wichita Busi-ness Journal*, October 8, 2012, http://www.bizjournals.com/wichita/feature/Health CareHeroes/2010/12/dr-donna-sweet.html.

7. Pat Munz, interview with the author, November 4, 2014. Recollections and quotations by Munz in this chapter are from this interview.

8. Cargill, "Beef North America," accessed June 2, 2017, https://www.cargill .com/meat-poultry/beef-na.

9. Wichita Art Museum, "Museum History," accessed December 30, 2016, https://www.wichitaartmuseum.org/about/museum_history.

CHAPTER 5. PIONEERS IN WESTERN KANSAS

1. LuAnn Kahl, interviews with the author, August 9, 2015, and August 16, 2015. Recollections and quotations by Kahl in this chapter are from these interviews.

2. Jenny Deam, "Doctor Struggles to Fill Role of Slain Kansas Abortion Provider," *Los Angeles Times*, March 5, 2012, http://articles.latimes.com/2012/mar/05/nation/la-na-kansas-abortion-20120305.

3. Anne Mitchell, interview with the author, November 16, 2014. Recollections and quotations by Mitchell in this chapter are from this interview.

4. Lindy Duree, interview with the author, September 1, 2015. Recollections and quotations by Duree in this chapter are from this interview.

5. Tanya Jantz, interview with Tami Albin, November 24, 2010, "Tanya Oral History," *Under the Rainbow: Oral Histories of Gay, Lesbian, Transgender, Intersex and Queer People in Kansas*, University of Kansas ScholarWorks, https://kuscholarworks.ku.edu/handle/1808/6892. All quotations and recollections by Jantz in this chapter are from this oral history.

6. Tim Vandenack, "Rainbow Flag Issue Starts Flap in Meade," *Hutchinson News*, August 5, 2006.

7. Associated Press, "Boy's Gift of Rainbow Flag Still Spawns Protests," *Topeka Capital-Journal*, August 29, 2006, http://cjonline.com/stories/082906/kan_flag.shtml#.V-Edlztg9mA.

8. Emily Behlmann, "Student, Group Offended by Wheeler's Remark," *Garden City Telegram*, February 14, 2008.

9. John P. Wheeler, Jr., "Sexual Crimes," PowerPoint presentation submitted in testimony of Thomas Witt, executive director, Kansas Equality Coalition, Senate Committee on the Judiciary, January 31, 2012, http://www.kslegislature.org/li_2012/b2011_12/committees/misc/ctte_s_jud_1_20120201_09_other.pdf.

10. Kristie Stremel, "Letter to the Editor," reproduced in Danny Alexander, "Standing Up for What's Real," *Take Em As They Come* (blog), February 24, 2008, http://takeemastheycome.blogspot.com/2008_02_24_archive.html.

11. Behlmann, "Student, Group Offended."

12. Isaac Unruh, interview with the author, September 9, 2015. Recollections and quotations by Unruh in this chapter are from this interview.

13. Shajia Ahmad, "Gay-Straight Alliance in Place at GCHS," *Garden City Telegram*, April 30, 2009.

14. Sharon Unruh, interview with the author, February 25, 2016. Recollections and quotations by Unruh in this chapter are from this interview.

15. Patricia Calhoun, "In the Age of Caitlyn Jenner, Trinidad Is No Longer World's Sex-Change Capital," *Westword*, July 29, 2015, http://www.westword.com /news/in-the-age-of-caitlyn-jenner-trinidad-is-no-longer-worlds-sex-change -capital-6965216.

16. Episode 5, *Sex Change Hospital*, November 11, 2008. The series is no longer online, but more information is available on IMDb.com: "Sex Change Hospital," IMDB, accessed June 2, 2017, http://www.imdb.com/title/tt0994543/.

PART THREE. THE COMEBACK

1. Jena McGregor, "Corporate America's Embrace of Gay Rights Has Reached a Stunning Tipping Point," *Washington Post*, April 5, 2016, https://www.washing tonpost.com/news/on-leadership/wp/2016/04/05/corporate-americas-embrace -of-gay-rights-has-reached-a-stunning-tipping-point/?utm_term=.4f2034a5fb3c.

2. Chad Griffin, "Letter from HRC Foundation President," *Corporate Equality Index 2015: Rating American Workplaces on Lesbian, Gay, Bisexual and Transgender Equality*, Human Rights Campaign, http://hrc-assets.s3-website-us-east-1.amazonaws .com//files/documents/CEI-2015-rev.pdf.

3. Human Rights Campaign, *Equality Forward: 2015 Annual Report*, 20, http:// hrc-assets.s3-website-us-east-1.amazonaws.com//files/documents/HRC-Annual Report-2015.pdf.

CHAPTER 6. THEY'LL TAKE MANHATTAN

1. Cora Holt, interview with the author, September 9, 2015. Recollections and quotations by Holt in this chapter are from this interview unless otherwise noted.

2. Alley Stoughton, interview with the author, August 27, 2015. Recollections and quotations by Stoughton in this chapter are from this interview unless otherwise noted.

3. James Carlson, "Order Extends Anti-Discrimination Policies to Gays," *Topeka Capital-Journal*, September 1, 2007, http://cjonline.com/stories/090107/sta _196188540.shtml#.Vj9RNWurGDU.

4. Diane Silver, "For the First Time in History, A Kansas Governor Stands Up for LGBT People," *In This Moment: An Uncommon Blog of Hope and Politics*, August 31, 2007, http://hopeandpolitics.blogspot.com/2007/08/for-first-time-in-history -kansas.html.

5. Alley Stoughton, email to Clyde Howard and Gary Leitnaker, April 17, 2008.

6. Gary Leitnaker, email to Alley Stoughton, February 8, 2008.

7. Alley Stoughton, email to Gary Leitnaker, August 25, 2008.

8. Gary Leitnaker, email to Alley Stoughton, August 25, 2008.

9. Gary Leitnaker, interview with the author, February 1, 2016. Quotations by Leitnaker in this chapter are from this interview unless otherwise noted.

10. Kansas State University Media Relations, "Professor Has High Hopes for Transgender Acceptance," *K-Statement*, August 21, 2008, https://www.k-state.edu /media/k-statement/vol31/82108stoughton.html.

11. Ibid.

12. "Jonathan Mertz: 'I'm from Manhattan, Kansas,'" *I'm From Driftwood: The LGBTQ Story Archive*, YouTube, September 26, 2010, https://www.youtube .com/watch?v=TKYDRIaIvIQ.

13. Jonathan Mertz, interview with the author, September 9, 2015. Unless otherwise noted, all recollections and quotations by Mertz in this chapter are from this interview.

14. Lukus Ebert, interview with the author, March 23, 2016. Recollections and quotations by Ebert in this chapter are from this interview.

15. Christopher Renner, "Historic March Draws over 200," *Kansas Free Press*, April 27, 2010, http://www.kansasfreepress.com/2010/04/historic-march-draws -over-200.html (site no longer active).

16. Ibid.

17. "What's the Problem?" *Awaken Manhattan*, accessed September 25, 2016, http://awakenmanhattan.com/the-ordinance/whats-the-problem/ (site no longer active).

18. Daniel Blomberg, "Legal Analysis of Proposed Ordinance," video at *Awaken Manhattan*, accessed September 25, 2016, http://awakenmanhattan.com/media -and-resources/videos/legal-analysis-of-proposed-ordinance/ (site no longer active).

19. Pastors' letter, November 2, 2010, *Awaken Manhattan*, accessed January 1, 2016, http://awakenmanhattan.com/the-ordinance/pastors-letters/ (site no longer active).

20. Minutes, City of Manhattan, Kansas, Commission Meeting, December 7, 2010, accessed September 25, 2016, http://cityofmhk.com/ArchiveCenter/View File/Item/2440.

21. Burk Krohe, "Ordinance's Repeal Approved," *Manhattan Mercury*, May 4, 2011.

22. Laura Thacker, "K-State Recognized for LGBT-Friendly Campus," *K-State Collegian*, July 30, 2013, http://www.kstatecollegian.com/2013/07/30/k-state -recognized-for-lgbt-friendly-campus/.

23. Brandon Haddock, interview with the author, August 15, 2015. Recollections and quotations by Haddock in this chapter are from this interview.

24. Kansas State University News and Communications Services, "Coordinator of University's LGBT Resource Center Earns National Award," March 5, 2013, accessed June 2, 2017, http://www.k-state.edu/media/newsreleases/mar13 /haddock3513.html.

CHAPTER 7. SPRINGTIME IN SALINA

1. Scott Graybeal, interview with the author, June 19, 2014. Recollections and quotations by Graybeal in this chapter are from this interview.

2. Sean Mune, testimony at Salina Human Relations Commission public forum, February 28, 2012.

3. Sean Mune, interview with the author, July 11, 2014. Recollections and quotations by Mune in this chapter are from this interview unless otherwise noted.

4. Chris Hunter, "Supporters, Opponents Speak about Proposed Ordinance Change," Salina Journal, February 29, 2012.

5. Jonathan Presley, testimony at Salina Human Relations Commission public forum, February 28, 2012.

6. Ron Boswell, testimony at Salina Human Relations Commission public forum, February 28, 2012.

7. David Martin, "Don Bell Believed that God Smiled on his Bank—But Now God's Frowning," Pitch, October 16, 2008, http://www.pitch.com/news/article/20 600282/don-bell-believed-that-god-smiled-on-his-bank-150-but-now-god146s -frowning.

8. Gary Martens, interview with the author, December 14, 2013. Recollections and quotations by Martens in this chapter are from this interview.

9. Janice Norlin, interview with the author, January 21, 2014. Recollections and quotations by Norlin in this chapter are from this interview.

10. Chris Hunter, "Mott Tells of Being a Man, Then a Woman," Salina Journal, February 27, 2012.

11. Ibid.

12. Beverly Cole, interview with the author, January 27, 2014. Recollections and quotations by Cole in this chapter are from this interview.

13. "'Religious Liberty' Rally Moved to BiCenter," Salina Journal, October 20, 2012.

14. Tim Unruh, "Salinans Rally to Repeal Ordinance," Salina Journal, October 23, 2012.

15. "Citizens Support Salina Mayor," KSAL, May 6, 2013, http://www.ksal.com /citizens-support-salina-mayor/.

16. "Mayors in Kansas and Arkansas Speak Out for the Freedom to Marry," Freedom to Marry, April 24, 2013, accessed June 2, 2017, http://www.freedomtomarry

.org/blog/entry/mayors-in-kansas-and-arkansas-speak-out-for-the-freedom-to-marry.

17. "Salina Gay Pride Month," KSAL, June 2, 2014, http://www.ksal.com/salina-gay-pride-month/.

CHAPTER 8. THE ONCE AND FUTURE HUTCHINSON

1. "Pauls HB2260 Hutch Forum Feb 18 2012," YouTube, uploaded February 20, 2012, accessed September 25, 2012, https://www.youtube.com/watch?v=njB0QFSbaXg.

2. "Redemption," *Hutchinson News*, August 30, 1991.

3. Jon Powell, interviews with the author, November 21, 2014, and December 6, 2014. Recollections and quotations by Powell in this and subsequent chapters are from these interviews.

4. "Easy Way Out," *Hutchinson News*, March 24, 1996.

5. "Kansas Democratic Party Chair Speaks Out against HB2260, Criticizes Rep Jan Pauls," YouTube, uploaded February 28, 2012, accessed September 25, 2016, https://www.youtube.com/watch?v=KjsA8YVPBuI.

6. Tom Witt, email to the author, April 14, 2017.

7. Erich Bishop, interview with the author, February 22, 2015. Recollections and quotations by Bishop in this chapter are from this interview.

8. Mary Clarkin, "Validity of New Pauls Home in Question—Walkthrough Planned to See if Church Meets Requirements to Be Home," *Hutchinson News*, June 15, 2012.

9. Lee Hill Kavanaugh, "Lawmaker Who Opposes 'Superior Rights' for Gays Fears Reprisals," *Kansas City Star*, October 23, 2012.

10. Kayla Regan, "Rival Meetings Tout, Oppose Measure—Anti-Bias Item's Impact on Religious Beliefs Is a Major Point at Two Events," *Hutchinson News*, October 26, 2012.

11. Eddie Ibarra, interview with the author, January 7, 2015. Recollections and quotations by Ibarra in this chapter are from this interview unless otherwise noted.

12. Kara Vaughn, interviews with the author, January 3, 2015, and February 7, 2015. Recollections and quotations by Vaughn in this chapter are from these interviews unless otherwise noted.

CHAPTER 9. ALL POINTS BULLETINS

1. "State Provides Tax Guidance for Same-Sex Couples Filing in Kansas," Kansas Department of Revenue, October 4, 2013, http://www.ksrevenue.org/CMS/content/10-04-2013-Same-Sex-Marriage.pdf.

2. Sam Brownback, "2014 State of the State of Kansas," January 15, 2014, https://governor.kansas.gov/2014-state-of-the-state-of-kansas/.

3. Kansas Legislature, Committee on Federal and State Affairs, House Bill No. 2453, Session of 2014, http://www.kslegislature.org/li_2014/b2013_14/measures /documents/hb2453_01_0000.pdf.

4. Ben Brumfield and Dana Ford, "Kansas House Passes Bill Allowing Refusal of Service to Same-Sex Couples," CNN, February 13, 2014, http://www.cnn .com/2014/02/13/us/kansas-bill-same-sex-services/.

5. Sarah Pulliam Bailey for Religion News Service, "Kansas, Arizona Bills Reflect National Fight over Gay Rights vs. Religious Liberty," Washington Post, February 21, 2014, http://www.washingtonpost.com/national/religion/kansas-arizona -bills-reflect-national-fight-over-gay-rights-vs-religious-liberty/2014/02/21/4827 c81e-9b42-11e3-8112-52fdf646027b_story.html.

6. Tim Carpenter, "Wagle Anxious Gay-Marriage Bill May Promote Discrimination," Topeka Capital-Journal, February 13, 2014, http://cjonline.com /legislature-state/2014-02-13/wagle-anxious-gay-marriage-bill-may-promote -discrimination.

7. Bobby Burch, "AT&T Speaks Out against 'Discriminatory' Kansas Bill," Kansas City Business Journal, February 14, 2014, http://www.bizjournals.com /kansascity/news/2014/02/14/att-speaks-out-against.html.

8. Bobby Burch, "Sprint: Kansas' Religious Freedom Bill Would 'Discriminate,'" Kansas City Business Journal, February 18, 2014, http://www.bizjournals .com/kansascity/news/2014/02/18/sprint-kansas-religious-freedom-bill.html ?page=all.

9. Sandra Meade and Thomas Witt, "Equality Kansas Urges LGBT Community to Respect Privacy of Phelps Family," Equality Kansas, March 16, 2014, http://eqks .org/post-5003/.

10. Thomas Witt, "UPDATED: Equality Kansas Urges LGBT Community to Respect Privacy of Phelps Family," Equality Kansas, March 16, 2014, http://eqks.org /post-5003/.

11. Jay Senter, "Equality Kansas Rally Shows Support for Roeland Park Anti-Discrimination Law after Westboro Baptist Protest," Shawnee Mission Post, March 17, 2014, https://shawneemissionpost.com/2014/03/17/equality-kansas-rally -shows-support-for-roeland-park-anti-discrimination-law-after-westboro -baptist-protest-25809.

12. Sandra Meade, interviews with the author, June 10, 2015, and August 11, 2015. Recollections and quotations by Meade in this and subsequent chapters are from these interviews.

13. Dan Blom, "Roeland Park Sets April Vote on Anti-Discrimination Ordinance for Sexual Orientation, Gender Identity," *Shawnee Mission Post*, March 4, 2014, https://shawneemissionpost.com/2014/03/04/roeland-park-sets-april-vote-on -anti-discrimination-ordinance-for-sexual-orientation-gender-identity-25466.

14. Ibid.

15. Minutes, City of Roeland Park, Kansas, Committee of the Whole Meeting, March 3, 2014, http://www.roelandpark.net/wordpress/wp-content/uploads/I-A -03032014-COW-Minutes.pdf.

16. Dan Blom, "Roeland Park Pushes Back Anti-Discrimination Vote Again after Another Lengthy Discussion," *Shawnee Mission Post*, May 6, 2014, http://shawnee missionpost.com/2014/05/06/roeland-park-pushes-back-anti-discrimination -vote-again-after-another-lengthy-discussion-27400.

17. Jenna Hanchard, "Mystery Flyer Causes Controversy over Roeland Park Ordinance," Channel 41 Action News, June 10, 2014, YouTube, https://www.you tube.com/watch?v=XHITWFd1mJM.

18. Michael Poppa, interview with the author, August 12, 2015. Recollections and quotations by Poppa in this chapter are from this interview.

19. Matt Canham, "Utah Governor Disappointed, but Ready to Uphold Gay Marriage," *Salt Lake Tribune*, last updated October 15, 2016, http://www.sltrib .com/info/staff/1677458-155/marriage-state-sex-herbert-reyes-utah.

20. "AG Schmidt Statement on Supreme Court's Decision Not to Decide Marriage Cases," *Attorney General Derek Schmidt*, October 6, 2014, accessed June 2, 2017, http://ag.ks.gov/media-center/news-releases/2014/10/06/ag-schmidt-statement -on-supreme-court-s-decision-not-to-decide-marriage-cases.

21. Julia and Gina Johnson, interview with the author, December 7, 2014. Recollections and quotations by the Johnsons in this chapter are from this interview.

22. Thomas Witt, update, EqualityKansas [closed group], *Facebook*, October 7, 2014, https://www.facebook.com/groups/EqualityKansas/search/?query="The %2010th%20Circuit%20ruling%20applies%20to%20Kansas%2C%20but%20 it's%20not%20self-executing%2C".

23. Angela Eichler and Kelli (last name withheld), interview with the author, August 25, 2015. Recollections and quotations by these two women in this chapter are from this interview.

24. Scott Rothschild, "Brownback Gets Heat for 'Real Live Experiment' Comment on Tax Cuts," *Lawrence Journal-World*, June 19, 2012, http://www2.ljworld.com /news/2012/jun/19/brownback-gets-heat-real-live-experiment-comment-t/.

25. Joe Rodriguez, "Deacons Offer Insight into Fox Resignation," *Wichita Eagle*, September 2, 2006.

26. Jerry Siebenmark, "Brownback Speaks at Rally Opposing Same-Sex Marriage in Summit Church Lot," *Wichita Eagle*, October 18, 2014.

27. Ibid.

28. Thomas Witt, update, EqualityKansas [closed group], Facebook, November 12, 2014, https://www.facebook.com/EqualityKansas/posts/966033090077068.

29. Dave Helling, "Same-Sex Marriage Licenses Can Be Issued in Johnson County," *Kansas City Star*, November 18, 2014, http://www.kansascity.com/news/politics-government/article4005322.html.

30. Peggy Lowe, "Brownback Won't Allow Marriage Rights to Gay Couples in Kansas," *KCUR*, November 20, 2014, http://kcur.org/post/brownback-wont-allow-marriage-rights-gay-couples-kansas.

31. Bryan Lowry, "ACLU to Amend Lawsuit to Force Kansas Agencies to Recognize Same-Sex Marriages," *Wichita Eagle*, November 20, 2014, http://www.kansas.com/news/politics-government/article4036105.html.

32. Associated Press, "Lawyer to Include Benefits in Same-Sex Marriage Suit in Kansas," *Topeka Capital-Journal*, November 21, 2014, http://cjonline.com/news/2014-11-21/lawyer-include-benefits-same-sex-marriage-suit-against-kansas#gsc.tab=0.

33. Lowry, "ACLU to Amend Lawsuit."

34. Eliot Sill, "County Issues 1st Same-Sex Marriage License," *Marion County Record*, November 27, 2014, http://marionrecord.com/direct/county_issues_1st_same_sex_marriage_license+4610samesex+436f756e74792069737375657320 3173742073616d652d736578206d61727269696765206c6963656e7365.

35. Derek Schmidt, "AG Schmidt Statement on Recent Court Rulings," *Attorney General Derek Schmidt*, June 26, 2015, accessed June 2, 2017, https://ag.ks.gov/media-center/news-releases/2015/06/26/ag-schmidt-statement-on-recent-court-rulings.

36. Equality Kansas, "UPDATE: IT'S DONE. Marriage Equality Comes to All 105 Kansas Counties," June 29, 2015, accessed June 2, 2017, http://eqks.org/meanwhile-in-kansas-the-struggle-continues/.

37. Bryan Lowry, "Brownback Defends Approach to Supreme Court's Same-Sex Marriage Decision," *Wichita Eagle*, July 2, 2015, http://www.kansas.com/news/politics-government/article26045212.html.

38. Equality Kansas, "UPDATE: Some State Agencies Recognizing Same-Sex Marriages, Governor's Office Contradicts," July 6, 2015, http://eqks.org/breaking-state-agencies-recognizing-same-sex-marriages/.

39. Ibid.

40. Ibid.

41. Kansas Office of the Governor, Executive Order 15-05, "Preservation and Protection of Religious Freedom," July 7, 2015, accessed June 19, 2017, https:// governor.kansas.gov/executive-order-15-05/.

42. Bryan Lowry, "Gov. Sam Brownback Issues Executive Order on Religious Liberty after Same-Sex Marriage Ruling," *Wichita Eagle*, July 7, 2015, http://www .kansas.com/news/politics-government/article26668207.html.

43. Ibid.

44. Peter Hancock, "State Seeks to Dismiss Gay Marriage Tax Lawsuit," *Lawrence Journal-World*, July 10, 2015, http://www2.ljworld.com/news/2015/jul/10/state -seeks-dismiss-gay-marriage-tax-lawsuit/.

45. Darci Pottroff and Joleen Spain, interview with the author, June 6, 2015. Recollections and quotations by Pottroff and Spain in this chapter are from this interview.

PART FOUR. THE TRANSFORMATION

1. Katy Steinmetz, "The Transgender Tipping Point," *Time*, May 29, 2014, http://time.com/135480/transgender-tipping-point/.

2. Michael Gordon, Mark S. Price, and Katie Peralta, "Understanding HB2: North Carolina's Newest Law Solidifies State's Role in Defining Discrimination," *Charlotte Observer*, March 26, 2016, http://www.charlotteobserver.com/news /politics-government/article68401147.html.

3. Sheryl Gay Stolberg, Julie Bosman, Manny Fernandez, and Julie Hirschfeld Davis, "How the Push to Advance Bathroom Rights for Transgender Americans Reached the White House," *New York Times*, May 21, 2016, http://www.nytimes .com/2016/05/22/us/transgender-bathroom-obama-schools.html?_r=0.

CHAPTER 10. KANSAS CITY ROYALTY

1. Mitch Kellaway and Sunnivie Brydum, "The 21 Trans Women Killed in 2015," *Advocate*, July 27, 2015, updated January 12, 2016, http://www.advocate .com/transgender/2015/07/27/these-are-trans-women-killed-so-far-us-2015.

2. Katy Steinmetz, "Why Transgender People Are Being Murdered at a Historic Rate," *Time*, August 17, 2015, http://time.com/3999348/transgender-murders-2015/.

3. Kansas Legislature, Session of 2016, Senate Committee on Ways and Means, Senate Bill no. 513, http://www.kslegislature.org/li/b2015_16/measures /documents/sb513_00_0000.pdf; and Kansas Legislature, Session of 2016, House of Representatives Committee on Federal and State Affairs, House Bill no. 2737, http://www.kslegislature.org/li/b2015_16/measures/documents/hb2737_00 _0000.pdf.

4. Edward M. Eveld, "Transgender Restroom Bill in Kansas Alarms LGBT Student Advocates," *Kansas City Star*, April 13, 2016, http://www.kansascity.com /news/politics-government/article71716992.html.

5. Thomas Witt, "The 2016 Legislative Session Is Drawing to a Close (Hopefully)," *Liberty Press*, June 2016.

CHAPTER 11. TRANS KANSAS

1. George W. Bush, Homeland Security Presidential Directive 9: Defense of United States Agriculture and Food, January 30, 2004, *Weekly Compilation of Presidential Documents* (February 9, 2004), 183–187, accessed via Homeland Security Digital Library, https://www.hsdl.org/?abstract&did=444013.

2. Justin Wingerter, "At National Bio and Agro-Defense Facility Groundbreaking, Federal and State Leaders Reflect on Its Importance," *Topeka Capital-Journal*, May 27, 2015, http://cjonline.com/news/2015-05-27/national-bio-and-agro -defense-facility-groundbreaking-federal-and-state-leaders.

3. Ibid.

4. Scott Rothschild, "Committee Considers Bill Prohibiting Discrimination Based on Sexual Orientation," *Lawrence Journal-World*, February 12, 2009, http:// www2.ljworld.com/news/2009/feb/12/committee-considers-bill-prohibiting -discriminatio/.

5. Stephanie Mott, interviews with the author, June 10, 2015; August 6, 2015; and July 2, 2016. Subsequent recollections and quotations by Mott are from these interviews unless otherwise noted.

6. "Topekan to Speak about Transgenderism," *Topeka Capital-Journal*, June 20, 2011, http://cjonline.com/news/2011-06-20/topekan-speak-about-transgenderism.

7. "Transgender Awareness Tour Kicks Off in Manhattan," KTKA ABC 49, July 1, 2011, http://www.clipsyndicate.com/video/play/2601073/transgender _awareness_tour_kicks_off_in_manhattan.

8. "Welcome to Stacy's Restaurant," *Stacy's Restaurant*, accessed January 1, 2017.

9. Erin Mathews, "Transition Period," *Salina Journal*, July 2, 2011.

10. Stephanie Mott, *God Loves Everyone (And Me): A Transgender Journey of Faith and Discovery*, 79, http://transfaithtour.org/book%20tft-150415.pdf.

11. Ibid., 79.

12. Stephanie Mott, update, Facebook, July 2, 2011, https://www.facebook.com /Topeka.Butterfly/posts/2200615339646.

13. Mott, *God Loves Everyone*, 83.

14. Mott, update, Facebook, July 3, 2011, https://www.facebook.com/Topeka .Butterfly/posts/2201205274394.

15. Mott, update, Facebook, July 3, 2011, https://www.facebook.com/Topeka.Butterfly/posts/2201222234818.

16. Mott, update, Facebook, July 3, 2011, https://www.facebook.com/Topeka.Butterfly/posts/2201570723530.

17. Mott, update, Facebook, July 3, 2011, https://www.facebook.com/Topeka.Butterfly/posts/2201808249468.

18. Mott, update, Facebook, July 3, 2011, https://www.facebook.com/Topeka.Butterfly/posts/2202153458098.

19. Mott, update, Facebook, July 3, 2011, https://www.facebook.com/Topeka.Butterfly/posts/2201815129640.

20. Mott, update, Facebook, July 4, 2011, https://www.facebook.com/Topeka.Butterfly/posts/2203500771780.

21. Mott, update, Facebook, July 4, 2011, https://www.facebook.com/Topeka.Butterfly/posts/2203727137439.

22. Mott, update, Facebook, July 4, 2011, https://www.facebook.com/Topeka.Butterfly/posts/2204342312818.

23. Mott, update, Facebook, July 4, 2011, https://www.facebook.com/Topeka.Butterfly/posts/2204414594625.

24. Mott, update, Facebook, July 4, 2011, https://www.facebook.com/Topeka.Butterfly/posts/2204930287517.

25. Mott, update, Facebook, July 5, 2011, https://www.facebook.com/Topeka.Butterfly/posts/2206254320617.

26. C. J. Janovy, "At Manhattan Gathering, Transgender Kansans Seek to Make Their State More Hospitable," KCUR, September 17, 2015, http://kcur.org/post/manhattan-gathering-transgender-kansans-seek-make-their-state-more-hospitable#stream/0.

27. Denise Neil, "Wichita's Transgender Community Strives to Become More Visible," Wichita Eagle, July 4, 2015, http://www.kansas.com/news/local/article26505787.html.

28. Elle Boatman, interview with the author, April 27, 2017.

29. Grayson Barnes, interview with the author, July 6, 2016. Recollections and quotations by Barnes in this chapter are from this interview.

30. Adam O'Brien, interview with the author, October 27, 2015. Recollections and quotations by O'Brien in this chapter are from this interview.

31. Michael Herman, "Let's Talk about Trans People," Manhattan Mercury, April 1, 2014.

32. Mott, update, Facebook, June 30, 2015, https://www.facebook.com/Topeka.Butterfly/posts/10207022739711669?match=bXVzdCBoYXZlIGJlZW4gaW4gdGhlIGVhcm55IDE5ODBzLDE5ODBzLGVhcm5yLGI1c3Q%3D.

EPILOGUE. FOREVER KANSAN

1. Kevin Stilley, interviews with the author, June 6, 2015, and May 29, 2016. Recollections and quotations by Stilley in this chapter are from these interviews.

2. Katie Jordan, interview with the author, February 7, 2016. Recollections and quotations by Jordan in this chapter are from this interview.

3. Opinion, "LGBT Inclusion Is a Step Forward," *Manhattan Mercury*, July 24, 2016.

4. US Department of Defense, "Secretary of Defense Ash Carter Announces Policy for Transgender Service Members," news release no. NR-246-16, June 30, 2016, https://www.defense.gov/News/News-Releases/News-Release-View/Article /821675/secretary-of-defense-ash-carter-announces-policy-for-transgender -service-members.

5. Dan Lamothe, "Trump Wants to Ban Transgender Military Troops. His Top General Feels Differently," *Washington Post*, September 26, 2017, https://www .washingtonpost.com/news/checkpoint/wp/2017/09/26/trump-wants-to-ban -transgender-military-troops-his-top-general-feels-differently/?utm_term=.2 cb19392b9d5; Chris Kahn, "Exclusive: Majority of Americans Support Trans- gender Military Service – Poll," *Reuters*, July 28, 2017, http://www.reuters.com /article/us-usa-military-transgender-poll/exclusive-majority-of-americans -support-transgender-military-service-poll-idUSKBN1AD2BL.

SELECTED BIBLIOGRAPHY

Albin, Tami. *Under the Rainbow: Oral Histories of Gay, Lesbian, Transgender, Intersex and Queer People in Kansas*. University of Kansas ScholarWorks. https://kuscholar works.ku.edu/handle/1808/5330.

Baker, Gilbert. Interview with Tami Albin, June 19, 2008. "Gilbert Baker Oral History." *Under the Rainbow: Oral Histories of Gay, Lesbian, Transgender, Intersex and Queer People in Kansas*. University of Kansas ScholarWorks. https://kuscholar works.ku.edu/handle/1808/6895.

Barrett-Fox, Rebecca. *God Hates: Westboro Baptist Church, American Nationalism, and the Religious Right*. Lawrence: University Press of Kansas, 2016.

Cenziper, Debbie, and James Obergefell. *Love Wins: The Lovers and Lawyers Who Fought the Landmark Case for Marriage Equality*. New York: William Morrow, 2016.

Crawford, Lucas. "Snorting the Powder of Life: Transgender Migration in the Land of Oz." In *Queering the Countryside: New Frontiers in Rural Queer Studies*, ed. Mary L. Gray, Colin R. Johnson, and Brian J. Gilley, 126–145. New York: New York University Press, 2016.

Drain, Lauren, and Lisa Pulitzer. *Banished: Surviving My Years in the Westboro Baptist Church*. New York: Grand Central Publishing, 2013.

Fejes, Fred. *Gay Rights and Moral Panic: The Origins of America's Debate on Homosexuality*. New York: Palgrave Macmillan, 2008.

Frank, Thomas. *What's the Matter with Kansas?: How Conservatives Won the Heart of America* New York: Metropolitan Books, 2004.

Gray, Mary L., Colin R. Johnson, and Brian J. Gilley, eds. *Queering the Countryside: New Frontiers in Rural Queer Studies*. New York: New York University Press, 2016.

Herring, Scott. *Another Country: Queer Anti-Urbanism*. New York: New York University Press, 2010.

Hirshman, Linda. *Victory: The Triumphant Gay Revolution*. New York: Harper Perennial, 2013.

Jantz, Tanya. Interview with Tami Albin, November 24, 2010. "Tanya Oral History." *Under the Rainbow: Oral Histories of Gay, Lesbian, Transgender, Intersex and Queer People in Kansas*. University of Kansas ScholarWorks. https://kuscholar works.ku.edu/handle/1808/6892.

Kaplan, Roberta, with Lisa Dickey. *Then Comes Marriage: United States v. Windsor and the Defeat of DOMA*. New York: W. W. Norton, 2015.

Mason, Carol. *Oklahomo: Lessons in Unqueering America*. Albany: State University of New York Press, 2015.

Mayer, Jane. *Dark Money: The Hidden History of the Billionaires behind the Rise of the Radical Right*. New York: Doubleday, 2016.

Miner, Craig. *Kansas: The History of the Sunflower State, 1854–2000*. Lawrence: University Press of Kansas, 2002.

Mott, Stephanie. *God Loves Everyone (And Me): A Transgender Journey of Faith and Discovery*. Accessed June 19, 2017. http://transfaithtour.org/book%20tft-150415.pdf.

Solomon, Marc. *Winning Marriage: The Inside Story of How Same-Sex Couples Took On the Politicians and Pundits—and Won*. Lebanon, NH: ForeEdge, 2014.

Witosky, Tom, and Marc Hansen. *Equal before the Law: How Iowa Led Americans to Marriage Equality*. Iowa City: University of Iowa Press, 2015.

INDEX

MAY 1 4 2019